THEORIZING
RELIGIONS PAST

COGNITIVE SCIENCE OF RELIGION SERIES

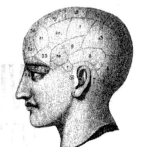

Series Editors: HARVEY WHITEHOUSE
and LUTHER H. MARTIN

The Cognitive Science of Religion Series publishes research into the cognitive foundations of religious thinking and behavior and their consequences for social morphology. The emphasis of the series is on scientific approaches to the study of religion within the framework of the cognitive sciences, including experimental, clinical, or laboratory studies, but works drawing upon ethnographic, linguistic, archaeological, or historical research are welcome, as are critical appraisals of research in these areas. In addition to providing a forum for presenting new empirical evidence and major theoretical innovations, the series publishes concise overviews of issues in the field suitable for students and general readers. This series is published in cooperation with the Institute for Cognition and Culture at Queen's University Belfast.

THEORIZING RELIGIONS PAST

Archaeology, History, and Cognition

EDITED BY
HARVEY WHITEHOUSE
AND LUTHER H. MARTIN

ALTAMIRA PRESS
A Division of Rowman & Littlefield Publishers, Inc.
Walnut Creek • Lanham • New York • Toronto • Oxford

AltaMira Press
A division of Rowman & Littlefield Publishers, Inc.
1630 North Main Street, #367
Walnut Creek, California 94596
www.altamirapress.com

Rowman & Littlefield Publishers, Inc.
A wholly owned subsidiary of The Rowman & Littlefield Publishing Group, Inc.
4501 Forbes Boulevard, Suite 200
Lanham, Maryland 20706

PO Box 317
Oxford
OX2 9RU, UK

British Library Cataloguing in Publication Information Available

Library of Congress Cataloging-in-Publication Data

Theorizing religions past : archaeology, history, and cognition / edited by
Harvey Whitehouse and Luther H. Martin.
    p. cm. — (Cognitive science of religion series)
    Includes bibliographical references and index.
    ISBN 0-7591-0620-7 (hardcover : alk. paper) — ISBN 0-7591-0621-5 (pbk. :
alk. paper)
    1. Religion. 2. Whitehouse, Harvey. 3. Archaeology and religion. 4.
Psychology, Religious. 5. Religions—History. I. Whitehouse, Harvey. II. Martin,
Luther H., 1937– III. Series.

BL48.T44 2004
200'.72—dc22   2004001817

Printed in the United States of America

♾ ™ The paper used in this publication meets the minimum requirements of American
National Standard for Information Sciences—Permanence of Paper for Printed Library
Materials, ANSI/NISO Z39.48-1992.

Dedicated to the memory of Keith Hopkins
who inimitably presented to the conference upon
which this volume is based his insights into the
causes of early Christianity's success

CONTENTS

Preface

IN 1995, IN HIS ETHNOGRAPHY of religious innovation and transmission among the Baining peoples of Papua New Guinea, the British anthropologist Harvey Whitehouse proposed a theory of two "modes of religiosity," a "doctrinal" and an "imagistic" (*Inside the Cult: Religious Innovation and Transmission in Papua New Guinea*), a theory he subsequently elaborated as a selectionist theory of human religiosity generally (*Arguments and Icons: Divergent Modes of Religiosity*). In brief, Whitehouse contends that a clustering of variables characterizes the doctrinal mode of religiosity, including a digital or discursive style of codification—which may be found in nonliterate contexts, but is most often characteristic of literate societies or of those influenced by them—a transmission of beliefs by means of routinized instruction and repetitive ritual, and a wide dissemination of tradition as constitutive of large, imagined communities in which meaning is controlled by some means of institutionalized orthodoxy, while group affinities are largely anonymous. By contrast, the variables characteristic of an imagistic mode of religiosity, according to Whitehouse, include an analogic or imagistic style of codification, transmission through infrequently performed rituals rendered memorable through intense sensory pageantry and heightened emotionality, and an enduring cohesion of small, face-to-face communities of participants (Whitehouse 1995: 197, table 5).

The two modes of religiosity Whitehouse proposes rely on and are cognitively constrained by different systems of memory. The catechetical instruction in and repetitive reinforcement of beliefs that are characteristic of the doctrinal mode become encoded as generalized scripts or schemas in the explicit memory system and rely upon this system for their transmission. The unique and personalized experiences characteristic of the imagistic mode are, on the other hand, encoded in the episodic, or autobiographical, memory system and rely upon this system for their transmission and meaning.

This volume is based upon the contributions to an international symposium of archaeologists, classicists, historians, and historians of religion held at the University of Vermont in August 2002, at which the predictions of the theory of two modes of religiosity were assessed. The Vermont symposium was the second of three; the first was held at Kings College, Cambridge, in December 2001 at which an international group of anthropologists assessed the predictions of the modes theory against differing domains of ethnographic data (*Ritual and Memory: Toward a Comparative Anthropology of Religion*, edited by H. Whitehouse and J. Laidlaw. Walnut Creek, Calif.: AltaMira Press, 2004) and the third was held at Emory University in August 2003 at which an international group of researchers in developmental and cognitive psychology assessed the psychological and cognitive foundations of religiosity and their implications for Whitehouse's modes theory (*Mind and Religion: Psychological and Cognitive Foundations of Religion*, edited by H. Whitehouse and Robert N. McCauley. Walnut Creek, Calif.: AltaMira Press, forthcoming).

It was anticipated that, because of the *longue durée* characteristic of historical data in addition to that data's ethnographic diversity, historians would find it more difficult than anthropologists and psychologists to focus their discussions in terms of a single theory. It was, however, precisely the theoretical focus articulated by Whitehouse in his modes theory that allowed a group of historically oriented scholars to dispute with one another topics ranging from prehistorical religiosity to Greco-Roman religions, to the beginnings of Christianity, to its medieval and Reformation developments, to diverse cases of modern religion and to debate the adequacy of this theory for accounting for the complexity of their data. We offer this volume on *Theorizing Religions Past: Archaeology, History, and Cognition* as a contribution to discussions about ways of theorizing the past, generally, and, specifically, as a contribution to the research project on the history of religions that is based on a scientific paradigm, rather than on the idiosyncratic agendas that have so dominated the study of religion since its founding as an academic field in the late nineteenth century.

We are grateful to the British Academy for providing the initial support, which made all three of the modes symposia possible. We are especially grateful to the John Templeton Foundation for its generous support of the Vermont and Emory symposia and to the Office of the Provost, the Dean of the College of Arts and Sciences, and the Department of Religion of the University of Vermont for their support of the Vermont symposium.

Luther H. Martin

INTRODUCTION $\quad$ I

The Wedding of Psychology, Ethnography, and History: Methodological Bigamy or Tripartite Free Love?

E. THOMAS LAWSON

SOME YEARS AGO I WAS ADVENTUROUS ENOUGH to publish an article in the journal *Historical Reflections/Réflexions Historiques* in which I argued for the relevance of cognitive science to the study of history (Lawson 1994). Much to my surprise and pleasure, I received very positive and encouraging responses from historians and, in fact, was invited to make my case in a graduate seminar offered by the history department at my own university. My rather simple, if not simpleminded, claim was that, if historians and other social scientists were willing to make claims about the transmission of traditions, then it would also be their job to help the rest of us identify the mechanisms that underwrite the processes of transmission.

Since the publication of this article, two books have been published that demonstrate willingness on the part of social scientists with a historical interest to do something like that. I refer to Harvey Whitehouse's *Arguments and Icons: Divergent Modes of Religiosity* (2000) and Steven Mithen's *Prehistory of the Mind* (1996). In Whitehouse's work we find a sophisticated wedding of cognitive psychology, ethnography, and history. In Mithen's work we find a powerful argument about how archaeology can not only be informed by cognitive psychology, but can, in turn, on the basis of information derived from archaeological research, make a fundamental contribution to our understanding of the working of the human mind.

These two volumes are genuinely interdisciplinary endeavors leading to coherent and compelling arguments about the origin, structure, and transmission of religious thought and practice. In the case of Mithen the claim is clear: We can only understand the present by knowing the past. In the long run this means gathering together everything we know about cognitive development, not only ontogenetically, but also through our knowledge of the evolutionary history of the mind, in order to relate the past to the present. Mithen has effectively accomplished the transformation of archaeology from a theoretical and empirical perspective on the past to a science of the mind in historical perspective thoroughly informed by evolutionary, cognitive, and developmental psychology.

The work of Harvey Whitehouse is equally ambitious. While pivotally ethnographic, his work is deeply sensitive both to psychological processes, particularly those that are mnemonic, as well as to historical facts. I do not know what historians and ethnographers make of his arguments, but I do know that those of us who are developing the cognitive science of religion have been persuaded about the importance of his insights, especially as these involve issues of the transmission of cultural forms.

The works of both Mithen and Whitehouse are scintillating examples of what I have jokingly called tripartite free love rather than methodological bigamy. Bigamy is a triangular relationship in which at the apex of the triangle is the bigamist and at the base of the triangle are the objects of bigamy. Essential to this triangular relationship is that the one member at the base is ignorant of the existence of the other member at the base. This ignorance spells trouble in the short or long run when the bigamy is discovered. And the consequent knowledge typically alienates all concerned.

In tripartite free love, each member of the relationship knows about the other. This does not necessarily spell trouble as long as mutual respect is present. However, the danger of subservience always looms. I do not want to overplay this metaphor because of its titillating character. The point I wish to make is that whether one is a psychologist, an anthropologist, or a historian, one has work to do that is respectively psychological, ethnographic, and historical. The virtual autonomy of those researchers grants them freedom to do what they do best while, of course, looking at what is going on in closely related disciplines. Their autonomy is qualified by their dependence on information generated by the practice of the other disciplines in the triangle.

A perusal of the indexes of the relevant journals demonstrates that the practitioners of these disciplines know when their work reflects the particular perspectives typical of their particular discipline and when their work creatively transgresses boundaries. One would not expect to find a discussion of historical questions, such as whether Caesar crossed the Rubicon, in a psychology or anthropology journal. Nevertheless, there are crucial moments in which the question of whether Caesar crossed the Rubicon is a psychological and ethnographic, and not simply a historical, problem. It is a psychological problem in the sense that whether the event is either remembered or imagined, and therefore communicated horizontally and vertically, depends upon its ability to command attention. Claims to historical knowledge presuppose mnemonic facts. It is also an ethnographic problem in the sense that this putative event plays a role in the lore of the traditions of the society in which it is remembered, discussed, and propagated. Claims to ethnographic knowledge all presuppose mnemonic processes. So, it is at that interdisciplinary moment that a wedding of perspectives between the three disciplines involved, freely entered into and with due respect for the integrity of each, is required.

Of course, this is also exactly the point at which methodological concerns arise. Is the historian, for example, knowledgeable enough about either psychology or ethnography to support his or her theoretical maneuvers? Is the ethnographer who appeals to mnemonic facts not guilty of reducing social facts to psychological facts? Charges of reductionism arise because it is inevitable that someone will ask which level of explanation is fundamental and which derivative.

Reductionism involves a relationship between different types and levels of theories. Sometimes theories of one kind can be reduced to better theories at the same level. So, for example, psychological theories that focus only on environmental variables might be capable of being reduced to theories that include internal variables such as cognitive states, which transform the external variables in novel, interesting, and predictable ways. Sometimes, of course, theories at one level of explanation can be reduced to theories at a deeper level. So, for example, psychological theories that focus on mental states might be capable of being reduced to nothing but brain states. I do not think that the relationships between psychology, history, and ethnography have been sufficiently clarified to decide yet whether ethnography and history (putatively higher level theoretical matrices) are grist for reduction to purely psychological categories. This is not to say that the facts that ethnographers and historians traffic in do not have psychological foundations (which I think they do), but there is a big difference between saying that cultural facts have psychological foundations and claiming that cultural facts are nothing but the foundations. There is always more to a building than its foundations. There may be more than one floor to the mansion, but good architectural design encourages the easy and efficient flow of traffic throughout the building.

Therefore, I want to claim that it will be possible for some considerable time to come to have a free, loving, and committed relationship (to revert to my metaphor) between psychology, ethnography, and history (including its archaeological dimensions), at least at crucial moments. The test of this claim is whether a coherent set of theoretical proposals that attend to psychological, ethnographic, and historical processes can be substantiated by logical analysis and empirical and experimental evidence. The playing field between these disciplines is still level. In fact, the interdisciplinary character of the modes project depends upon conceiving of the players as being not only on the same turf, but in the same game. Interdisciplinary projects can lead to the establishment of new disciplines.

A prime candidate for such an interdisciplinary theory that combines the insights of psychology, ethnography, and history is the work of Harvey Whitehouse. Whitehouse's postulation of doctrinal and imagistic modes of religiosity provides important heuristic tools for unpacking some of the critical features informing the trajectory of religious change and development. In short, with this perspective it is possible for us to understand more deeply the processes of the transmission of both concepts and practices not only horizontally, but also vertically. Whitehouse has made a fundamental epidemiological contribution to the factors involved in the spread of religion across cultures and through time.

Such heuristic tools not only enable us to develop an explanatory understanding of the contents of our history books about the successes and failures of religious institutions, but also open up new avenues of investigation in fieldwork. Furthermore, by focusing upon ritual practices and not just upon religious ideas, Whitehouse brings an observable and empirical dimension to theoretical claims about cognitive processes.

While the initial claims that Whitehouse makes involve a small geographical area, they enable the theoretician to examine the possibility of making claims about other geographical areas and ultimately about proposing cross-cultural and historical generalizations.

In any such project there is always the chance that important ideas will be missed. I think that participants in the modes project inspired by the theorizing of Whitehouse need to take additional theoretical perspectives and the empirical and theoretical work that accompanies them into account. The first of these is the psychological studies on theological correctness by Justin Barrett and Frank Keil (1996) and later Barrett (2000). Such work should be synthesized with the ideas entertained in the modes project because it is clear that the doctrinal mode is infused with theological correctness and, as such, has implications for the processes of cultural transmission. These studies also point to the fact that offline reflective thinking is difficult to transmit, even when the necessary institutions are established to perpetuate these modes of thought. Theology is not easy to come by.

The second of these is Pascal Boyer's (2001) work on intuitive ontology, which is important because it focuses upon the kinds of templates that typically underwrite our variable concepts and have, therefore, a significant impact on our explanatory understanding of the processes of acquiring and transmitting information within and across cultures and through the historical process.

The third of these has do with the notion of balanced and unbalanced religions and the role that conceptual control plays in the evolution of religious systems in general and religious ritual systems in particular. Robert McCauley and I have tried to show that a small number of variables exerts selection pressures on all religious ritual systems and how these systems meet the mnemonic and motivational demands necessary for their transmission (McCauley and Lawson 2002).

The interdisciplinary study of religion, infused with the insights provided by psychology, ethnography, and history are opening up new avenues of knowledge that promise to expand our understanding of human thought and behavior in interesting new ways. Such a wedding should provide a welcome sense of pageantry to those participants eager to enjoy the party.

References

Barrett, Justin L. 2000. "Exploring the Natural Foundations of Religion." *Trends in Cognitive Science* 4: 29–34.

Barrett, Justin L., and Frank Keil. 1996. "Conceptualizing a Non-natural Entity: Anthropomorphism in God Concepts." *Cognitive Psychology* 31: 219–47.

Boyer, Pascal. 2001. *Religion Explained: The Evolutionary Origins of Religious Thought.* New York: Basic Books.

Lawson, E. Thomas. 1994. "Counterintuitive Notions and the Problem of Transmission: The Relevance of Cognitive Science for the Study of History." *Historical Reflections/ Réflexions Historique* 20(3): 481–95.

McCauley, Robert N., and E. Thomas Lawson. 2002. *Bringing Ritual to Mind: Psychological Foundations of Cultural Forms.* Cambridge: Cambridge University Press.

Mithen, Steven. 1996. *The Prehistory of the Mind: The Cognitive Origins of Art, Religion, and Science.* London: Thames and Hudson.

Whitehouse, Harvey. 2000. *Arguments and Icons: Divergent Modes of Religiosity.* Oxford: Oxford University Press.

Toward a Scientific History of Religions 2

LUTHER H. MARTIN

> *There must in the nature of human institutions be a mental language common to all nations, which uniformly grasps the substance of things feasible in human social life and expresses it with as many diverse modifications as these same things may have diverse aspects. . . . This common mental language is proper to our Science, by whose light . . . scholars will be enabled to construct a mental vocabulary common to all.*

—VICO 1744: ¶ 161

A T THE TURN OF THE MILLENNIUM, the Musée d'art contemporain de Montréal sponsored the exhibit "Around Memory and Archive," which explored the various mechanisms and strategies for encoding, in imagination and in object, the various behaviors, situations, and recollections that have been considered to be laden with varying degrees of meaning and significance. The participants in this exhibit considered the relationships between the alternatively enduring, fleeting, and intangible impressions of memory, the concern with the retention and transmission of information by historians, and the choices that must be made in consideration of finite constraints upon archival storage (MACM n.d.; see Charbonneau 2000). It is just such relationships between the ways in which cultural information is conserved, recalled, and transmitted that are central to the comparative and historical study of religions, and it is precisely these issues that are central to the researches of the British anthropologist Harvey Whitehouse (1995, 2000, 2002, 2004).

Suggestions that the cognitive sciences might provide a theoretical foundation for the study of religions have appealed rather more to anthropologists than to historians of religion, and ethnographic data have more often been elicited than have historical materials to illustrate or to assess the analyses of and the predictions about religion by cognitive theorists (e.g., Guthrie 1980, 1993; Sperber 1975, 1996; Boyer 1994, 2001; Whitehouse 1995, 2000; Atran 2002). The promises and problems confronting ethnography and historiography are, however, quite similar in principle; as summarized by the Princeton historian Robert Darnton, the issue is how "to make contact with the otherness in other cultures" (1984: 261)—whether that otherness is defined by spatial or by temporal remove, or by both. Darnton proposed an "anthropological mode of history" that, reminiscent of Vico's prescient requisite, would show how ordinary people "construed the world . . . and infused it with emotion," how they "organized reality in their minds and expressed it in their behavior" (1984: 3, 6). Darnton identified this "history in an ethnographic grain" with what the French call *l'histoire des mentalités* (1984: 3)—an ethnographically influenced approach to history that can be traced back to Lucien Lévy-Bruhl (Burke 1986: 444). Lévy-Bruhl's notion of *représentations collectives*, together with that of his colleague Emile Durkheim, provided the theoretical basis for interest by Lucien Febvre and Marc Bloch in what they called *mentalités collectives* or *outillage mental*—the workings of "everyday thought" (Burke 1986: 439), in how people think as well as what they think (Darnton 1984: 3).

Lévy-Bruhl is perhaps most famously remembered for his view, expressed in an early philosophical work, that "humanity everywhere went through [a primitive or prelogical period of thought] as a necessary stage of its evolution" (1899: 135; Preus 1987: 53). In his mature work, however, Lévy-Bruhl came to reject such social evolutionary views and to insist that "[p]relogical thought is not a stage antedating logical thought" and concluded that "we shall no longer define the mental activity of primitives . . . as a rudimentary form of our own" (1923: 33; Cazeneuve 1968: 264). Rather, Lévy-Bruhl emphasized that the fundamental structures of the human mind are everywhere the same (Cazeneuve 1968: 265; Gardner 1987: 258, 255, 224). The minds of "primitives" are "quite as capable of scientific thought as those of Europeans," he wrote. Rather, it is the social world and customs of others that differ from one another as from our own (Lévy-Bruhl 1923: 22).

It is the social world of difference and not the common mental structures of human cognition that subsequently came to be emphasized by social scientists as by historians generally. In a recent review of Pascal Boyer's *Religion Explained*, for example, W. G. Runciman compliments Boyer for his careful consideration of "the ethnographic record and the findings of recent psychology," but criticizes Boyer for emphasizing human universals at the expense of the explanatory effects of particularistic histories. "[T]here is," Runciman writes, "a *historical dynamic* which explains why, under specific sociological conditions, the members of different cultures will adopt or discard belief systems of different kinds" (2002: 24, emphasis added). E. Thomas Lawson has concluded, however, in one of the earliest suggestions concerning the relevance of cognitive science for historical study, that even when historians confine their inquiries to such political, economic, or intellectual dynamics, they "still have not identified structures capable of accounting for . . . [the] emergence, development and persistence" of the different "ideas and the practices" that might emerge from "the same constrained context" (1994: 483). The focus of Lawson's argument, in other words, is that history cannot be an *explanans*, but must be the *explanandum*; it is precisely the "emergence, development and persistence" of particularistic historical contexts that begs for explanation (see also Lawson and McCauley 1993).

A fruitful explanatory exploration of particularistic historical contexts might begin with a consideration of such contexts in the way that cognitive scientists think about culture. Scott Atran, for example, writes that cultures "are not ontologically distinct 'superorganisms' or 'independent variables' with precise contents or boundaries. They are no more things in and of themselves, or 'natural kinds' with their own special laws, than are cloud or sand patterns" (2002: 10).

The task then, Atran concludes,

> is not to account for ideas and practices in terms of culture. . . . Rather, it is to scientifically explain cultures . . . in terms of material causes. Cultures . . . exist, and are explained, to the extent that they reliably express structurally enduring relationships among mental states and behaviors and where these material relationships enable a given population of individuals to maintain itself in repeated social interactions with a range of ecological contexts (2002: 10, 112; see Sperber 1996).

Similar to the case of culture, we might conclude that there are no historical contexts apart from "structurally enduring relationships" among the mental states and behaviors of individual historical and historiographical agents.

Historical agents are those human agents from the past who, like all human agents, represent themselves and their environment, to themselves and to others (*res gestae*), in ways that some relic of their representations are left behind, whether intentionally (e.g., in texts) or unintentionally (e.g., in the material remains of everyday culture). (Representations can, of course, also be preserved unintentionally in texts and deliberately as material remains.) Historiographical agents, on the other hand, are the historically minded who subsequently seek to represent historical remains systematically (Gaddis 2002: 9), and usually in the form of narrative (*historia rerum gestarum*) (Gaddis 2002: 15; on the cognitive salience of narrative, see Turner 1996).

"History," in the sense of "historiography," represents, in other words, a "way of knowing" (from the Greek *historia*, "inquiry"; see Herodotus 1.1); but the way of knowing that has privileged itself above all other modes of inquiry is science (Boyer 2001: 320–21). In the estimation of one historian, science "has shown itself more

capable than any of the other [ways of knowing] . . . at eliciting agreement on the va-
lidity of results across cultures, in different languages, and among highly dissimilar
observers" (Gaddis 2002: 37). For historiography to be a reliable way of knowing,
then, its methods must at least approach the standards for verification that exist
within science (Gaddis 2002: 17), especially the nonexperimental "historical" sciences like astronomy, geology, paleontology, and evolutionary biology (Gaddis 2002:
39–40, 43). As Louis Gottschalk argued some forty years ago, historiographical interpretation "must be subject to certain general standards and tests—of human behavior, of logical antecedents and consequences, of statistical or mass trends" (1963:
vi; for an extended discussion of the issue of historical objectivity, see Appleby, Hunt,
and Jacob 1994). Whitehouse has now proposed an explanatory theory, based in the
cognitive sciences, that explains how (religious) actors conserve, recall, and transmit
information in ways that have predictable sociopolitical consequences. And, this theory is amenable to testing not only against a wide range of ethnographic data, in
terms of which it was formulated, but against that of historical data as well.

Like numerous social scientists before him, Whitehouse has recognized that
religious data can be described in terms of "two very different sets of dynamics"
(2002: 293–94). His own designations for these dynamics—what he terms "two
modes of religiosity"—are "imagistic" and "doctrinal." The imagistic mode of religiosity refers, in Whitehouse's description, to a convergence of analogical pre-
cepts and practices encoded in the episodic memory system, spontaneously
expressed, and transmitted through infrequently performed, but emotionally
salient, rituals by small-scale, face-to-face groups. He distinguishes this imagistic
mode of religiosity from a doctrinal mode, which is associated with the widespread affirmation and transmission of a commonly held set of standardized beliefs and teachings that have been encoded in the semantic memory system,
reflectively expressed, and cogently argued. The often-complex set of beliefs and
teachings characteristic of this mode is controlled by some centralized authority
and maintained through routinized review and frequent repetition. Driven by selectionist mechanisms, these two distributions of cognitive effects have, according
to Whitehouse, major consequences for the nature of religious experience and action and for the way in which religions are organized. If confirmed, Whitehouse's
model would provide "a fruitful theoretical framework for gathering in and organizing a great range of research currently being pursued by other cognitivists,"
as well as by anthropologists and historians working in the field of religion (Tremlin 2002: 326, 346). Furthermore, it would accurately predict general features of
religion that should appear in different cultures and throughout the course of human history, and it offers an explanation for these features in terms of a universal
set of interdependent variables. Table 2.1 presents these variables as summarized
by Whitehouse (2002: 309).

Table 2.1.   Modes of Religiosity Contrasted

Variable	Doctrinal	Imagistic
	Psychological Features	
1. Transmissive frequency	High	Low
2. Level of arousal	Low	High
3. Principal memory system	Semantic schemas and implicit scripts	Episodic/flashbulb memory
4. Ritual meaning	Learned/acquired	Internally generated
5. Techniques of revelation	Rhetoric, logical integration, narrative	Iconicity, multivocality, and multivalence
	Sociopolitical Features	
6. Social cohesion	Diffuse	Intense
7. Leadership	Dynamic	Passive/absent
8. Inclusivity/exclusivity	Inclusive	Exclusive
9. Spread	Rapid, efficient	Slow, inefficient
10. Scale	Large scale	Small scale
11. Degree of uniformity	High	Low
12. Structure	Centralized	Noncentralized

In contrast to social scientists, who have traditionally attributed human behavior to one or two independent variables, historians are much more familiar with organizing their data in terms of an "interdependency of variables" (Gaddis 2002: 53–54).

Most simply, historians can assess the degree to which characteristics of the group or tradition they are researching conform to the set of variables associated with one or the other mode of religiosity described by Whitehouse's theory. Do the specific predictions of this theory stand up? That is to say, do the variables the theory is concerned with tend to coalesce in the manner predicted across the range of religious traditions we know about? Are there historical examples of variables that apparently conform to neither of those predicted for the two modalities? Such historiographical decisions are, of course, generalizations based upon assessments of the available data, and generalizations are always characterized by exceptions, especially in the human sciences. Can the modes theory account for them? Must the theory be modified? Historiographical assessments of any theory, such as that proposed by Whitehouse, will likely provide counterexamples as well as confirmations of the proposed model. But are these counterexamples based upon incomplete or interpretatively biased historical data? Are they based upon variables not addressed by the theory, but that may belong to the enormously complex array of historical data? Justin Barrett has concluded, specifically with regard to the modes theory, that "[i]n any social-scientific model, the best we can hope for is to explain more of the data than other competing theories and at a rate both significantly and meaningfully greater than chance" (private communication 2003).

Even the most positivistic historians recognize, of course, that they will never attain certainty about the past; their goal, rather, is to make decisions about probability in the face of historical possibility (see Bloch 1953: 124).

In addition to assessing the predictions of the modes theory, a more venturesome question for historians is whether this theory can offer historians an infrastructure for explaining their data with greater confidence. Historians have always been more comfortable with description than they have been with theory—even though the latter always lurks implicitly below the surface of the former. But, it can be asked, to what extent might formal theoretical predictions, such as those proposed by Whitehouse, help clarify the complexities of the historical data? If, for example, one or more apparent exceptions to the predicted set of variables were characteristic of one or the other modality and were not based upon incontrovertible data—a rarity in historical research—but upon historiographic interpretation, might historical plausibility best be established if these ambiguities were interpreted in conformity with the otherwise interdependent set of predicted variables? Or even in the absence of sufficient historical data, might some historiographical reconstructions be completed on the basis of theoretical models that have elsewhere been substantiated (Martin 2004)?

If the theory proposed by Whitehouse emerges relatively unscathed from ethnographical and historical assessments, we are then motivated to ask questions about whether and how that theory might be refined, and we are even emboldened to ask questions about aspects of religious transmission that fall outside the original ambit of the theory. The rich historical data and theoretical arguments presented in this volume suggest that we can make significant progress in responding to all of these issues—progress, it might be suggested, that will lead toward the development of a scientific paradigm for the history of religion.

References

Appleby, Joyce, Lynn Hunt, and Margaret Jacob. 1994. *Telling the Truth about History*. New York: W. W. Norton.
Atran, Scott. 2002. *In Gods We Trust: The Evolutionary Landscape of Religion*. New York: Oxford University Press.
Bloch, Marc. 1953. *The Historians' Craft*, translated by P. Putnam. New York: Vintage Books.
Boyer, Pascal. 1994. *The Naturalness of Religious Ideas: A Cognitive Theory of Religion*. Berkeley: University of California Press.
———. 2001. *Religion Explained: The Evolutionary Origins of Religious Thought*. New York: Basic Books.
Burke, Peter. 1986. "Strengths and Weaknesses of the History of Mentalities." *History of European Ideas* 7(5): 439–51.

Cazeneuve, Jean. 1968. "Lévy-Bruhl." In *Encyclopedia of Social Science*, edited by D. L. Sills. Vol. 9, 263–66. New York: Macmillan.

Charbonneau, Charntal. 2000. *Définitions de la Culture Visualle IV: Mémoire et Archive*. Montréal: Musée d'art contemporain de Montréal.

Darnton, Robert. 1984. *The Great Cat Massacre and Other Episodes in French Cultural History*. New York: Basic Books.

Gaddis, John Lewis. 2002. *The Landscape of History: How Historians Map the Past*. Oxford: Oxford University Press.

Gardner, Howard. 1987. *The Mind's New Science*. New York: Basic Books.

Gottschalk, Louis. 1963. "Forward." In *Generalization in the Writing of History*, edited by L. Gottschalk, v–xii. Chicago: The University of Chicago Press.

Guthrie, Stewart. 1980. "A Cognitive Theory of Religion." *Current Anthropology* 21(2): 181–203.

———. 1993. *Faces in the Clouds: A New Theory of Religion*. New York: Oxford University Press.

Lawson, E. Thomas. 1994. "Counterintuitive Notions and the Problem of Transmission: The Relevance of Cognitive Science for the Study of History." *Historical Reflections/Réflexions Historiques* 20(3): 481–95.

Lawson, E. Thomas, and Robert N. McCauley. 1990. *Rethinking Religion: Connecting Cognition and Culture*. Cambridge: Cambridge University Press.

———. 1993. "Crisis of Conscience, Riddle of Identity: Making Space for a Cognitive Approach to Religious Phenomena." *Journal of the American Academy of Religion* 61: 201–23.

Lévy-Bruhl, Lucien. 1899. *History of Modern Philosophy in France*. Chicago: Open Court Publishing Company.

———. 1923. *Primitive Mentality*, translated by L. A. Clare. New York: Macmillan.

MACM. n.d. "Around Memory and Archive." Musée d'art contemporain de Montréal, December 11, 1999–March 26, 2000, at www.macm.org/expositions/iti_view.cfm?exposition_id=43 (last access February 2002).

Martin, Luther H. 2004. "Towards a Cognitive History of Religions." In *Unterwegs. Neue Pfade in der Religionswissenschaft. Festschrift für Michael Pye zum 65 Geburtstage*/On the Road. New Paths in the Study of Religions Festschrift in Honour of Michael Pye on His 65th Birthday, edited by C. Kleine, M. Schrimpf, and K. Triplett, 73–80. München: Biblion.

Preus, J. Samuel. 1987. *Explaining Religion*. New Haven, Conn.: Yale University Press.

Runciman, W. G. 2002. "Why Are We Here. Review of Pascal Boyer, *Religion Explained: The Human Instincts That Fashion Gods, Spirits and Ancestors*." *London Review of Books* 24(3) (February 7): 23–24.

Sperber, Dan. 1975. *Rethinking Symbolism*, translated by A. L. Morton. Cambridge: Cambridge University Press.

———. 1996. *Explaining Culture: A Naturalistic Approach*. Cambridge, Mass.: Blackwell.

Tremlin, Todd. 2002. "A Theory of Religious Modulation: Reconciling Religious Modes and Ritual Arrangements." *Journal of Cognition and Culture* 2: 309–47.

Turner, Mark. 1996. *The Literary Mind: The Origins of Thought and Language*. New York: Oxford University Press.

Vico, Giambattista. [1744] 1961. *The New Science of Giambattista Vico*, edited by T. G. Bergin and M. H. Fisch. Ithaca, N.Y.: Cornell University Press.

Whitehouse, Harvey. 1995. *Inside the Cult: Religious Innovation and Transmission in Papua New Guinea*. Oxford: Oxford University Press.

———. 2000. *Arguments and Icons: Divergent Modes of Religiosity*. Oxford: Oxford University Press.

———. 2002. "Modes of Religiosity: Towards a Cognitive Explanation of the Sociopolitical Dynamics of Religion." *Method & Theory in the Study of Religion* 14(7): 293–315.

———. 2004. *Modes of Religiosity: A Cognitive Theory of Religious Transmission*. Walnut Creek, Calif.: Alta Mira Press.

THE ARCHAEOLOGICAL EVIDENCE II

From Ohalo to Çatalhöyük: The Development of Religiosity during the Early Prehistory of Western Asia, 20,000–7000 BCE 3

STEVEN MITHEN

EVER SINCE KATHLEEN KENYON UNDERTOOK her 1952 to 1958 excavations at Jericho and proposed a "skull cult" on the basis of plastered crania and headless burials, the origin of farming economies has been related to the development of new religious ideologies. In the decades that followed Kenyon's work, substantial evidence accumulated about the emergence of domesticated plants and animals, the establishment of sedentary villages and towns, and the development of religious practices. The idea of a "Neolithic revolution" (e.g., Childe 1958) was replaced by the acceptance of long-term continuities and a blurring of the distinctions between later Pleistocene hunter-gatherers and early Holocene farmers (e.g., see Bar-Yosef 1998). Nevertheless, the period between the late glacial maximum at 20,000 BCE and the climatic optimum at c. 7000 BCE is a time of critical social and economic change, one that laid the foundations for the first civilizations.

The striking nature of Jericho's plastered skulls has been matched by a succession of new discoveries that relate to past religious practices, notably the plaster statues of 'Ain Ghazal (Schmandt-Besserat 1997), the burials of Jerf el Ahmar (Stordeur, Helmer, and Wilcox 1997), and the carved stone pillars of Göbekli Tepe (Hauptmann 1999). These recent discoveries, however, remain eclipsed by the site of Çatalhöyük with its array of paintings, sculptures, and burials within which bulls and predatory birds are prominent (Mellaart 1967). All such evidence supports the idea that the economic changes that led from hunting and gathering to farming were intimately related to changing religious ideologies. The nature of this relationship has received limited attention from archaeologists with the exception of Jacque Cauvin, although there has been extensive consideration of the relationship between the changes in mortuary practices and social organization (e.g., Belfer-Cohen 1995; Byrd and Monahan 1995; Goring-Morris 2000; Kuijt 1996, 2000, 2001; Rollefson 2000).

In his 1994 publication *Naissance des devinités, naissance de l'agriculture, la révolution des symboles au Néolithique,* Cauvin argued that Neolithic religion was organized around two divinities, a female goddess and a subordinate bull god. Substantial emphasis was placed on the former, with the appearance of anthropomorphic figurines being contrasted with the zoomorphic art of the preceding hunter-gatherer periods. Both deities arose, Cauvin suggested, in the very earliest stages of the Neolithic age, as evidenced by the appearance of figurines and ritualistic treatment of bovine bones at Mureybet, the site he excavated in the northern Levant. From that origin, Cauvin claimed, the deities spread and became elaborated throughout the Near East, influencing the religions of Europe and Mesopotamia.

Cauvin's arguments have not fared well with the new archaeological discoveries. While additional female figurines and evidence for the involvement of bulls in religious ritual and belief have arisen, so too have male figurines and evidence for a great variety of zoomorphic art in the Neolithic, notably at Nevali Çori and Göbekli Tepe (Hauptmann 1999). Cauvin made reference to such discoveries in the 2000 English translation of his work, but appears not to have appreciated how these undermine the claim for the dominance of a single female goddess and a switch from a zoomorphic to an anthropomorphic art coincident with the start of farming.

Cauvin made little attempt to relate archaeological evidence for religious practices to anthropological theories for religious behavior. Although others have drawn on ethnographic analogies to facilitate the interpretation of specific sites (e.g., Kuijt 1996), the need persists to draw on anthropological theory and to make more extensive use of ethnographic analogy. This has become more pressing as the quantity and diversity of the archaeological evidence has increased, especially during the past decade. Fortunately, the possibility of doing so has arisen with the new willingness of anthropologists to develop general models of religious behavior that draw upon universal features of human cognition (e.g., Boyer 1994, 2001; Whitehouse 2000) and the life cycle (e.g., Bloch 1992).

In this chapter I examine the evidence for changing religious practices in western Asia between 20,000 and 7000 BCE in light of Harvey Whitehouse's modes of religiosity theory (2000).[1] I do not pretend that this theory can reconstruct the prehistoric religious ideologies in any meaningful sense—the archaeological evidence is far too sparse, biased, and ambiguous. It can, however, enrich our interpretations of specific aspects of the archaeological record, make some interpretations more plausible than others, and help us identify previously unrecognized causal links between religious practices and political structures. A framework of anthropological theory also provides a necessary context for the inevitable use of ethnographic analogy.

Reciprocally, it is unlikely that archaeological evidence can provide a formal test of anthropological theory regarding religion. But it can provide a longer-term perspective on how religiosity develops in relation to economy and society than is possible from the ethnographic record alone. Along with an attempt to engage anthropological theory and archaeological data, a key aim of this article is to explore the extent to which the religious themes evidently present at Çatalhöyük can be located in the earlier prehistory of western Asia.

I begin by providing a brief summary of the pertinent aspects of Whitehouse's theory from an archaeological perspective and comment on the immense problems facing archaeologists in their study of prehistoric religion. I then undertake a chronological review and interpretation of the archaeological record, beginning at Ohalo in 19,000 BCE and finishing at Çatalhöyük in c. 7000 BCE. In light of this vast time span, only selective aspects of the archaeological evidence can be covered. With regard to geographical range, my focus is on the Levant (present day Israel, Palestine, Jordan, and Syria) owing to its concentration of sites, but I do make some reference to sites in northern Mesopotamia and eastern Anatolia (present day Iran, Iraq, and Turkey). Finally, I attempt to draw out some generalizations regarding the development of religiosity during this critical period of human prehistory.

Any consideration of prehistoric religion necessarily involves some speculation. I have attempted to keep this to a minimum here, having provided elaborate and imaginative interpretations of this archaeological record of western Asia (and for the rest of the world) for 20,000 to 5000 BCE elsewhere (Mithen 2003).

Modes of Religiosity

Archaeologists have been dependent upon the use of ethnographic analogies for interpretation of their data. Kenyon herself referred to the Sepik River people of New Guinea when considering the skull cult of Jericho (1957). The problem, of course, is the applicability of such analogies; archaeologists always face the risk of imposing an inappropriate ethnographic present onto a quite different prehistoric past. Anthropological theories that attempt to provide general models of religious behavior by drawing on universal features of human cognition are, therefore, attractive to archaeologists.

Whitehouse's (2000) theory of modes of religiosity relates the diversity of religious practices to two dimensions of human memory, these being assumed as universal for all *H. sapiens* (Tulving 1972). Whitehouse's imagistic mode draws primarily on episodic memory—knowledge that is recalled in the context of one's own past events and experiences. Imagistic religion involves irregularly occurring, highly emotive, revelatory experiences that are open to rich idiosyncratic exegesis. The doctrinal mode, in contrast, relies on depersonalized religious experiences and depends upon semantic memory for the nature of religious knowledge. Semantic memory provides knowledge about the world that has been abstracted and generalized from either one's own or someone else's experiences. Doctrinal religion involves the frequent repetition of specific rituals and acceptance of a shared set of beliefs. Such doctrines often derive from a charismatic religious leader, while the religious practices are monitored by designated persons—a priesthood.

Whitehouse proposes that the first religions to have appeared in human prehistory were imagistic in nature, this religious mode being found in small scale, nonliterate societies. He suggests that the religion of the Upper Palaeolithic in southwestern Europe, as far as this can be inferred from cave paintings, was imagistic in nature. Doctrinal religions entail, according to Whitehouse, a centralized political organization and may be dependent upon a literate culture—although the specific role of literacy remains unclear. He suggests that the emergence of the first civilizations marked the appearance of large-scale routinized religions, monitored and policed by a priestly hierarchy. The association of specific modes of religiosity with specific patterns of political and economic organization provides some expectations for patterns in the archaeological record.

Whitehouse's theory is weakened by the fact that the preliterate societies for which an imagistic mode of religion is proposed encompass an immense degree of economic and political variability, which, in western Asia, for instance, ranged from small-scale, egalitarian, highly mobile hunter-gatherers, to hierarchically organized, sedentary hunter-gatherers, to farmers living in permanent villages with two-storey mud-brick architecture. Is there, one must ask, systematic variation between such political and economic variability and religious practices within the imagistic mode of religion? Or might features of the doctrinal mode arise prior to the invention of writing?

Archaeologists face the difficulty that any such variation in religious behavior, whether within or between Whitehouse's religious modes, might be quite undetectable in the archaeological record owing to poor preservation, limits of inference, and the simple absence of any material residues from religious behavior. Colin Renfrew (1985, 1994) has outlined the problems that the study of religion poses to archaeologists, stressing its embeddedness in the other activities of daily life and the need for explicit criteria to recognize religious activity in the archaeological record. We can simply note that Whitehouse's (2000) descriptions of the types of initiation rites involved in imagistic religions, such as the terrifying experiences of being isolated for several months in huts before being brutally attacked, penis bleeding, the piercing of the nasal septum, and the burning of forearms, would leave either no archaeological trace or residues that are more likely to be interpreted in functional than religious terms, such as living structures and utilitarian artifacts.

Many of the artifacts from the archaeological record remain quite ambiguous as to their meaning; scratched pieces of bone and stone might be replete with symbolic and religious connotations or purely mundane (e.g., see D'Errico and Now-ell 2000 for the debates about the Berekhat Ram figurine). Even when archaeolo-gists have well preserved representational art, such as ice age cave paintings or the carved pillars from Göbekli Tepe, which I describe below, the meaning of such im-ages remains unclear. One assumes that they are likely to be multivalent in a sim-ilar fashion to ethnographically documented hunter-gatherer art, such as that of the Australian aborigines (Morphy 1989). If so, archaeologists are likely to have more success at gaining access to the mundane, "outside," or public meaning of such images, rather than the "inside" meaning, which is likely to remain quite un-known without the aid of informants. For ice age cave paintings, for instance, de-pictions of horse and bison may have been undertaken because these animals were good to hunt and the rituals associated with these paintings function to transmit ecological knowledge (e.g., Mithen 1988); such ideas can be validated by analysis of the specific imagery and evidence for subsistence behavior. The images are also likely to have metaphorical meanings, perhaps relating to an ice age spirit world that remains inaccessible to us today.

It is, however, comforting for archaeologists to learn that even if such in-formants were present, such inside meanings might remain elusive. Whitehouse (2000) explains that one should expect a lack of verbally transmitted exegesis about the meaning of rituals within imagistic modes of religion, as this would de-tract from the highly personalized, emotive nature of the experience. Pascal Boyer (2001: 33) has also emphasized how in many societies, participants in religious rituals are left with "free interpretation" as to their meaning, while Marc Bloch (1992) has described how the language of many rituals is so archaic that no one has a clear idea of what they mean. Renfrew's (1994: 48) claim that "[e]very re-ligion, by definition, involves a system of beliefs which offers answers to profound existential questions . . . a coherent view of the nature of the present world, of the origins of the world and of future human destiny" appears not to be the case; such comprehensive, shared belief systems are most likely restricted to those religions falling into Whitehouse's doctrinal religious mode. Consequently, archaeologists' frustration at being unable to establish what formal religious ideology may have existed behind figurines, cult buildings, or burial practices may be unnecessary; there may have been no more than highly personal interpretations and experiences of ritual performances, which were loosely allied to a set of shared beliefs that re-mained largely undiscussed.

While this aspect of Whitehouse's imagistic mode of religion is encouraging to archaeologists, his comments about the significance of burial practices are less so. Mortuary evidence is often the only surviving trace of recognizable ritual be-havior. Whitehouse (2000: 20) suggests that within the imagistic religious mode, the social and political role of mortuary rites may take priority over any attempts to trigger religious revelations. Archaeologists implicitly recognize this, as burials have been predominately interpreted with regard to past social and political organization rather than burial ritual and religious beliefs.

The Archaeology of Religion in Western Asia, 20,000 to 7000 BCE

I am now going to turn to the archaeological evidence for religious behavior in western Asia throughout the period of environmental, economic, and social change associated with the end of the Pleistocene and the origins of agriculture, towns, and trade. This is a climatically turbulent period with global warming leading to a particularly warm and wet phase between 12,700 and 10,800 BCE, the late glacial interstadial, followed by a return to ice age conditions during the 1,000 years of the Younger Dryas and then dramatic global warming after 9600 BCE, the date used to demarcate the start of the Holocene. Throughout this period there are many minor fluctuations of climate, the complexity of which have become apparent through the study of ice cores.

The cultural developments of this period make an approximate fit onto this climatic sequence, reflecting how people responded to the marked environmental change that it induced (Mithen 2003). Archaeologists have adopted a range of cultural labels for collections of sites that share similar features (such as architectural styles, tools types, and food remains) and are broadly contemporary. Quite what such cultural entities mean in behavioral terms is unclear, but this remains a useful manner in which to organize study of this period. Consequently, I follow convention and discuss the archaeological evidence for religious practices in the succeeding Kebaran, Early Natufian, Late Natufian, Pre-Pottery Neolithic A, and Pre-Pottery Neolithic B periods in light of the anthropological models described above. I stress, however, that there are very strong continuities between these periods and considerable regional variation in cultural change. An overview of these periods for the Levant can be found in T. Levy (1995), for the equivalent periods in northern Mesopotamia in R. Matthews (2000), and for Anatolia in M. Özdoğan and N. Başgelen (1999).

Kebaran Hunter-Gatherers, 20,000 to 12,700 BCE

From the late glacial maximum until the late glacial interstadial, people throughout western Asia lived as mobile hunter-gatherers characterized as the Kebaran culture; this has been subdivided into the Kebaran and geometric Kebaran, and the latter further divided into a multitude of cultures on the basis of variations in the style of chipped stone tools (Goring-Morris 2000). The meaning of such cultural variation is unknown—the implicit assumption that these represent groups with distinct ethnic identities is most unlikely to be correct. Consequently, I deal with all of these late Pleistocene, or epipaleolithic, hunter-gatherers together. In any case the evidence for religious practices is extremely sparse.

The vast majority of archaeological evidence consists of scatters of chipped stone artifacts: animal bones, plant remains, dwellings, fireplaces, and any other potential aspect of the archaeological record are extraordinarily sparse and, when known, poorly preserved. The one exception to this generalization is the site of Ohalo II, dated to c. 19,000 BCE and located on the edge of the Sea of Galilee. Owing to the extensive charring of plant remains and animals bones, followed by the flooding of the site soon after abandonment, Ohalo II has allowed an exceptional insight into the hunter-gatherer economy of western Asia close to the last glacial maximum. Its occupants had constructed circular huts from brushwood, gathered an immense variety of wild plants, and hunted gazelle and other mammals (Nadel and Hershkovitz 1991; Nadel and Werker 1999). Their tools utilized small blades of chipped stone referred to as microliths that—although changing in their design—remained as the standard feature of human technology for at least the next 10,000 years (Goring-Morris 2000).

Amidst all of this evidence for subsistence and domestic activities, that relating to religious practices is practically nonexistent. Just one burial has been discovered at Ohalo II, that of a man placed in an extended position within a shallow grave with no grave goods (Nadel 1994). The grave was located close to the huts within an area used for domestic activity. There are no traces of art that might depict supernatural beings or encode religious concepts or any other signs of ritual behavior. Of course, it is quite possible that a vast amount of ritual activity took place at the site, involving animal and plant materials that have not survived or have been interpreted as utilitarian. Whitehouse's (2000: 65) descriptions of the metaphorical significance of pig fat and hair to the Baktaman people of New Guinea can only make us wonder about that of gazelle fat and hair to those who lived at Ohalo.

The Ohalo burial is similar to the few others found in the Kebaran period; their scarcity most likely reflects a combination of poor preservation, lack of discovery, and mortuary practices that leave no archaeological trace. Only close to the end of the Kebaran period, at a time when a less mobile lifestyle may have been emerging, do we find a more complex burial. This was excavated at Neve David, a site at the foot of the western slopes of Mt. Carmel, and most likely dates to around 15,000 BCE. A twenty-five- to thirty-year-old male was buried in a tightly flexed position on his right side between two rows of large stone. A fragment of a broken mortar that would have been used for grinding plants was placed directly over the skull, and one of a broken stone bowl was placed behind the neck and shoulder (Kaufman 1986).

With such sparse evidence for any behavior likely to be of a religious nature, we can do no more than assume that the religiosity of the Kebaran hunter-gatherers conformed to the imagistic mode as described by Whitehouse in light of the small group size, egalitarian social structure, and highly mobile nature of these hunter-gatherers.

Sedentary Hunter-Gatherers of the Early Natufian, 12,700 to 10,800 BCE

The dramatic increase in rainfall and temperature that marked the start of the late glacial interstadial appears to have had a major impact on hunter-gatherer groups in the Levant, although the archaeological record is heavily biased to the central Levant. Several settlements are known from this region in which circular semisubterranean dwellings with stone walls make an appearance, together with a vast increase in the quantity and size of grinding equipment, such as mortars, pestles, and grinding stones. It is assumed that these were used for plant processing, although the only direct evidence relates to the grinding of limestone and ochre. Numerous flint blades have "sickle gloss" suggesting the intensive harvesting of wild cereals. Microliths remain a key feature of the chipped-stone technology, many now being manufactured in a distinctive lunate shape. When such lunates dominate the microlith assemblage, the site is designated as part of the Natufian culture, a period reviewed by O. Bar-Yosef (1998, and substantially covered by Bar-Yosef and Valla [1991]). This cultural period is often divided into two phases—early and late. The former is associated with the late glacial interstadial, a time when wild plant foods and game were relatively abundant. Plant remains, however, are extremely sparse on Early (and Late) Natufian sites, while those of animals indicate intensive gazelle hunting. Seasonality evidence, along with the investment in architecture and massive grinding equipment, has been used to argue for a sedentary hunter-gatherer lifestyle (Lieberman 1993), although this remains contentious (Edwards 1989).

Two elements of the Early Natufian archaeological record may be informative about religious behavior: burial patterns and art. Burials are found in substantial numbers, notably at three major Early Natufian sites that have distinct cemeteries: Ed Wad, 'Ain Mallaha, and Hayonim Cave. These cemeteries also contain burials from the succeeding Late Natufian, which has complicated the reconstruction and interpretation of Early Natufian mortuary practices. Initial studies (e.g., Wright 1978) concluded that substantial status differentiation had existed in light of variation in grave goods. A. Belfer-Cohen (1995) and B. F. Byrd and C. M. Monahan (1995) challenged this interpretation by differentiating between the Early and Late Natufian mortuary practices. Those of the earlier period were predominantly group burials, either of several bodies buried at once or in graves that had been reopened for additional burials. The majority comprised primary burials (i.e., there had been no disturbance after the initial burial had taken place). About 25 percent of the Early Natufian burials had grave goods of shells, pierced animal teeth, gazelle horn cores, and red ochre. Some individuals were buried with elaborate decorations, such as headdresses made from dentalium shell beads.

While there has been considerable discussion as to the social and political significance of these burial practices, their implications for religious beliefs remain unclear; indeed, it may be quite impossible to draw any such implications at all. There certainly appears to be a considerable degree of latitude in burial practices, as there is a general lack of patterning between age, grave construction, and burial goods. Byrd and Monahan (1995) suggest that the distribution of grave goods was generated by a series of local factors, including local traditions, age-set membership, and sentimentality with regard to the inclusion of grave goods with the very young. We gain the impression that burial practices were open to individual or family interpretation as would be expected in an imagistic mode of religion, as opposed to the imposition of a doctrinally defined procedure that would create greater uniformity in the burial record.

Natufian Art

Compared to the preceding Kebaran period, the Natufian has an abundance of "art" objects (Bar-Yosef and Belfer-Cohen 1998). With regard to representational imagery, animals are more frequently depicted than humans, being found incised on stone and bone surfaces as well as carved in the round. The most frequent image is that of a young ungulate (probably gazelle) as found sculptured on the haft of sickles from El Wad and Kebara Cave, and carved in stone at the site of Nahal Oren. Other depicted animals include a baboon, a dog, and an owl. Human depictions are scarce; other than highly schematic and ambiguous images, there is a naturalistic human head and face from El Wad and a pair of humans in a face-to-face pose apparently engaging in sexual intercourse from the site of 'Ain Sakhri.

Complex geometric designs with no apparent representational status are found incised on utilitarian objects, such as stone mortars, bowls, and bone spatulas, as well as on pieces of shell and stone with no evident functional purpose. Some designs have been found repeatedly, notably a ladder design depicted on bone spatulas from both Hayonim Cave and Kebara (Bar-Yosef and Belfer-Cohen 1998). Several incised stone slabs are also known. These carry complex designs that have been described as "notational in character" (Bar-Yosef and Belfer-Cohen 1998: 255).

Whether any or all of these "art" objects relate to ritual practices and religious ideas remains unclear. It is well known from the art of ethnographically documented hunter-gatherers that even simple geometric designs may encode complex religious notions and mythological events, while naturalistic depictions of animals may encode abstract concepts (e.g., see Faulstich 1992 for Warlpiri art). It may be possible that artifacts such as the horn core from Nahal Oren, which depicts a human head at one end and an ungulate at the other, might be representing the possibility of transformation between these species, this being a common feature in many hunter-gatherer mythologies and exemplary of the counterintuitive features that Boyer (2001) describes (i.e., one species cannot turn into another).

When considering the Early Natufian record, the impression we gain is of settlements in the central Levant sharing a range of cultural attributes and religious ideas, but having the opportunity of practicing and interpreting these in their own fashion. As Belfer-Cohen (1995: 16) concluded when studying the burial evidence, "it seems that besides some broad similarities in the treatment of the dead, every site had its very own local set of traditions as regards the burials. Such a pattern of variation has been observed for the jewellery and decorative items of the various Natufian base camps." This sounds most similar to Whitehouse's characterization of local communities that adopt an imagistic mode of religiosity as developing their own distinctive versions of religious traditions (2000: 49) and perhaps corresponds to what he means by a "fragmented political landscape" (2000: 31).

Hunter-Gatherers of the Younger Dryas, 10,800 to 9600 BCE

The Late Natufian corresponds to the period of the Younger Dryas—a millennium of low temperatures and drought that led to a substantial reduction in the availability of plant and animal foods. This had a substantial impact upon settlement patterns: the abandonment of the (semi-) sedentary sites such as 'Ain Mallaha and a return to a highly mobile existence, not dissimilar to that of the Kebaran period. Whether the Younger Dryas was the only cause of this settlement change remains unclear. There may have been substantial population growth during the Early Natufian, resulting in an overexploitation of the wild foodstuffs around settlements, along with a deterioration of human health (Belfer-Cohen, Schepartz, and Arensburg 1991; Smith 1991). Climate change and resource depletion most likely provided a potent combination that forced people to return to a mobile lifestyle. Late Natufian settlement sites are extremely sparse; those known, such as Salibiya I in the Jordan Valley (Crabtree et al. 1991) are poorly preserved, but suggest a broadening of the diet to include a wider range of small game.

Belfer-Cohen (1995) and Byrd and Monahan (1995) identified significant changes in burial practices that appear to be a direct reflection of a more mobile lifestyle, although Ian Kuijt (1996) believes that changing social attitudes are of greater significance. There are three key developments: (1) a marked reduction of the placement of grave goods with the complete absence of any decorated burials, (2) the predominance of individual over group burial, and (3) a marked increase in secondary burial. The latter often involves the removal of crania from primary burials and their reburial within a skull cache.

Many of the individual, secondary burials are located within the Early Natufian cemeteries. One scenario for Late Natufian mortuary practices involves occasional gatherings of Late Natufian groups at the abandoned Early Natufian settlements, which may have had dilapidated houses overgrown with weeds. Each group may have arrived with the bones, or perhaps just the skulls, of their deceased members that had been exhumed from their primary burial locations. The Early Natufian cemeteries may have been reopened and the bones positioned adjacent to their ancestors who had once lived at the now abandoned sites. Such occasions can be readily imagined as highly emotive events, the type of revelatory experiences that become embedded in episodic memory and that Whitehouse describes as the key to imagistic religiosity. This would especially be the case if such gatherings occurred infrequently, perhaps every decade, so that each person would remember just one occasion from his or her childhood—a memory involving who else was present and perhaps stories about the people who had once lived all year round at the now abandoned settlements.

While this is a speculative interpretation of the archaeological data, there can be no question that the reburial of bones and the creation of skull caches within Early Natufian cemeteries would have been highly emotive experiences. There is considerable variability in how such bones were arranged, suggestive of the subtle innovations in ritual practices that Whitehouse (2000: 93) argues are important in shaping religious episodes within the imagistic mode.

Hunter-Gatherer-Cultivators of the Pre-Pottery Neolithic A, c. 10,000 to 8500 BCE

While permanent settlement may have arisen at Hallan Çemi during the late Pleistocene, it did not reappear in the Levant until the dramatic climatic change that marked the end of the Pleistocene. This occurred at c. 9600 BCE with a substantial increase in rainfall and temperature, enabling the establishment of permanent villages in the Jordan and Euphrates Valleys. These have circular dwellings reminiscent of the Early Natufian, but are predominantly located on alluvial soils, where cereal and legumes could have been cultivated. Such plants most likely remained biologically wild for much, perhaps all, of the Pre-Pottery Neolithic A (PPNA), with the domestic varieties arising from the cultivation practices that were now employed, such as weeding, watering, pest control, and reseeding. While direct evidence remains scarce, substantial experimental and ethnoarchaeological research has been undertaken to explore the transition to domesticated crops (e.g., Hillman and Davies 1990; Anderson 1991).

The first identified of these new settlements was Jericho—a series of circular mud-brick dwellings located at the base of the Tell and partly surrounded by a wall with a massive stone-built tower. Kenyon's excavations found a large number of burials, indicating similar mortuary practices to those of the Late Natufian—many lacked their skull, while secondary burials and skull caches were located. Similar burial practices were found at other PPNA sites, such as Netiv Hagdud, also located in the Jordan Valley (Bar-Yosef and Gopher 1997).

When reviewing Natufian and PPNA mortuary practices in 1996, Kuijt argued that although continuities are substantial, burial in the PPNA was relatively more standardized. Its key features were individual burials, an absence of grave goods, and the removal of skulls from almost all adults, but only from a small proportion of children. The majority of PPNA burials are located below floors, in the fill of abandoned houses, or in open spaces. They are all closely associated with domestic architecture—the dead are kept in very close vicinity to the living.

Kuijt (1996) argues that such mortuary practices in both the Natufian and PPNA derive from ritual events organized for the veneration or worshipping of ancestors, while serving to reaffirm community identity and egalitarian beliefs, the latter achieved by the denial of social differences via the absence of grave goods and the homogeneity of grave construction. He recognized that burials located within the Jericho tower were an anomaly (Kuijt 1996: 324–25). Twelve bodies (men, women, and children) had been pushed through a hole cut in the wall of the tower as a single mass burial after the tower's internal passageway had fallen into disuse. There was no secondary burial for these individuals, the only group of adults cached together at Jericho without skull removal.

The Jericho tower burials challenged Kuijt's (1996: 325) notion of a "highly standardized mortuary system." Excavations undertaken during the late 1990s have further enhanced the impression of diversity, rather than standardization, of mortuary practices during the PPNA. The excavation at Wadi Faynan 16 (WF16) in the southern Levant has provided a primary burial of an adult with the skull intact, but apparently wrenched out of place to lie upon a stone pillow and partially exposed above the dwelling floor (Bill Finlayson, personal communication). At Jerf al Ahmar, located in the northern Levant, a skull cache involved placing three skulls within a pit where a fire had recently been burning, or may still have been alight, and then sealing the pit with pebbles and stones (Stordeur et al. 1996; Stordeur, Helmer, and Willcox 1997).

Göbekli Tepe: An Early Neolithic Hilltop Sanctuary

Göbekli Tepe is entirely unique in the Early Neolithic archaeology of western Asia and is requiring archaeologists to reconsider their understanding of Neolithic religion and the origin of agriculture. Although excavated since 1996 (Schmidt 1994, 1996, 1998, 2001), the nature of the site has only revealed itself in the most recent field seasons of work. It has become apparent that several semisubterranean circular structures were constructed into the summit of a limestone hill during the PPNA, most likely around 9500 BCE (Schmidt, personal communication). These were up to ten meters in diameter and had stone-built walls. In the center of each structure, two massive stone pillars were erected, each weighing around seven tons. Additional pillars were erected at regular intervals around the walls and separated by benches. The pillars had been quarried from local limestone. Their surfaces were carefully prepared and then carved with wild animals, including foxes, snakes, boars, aurochs, and water birds. Various abstract symbols were also engraved upon their surfaces.

There are no traces of domestic activity at the site, leading the excavator to describe it as a Neolithic hilltop religious sanctuary—an assessment that cannot be challenged on present evidence. Its construction required a vast amount of time and effort. The ambition of those who undertook the work is evident from one of the stone pillars that was not completely removed from the bedrock; it would have weighed at least thirty tons and stood seven meters high.

Schmidt (personal communication) suggests that Göbekli Tepe functioned as an aggregation site to which people came from a radius of perhaps up to 200 kilometers for their joint religious practices. The scale of undertaking would certainly appear to be far beyond that of a single hunter-gatherer community; in fact, it is quite staggering to behold even for a joint effort by many hunter-gatherer groups. The quantity of food to feed such gatherings and the numbers of those who built the structures and then quarried, prepared, and carved the pillars must have been substantial. It is interesting to note, therefore, that the Karacadağ Hills are no more than thirty kilometers from Göbekli Tepe and can be seen from its summit. Geneticists have pinpointed the location as the most likely origin of domestic wheat owing to its close genetic similarity to the wild strains that still grow in those hills (Heun et al. 1997). The possibility arises, therefore, that it may have been from the intensive cultivation of wild cereals to feed those who worked and gathered for religious ceremonies at Göbekli Tepe that the domestic strains arose. The seed grain from these may have then spread around the Fertile Crescent by people dispersing from Göbekli Tepe to their own settlements.

This scenario places the developments of religious ideology as the cause of plant domestication and, hence, farming economies, just as Cauvin (1994) proposed. In contrast to Cauvin's views, however, it suggests that domesticated wheat arose as an accidental by-product of the intensive cultivation required to support the aggregations of people at a religious site, rather than from changing attitudes toward the natural world brought about by new religious beliefs.

The animal depictions on the pillars at Göbekli Tepe have clear links to the art of Jerf el Ahmar and Nemrik and to the raptor-dominated bird remains from Zawi Chemi Shanidar and WF16. Quite different, however, is the investment made into such artwork and the religious infrastructure. It is difficult to imagine that this may have occurred without coordination by priests and in light of a strongly held, shared doctrine of religious beliefs. This would place the religious activity closer to the doctrinal than to the imagistic mode of religion as proposed by Whitehouse, or cause us to recognize that the amount of diversity within the imagistic mode calls this dualistic model into question.

Farming Villages of the Pre-Pottery Neolithic B, c. 8500 to 6500 BCE

Within a millennium of the first Levantine farming villages being established, there was a major and widespread transformation in architectural styles, technology, and economy that is denoted as the start of the Pre-Pottery Neolithic B (PPNB). Small circular dwellings were replaced by rectangular buildings constructed from stone or mud brick, some of which were internally partitioned and had two storeys. Floors and walls were plastered. The sizes of such rooms vary, suggesting a differentiation of function, but the rarity of occupational debris confounds any clear insight. Some are likely to have been storerooms and others dwellings for extended families. Along with this new architecture, settlement size increased dramatically, although population numbers are difficult to ascertain, as houses may not have been contemporaneously occupied. 'Ain Ghazal was one of the largest of the new Pre-Pottery Neolithic B villages and covered thirty acres, perhaps with a population of 3,000 people (Rollefson and Simmons 1987). Such settlements complemented much smaller villages and hamlets, especially in environmentally marginal areas. Hunting and gathering is likely to have continued, perhaps by townspeople on a seasonal basis or by people who traded wild game for cereals and other items from the farming settlements. Trade networks were extensive, especially involving obsidian and seashells.

These developments are associated with the appearance of mixed farming economies—domesticated cereals, legumes, sheep, goat, and cattle. Several new types of stone points appear, which are larger and more standardized than the El Khiam points characteristics of the PPNA. But, in spite of the immense technological advances associated with the architecture and production of plaster, these societies remain aceramic, making bowls from stone and (one assumes) organic materials. PPNB settlements are found throughout the Levant and show a remarkable degree of architectural homogeneity. It would be surprising if such towns developed and functioned without some form of leadership, but—other than in the possibility of selective mortuary treatment—there is no evidence for social differentiation as one might find in the form of rich burials or particularly grand domestic dwellings. Nevertheless, the sociopolitical features of the PPNB tend toward those that Whitehouse (2000) associates with a doctrinal mode of religiosity: large in scale with high degrees of uniformity and centralization. There are no traces of literacy, although D. Schmandt-Besserat (1992) argued that geometric clay tokens used at 'Ain Ghazal provided the foundation from which writing systems developed.

Mortuary Practices and Plastered Skulls

PPNB mortuary practices show substantial continuities with those of the PPNA and have been summarized by Kuijt (2000, 2001), who interprets them as serving to reinforce a collective ethos to encourage social cohesion and solidarity. Adults were predominately buried on their sides in individual graves without any grave goods and located within courtyards and middens. The graves were plastered over, but marked, so that after sufficient time had elapsed for defleshing, they could be reopened and the skulls removed. Secondary burials were also created in courtyards and middens, along with skull caches that were sometimes located within wall niches. Children were buried in similar locations as well as under house walls and in postsockets for interior supports. They were left undisturbed and intact.

The manner in which some of the exhumed skulls were treated represents an elaboration upon earlier practices. Some were painted and others elaborately modeled into faces with plaster, paint, and shells for eyes. They may even have been given wigs in light of an absence of plaster on the cranium itself. Notable specimens come from Jericho, 'Ain Ghazal, Kfar HaHoresh, and Beisamoun, all of which have recently been analyzed in detail by Y. Goren, N. Goring-Morris, and I. Segal (2001). They identified significant differences in the specific construction methods used at different sites, even though the plastered skulls conformed to the same general design and described their manufacture as "non-canonized technical production."

The plastered skulls have been found within pits, sometimes as part of a cache, and it is unclear whether they were displayed prior to burial. Two specimens from Beisamoun were found on the floor of a dwelling and appeared to be associated with a collection of arrowheads. It seems unlikely that any were intended to be lifelike portrayals of the deceased (Goren, Goring-Morris, and Segal 2001); some are distinctly nonlifelike as the face has been modeled over the cranium and upper jaw alone, although one specimen from Jericho made use of the lower jaw and achieved a naturalistic appearance. The non-portrait-like nature of the plastered skulls recalls Boyer's (2001) suggestions that the latter stages of mortuary practice occur after the cognitive "person files" of the deceased have been turned off.

Another form of skull treatment has been identified from the material excavated in the cave of Nahal Hemar, located in the Judean desert far from any known settlement (Bar-Yosef and Schick 1989). These skulls lacked any plaster additions, but the crania had been decorated with strips of bitumen arranged in a network of diamonds, perhaps to attach hair that has since decayed. The cave itself provided a remarkable array of items likely to have been involved in ritual, including a stone mask painted in red and green, plaster faces with human hair attached, and fragments of plaster statues modeled on armatures of reeds. These statues are assumed to have been similar to the well-preserved statues from 'Ain Ghazal, as is described below. Numerous fragments of woven material survived, including part of a conical woven cap.

One interpretation of the Nahal Hemar collection is that these were to be used in ritualistic ceremonies and kept in a secret or sacred location, perhaps with a guardian. This might be expected if the religiosity of this period remained imagistic in nature. Whitehouse (2000: 63) describes how mystery, excessive secrecy, and danger are essential in ethnographically documented rituals, such as the male initiation rites of the New Guinea Baktaman.

Plaster Statues and Figurines

Thirty-two plaster statues were discovered at 'Ain Ghazal in two separate caches, each buried within a pit inside an abandoned building and dating a few centuries apart (Schmandt-Besserat 1998). The earlier cache contained twenty-five specimens—thirteen complete figures and twelve heads and busts. Some were a meter tall, substantially larger than any other "art" item from the PPNB, and have been described by Schmandt-Besserat as "monumental." The second cache contained seven statues, three of which were two-headed busts. All of the statues were made by covering reed armatures with plaster; traces of paint survive, while in some cases the eyes were strikingly depicted with bitumen. The heads and necks were disproportionately large compared to the body, genitals were omitted, and, although practically two dimensional, the statues were balanced so that they could have stood up. Their discovery allowed the Nahel Hemar plaster fragments as well as two collections from Jericho to be interpreted as the remnants of similar statue caches. There are some striking similarities between the Jericho and 'Ain Ghazal figures, such as the presence of a modeled foot with six toes in both collections.

Various interpretations have been proposed for the plaster statues—venerated ancestors, representations of ghosts and of deities. Their size alone suggests that any related ritualistic ceremony had a more public nature than those involving plastered skulls and burial, both of which appear to have been associated with domestic contexts, perhaps involving collective households (Kuijt 2000)— G. Rollefson (2000) suggests that there was a hierarchy of ritual organization. Schmandt-Besserat (1998) has suggested the statues might represent a pantheon. She is impressed by their similarities to the cuneiform descriptions and depictions of Babylonian deities, notably the two-headed figures and postures with hands framing breasts.

Schmandt-Besserat (1997) has also looked to cuneiform texts as a means of interpreting the animal figurines found at 'Ain Ghazal and other PPNB sites in the Levant. Of these, 126 have been recovered from 'Ain Ghazal ranging in size from three to five centimeters with great homogeneity in form and manufacturing technique. The majority depicts bulls, while goats, rams, gazelle, and a boar are also represented. They were made from coarse clay that was simply coiled and then pinched into the chosen form. The animals have short, schematic legs and exaggerated foreparts with large heads and sweeping horns, powerful necks, and withers. While such figures have been interpreted as children's toys, some appear to have been used in ritual activity and all might have been of a religious significance. Two bull figures were found in a small pit sealed by a limestone slab in the corner of a room. Both had been stabbed with flint blades in the throat and abdomen. Another pit at 'Ain Ghazal contained twenty-four bull figures, all but one of which appeared to have been made by the same hand and discarded almost immediately along with unused clay. Another bull figurine was found at the base of a plaster-lined pit below three cattle metacarpals, one of which had been deliberately incised with crosshatchings and another with long striations (Rollefson and Simmons 1987). Many other bull figurines were discarded into fireplaces. Schmandt-Besserat (1997) suggests that the animal figurines may have been used in similar rituals to those documented in cuneiform texts from the third to the first millennium BCE. Such rituals were used for tasks such as counteracting bad omens or to bring good luck.

Forty human figurines were also recovered from 'Ain Ghazal, and they have been found in other PPNB settlements. Some are clearly female, but the majority lack any sexual characteristics. All but one of the 'Ain Ghazal figurines consist either of a headless body or a detached head—the figurines were manufactured and then decapitated (Rollefson 2000), a direct parallel with mortuary practices.

Rituals involving animal and human figurines appear compatible with the imagistic-type religiosity suggested by the mortuary practices and plastered skulls. But the appearance of buildings that are most likely temples toward the end of the PPNB period supports the interpretation of the plaster statues as suggesting more

communal, perhaps doctrinal-type, religious activity. Such a purpose has been suggested for buildings in Jericho (Kenyon and Holland 1981) and Beidha (Kirkbride
1968), but the most convincing examples come from 'Ain Ghazal. Toward the end
of this settlement's existence, three new types of building appeared, diversifying
what had been a remarkable degree of architectural homogeneity of rectangular,
domestic dwellings. Rollefson (1998) describes the appearance of buildings with
apsidal ends that became scattered within neighborhoods of the domestic
dwellings; small circular buildings were also constructed. These were repeatedly re-
floored and interpreted by Rollefson as shrines associated with several families or
a lineage. Two special buildings are also known from the final phases of 'Ain
Ghazal. The most impressive of these is located high on a slope in full view of the
whole settlement. It is unique in lacking a plaster floor and in the nature of its
surviving fittings and furniture. A square, red-painted hearth was positioned in the
center of the room surrounded by seven flat limestone slabs; there were several
standing blocks of limestone and an anthropomorphic orthostat. Rollefson
(1998) suggests that the building may have functioned as a temple for the whole
community.

Ancestor Worship and Religious Leaders

If we take the evidence for religiosity in the PPNB from the central and southern
Levant as a whole, we find both strong continuities with that of the PPNA and
Natufian, especially in mortuary practices, along with significant developments involving "monumental" statues, dedicated buildings, and funerary centers. It would
indeed be remarkable if the nature of religiosity had not evolved in light of the
major changes in settlement and economy. Whether the new developments suggest
a trend toward a doctrinal mode of religiosity remains unclear.

One common interpretation is that the mortuary practices indicate a cult of
the ancestors or even ancestor worship (e.g., Goring-Morris 2000; Kuijt 2000;
Rollefson 2000). When the archaeological evidence is seen in light of Whitehouse's model of imagistic religiosity, this interpretation might be questioned, or
at least seen from a different perspective. People's primary concern is frequently
what to do with a dead body; while their rituals are about sending the dead into
another world, they often have extremely vague notions about the nature of their
other world and the ancestors who live within it. Boyer (2001: 210) cites the example of the Kwaio people. Very few of them thought about the exact process
whereby people who died became ancestors; those who did tended to have rather
incoherent personal intuitions. Such vagueness, however, did not prevent the
Kwaio from talking to their ancestors everyday and interpreting most events in
their lives in terms of what the ancestors wished to happen.

From this perspective we should avoid thinking of the Pre-Pottery Neolithic people of western Asia as engaging in some formal worshipping of their ancestors. Instead, we should envisage a constant dialogue with the dead, with ancestors whose state of being is left undiscussed and whose presence in the world is more tolerated than venerated.

This imagistic interpretation of the archaeological evidence implies the absence of a formal priesthood. There are no archaeological traces of such priests, unless it was the skulls of such people that were inserted into caches or underwent the special treatment of plastering and decoration. Several specialists of the PPNB period have argued the likelihood that some form of priesthood existed. In addition to Goring-Morris's suggestion of site guardians at Kfar HaHoresh, Kuijt (2001: 94) has proposed that "ritual practitioners must have served a central role within these communities, for through the use and construction of skulls as masks they facilitated contact with the ancestors in a way that must have been distinct from that of merely participating in primary and secondary mortuary rituals." Rollefson (1998: 57) has suggested, "Community-wide observances might have been more seasonally oriented, and here once could argue that some panel of full-time 'priests' may have been in charge of solemn rites and festivities." I remain unconvinced, however, preferring to envisage rituals being conducted and interpreted on familial and individual bases.

Religion and Ritual at Çatalhöyük

Çatalhöyük is a large mound on the Konya Plain, a small fraction of which was excavated by James Mellaart in the 1960s. He revealed a remarkable series of buildings with elaborate murals and sculptures that entirely transformed our understanding of the Pre-Pottery Neolithic. These included plaster models of bulls' heads emerging from walls, paintings of what appear to be hunting scenes with massive animals and diminutive people, paintings of schematic vultures attacking headless people, handprints, and many abstract designs. Sculptures included many female figurines, some of which were particularly impressive, such as one depicting a seated woman flanked by two leopards, which was found in a grain bin (Mellaart 1967).

When discovered in the 1960s, the images at Çatalhöyük were without precedent in the prehistory of western Asia. It is now possible to trace certain themes back into the early Holocene and even the late Pleistocene. This is certainly the case with much of the mortuary ritual that involves skull caching and the placement of primary and secondary burials in contexts associated with domestic activities. The depiction of raptors at Çatalhöyük is now known to follow their representation at Göbekli Tepe, Nevali Çori, and Nemrik and a likely ritualistic role in PPNA settlements and the late Pleistocene site of Zawi Chemi Shanidar. As Cauvin (1994) argued, the auroch or bull appears to have been associated with ritual throughout the earlier Neolithic of western Asia.

Mellaart interpreted the Çatalhöyük as containing two types of structures: domestic dwellings and shrines. He argued for a mythological and ritual system centered on the Great Goddess, who "as the only source of life . . . became associated with the processes of agriculture, with the taming and nourishing of domesticated animals, with the ideas of increase, abundance and fertility" (1967: 202). More recently, he described this goddess as the "source and mistress of all life, the Creatress, the Great Mother, the symbol of life itself" (Mellaart, Hirsch, and Balpinar 1989: 23) (both quotes cited in Voigt 2000: 253–455). The large number of burials that Mellaart excavated provided some indication of social differentiation, but there was no clear evidence for particularly powerful or wealthy individuals. Nevertheless, he has recently argued, "Evidently Çatalhöyük had established rules of some sort. Shrine after shrine was rebuilt along essentially the same lines though the decoration of paintings and relief might vary greatly" (1998: 36–38).

The sheer size of the settlement, the suggestion of a deity and rulers, and the architectural conformity of the structures would suggest that we are dealing with a type of religiosity that tends toward the doctrinal rather than imagistic mode in Whitehouse's terms, even though there is no evidence of literacy. There are, however, substantial doubts regarding the veracity of Mellaarts interpretations, partly derived from the new excavation and research program directed by Ian Hodder (1996, 1999, 2000) and partly from a reevaluation of Mellaart's evidence. Hodder has argued that the term *shrine* is inappropriate, as each structure appears to blend a rich mix of domestic and nondomestic activities, these being carefully segregated in space. He questions the idea of an all-powerful goddess and a priestly elite, arguing for "daily domestic rituals and a set of beliefs in which both men and women play a role" (1996: 11), while the imagery may "have little to do with representation and symbolism at all. It may be more like a tool, used to control or communicate with animals, spirits, and ancestors" (1999: 190). A great deal of the Çatalhöyük imagery has a violent aspect to it—vulture beaks, bull horns breaking through walls, modeled female breasts split open to hold the jaws of fox and weasel. One can easily imagine such imagery being used in the types of rites of terror described by Whitehouse (2000).

In these regards, therefore, the interpretations of Çatalhöyük emerging from the 1990s research appear more compatible with an imagistic mode of religiosity. But one key aspect of Mellaart's interpretation remains valid—the extent of architectural conformity among buildings regarding the locations of domestic fittings and wall art. Hodder's program of work has verified claims for annual replastering of walls within the main rooms, and in some cases at much more frequent intervals, along with regular replastering of the bull-head sculptures (W. Matthews, personal communication). From this, one gains an impression of immense conformity and routinization in people's lives that seems more compatible with Whitehouse's notion of doctrinal religiosity. Whether this impression will be verified by full publication of the new research remains to be seen.

Conclusion

When taken as a whole, the archaeological evidence from the early prehistory of western Asia appears more compatible with Whitehouse's imagistic, rather than doctrinal, mode of religiosity. There is a considerable degree of intra- and inter-site variation in any one period with regard to how particular rituals were undertaken within a regional framework of shared ideas. Many of these are readily interpreted as having been highly emotive experiences that would have become embedded in episodic memory. Much of the imagery from the later periods seems compatible with ideas about rites of terror.

Characterizing religion through this period as imagistic in nature suggests that we should avoid terms such as *ancestor worship*, which implies a more formally defined concept of the afterlife and of ancestors themselves and is frequently used in archaeological texts. Notions about the afterlife are likely to have remained nondiscursive so as to maintain the significance of episodic and emotive memories; individuals and families likely had considerable freedom to develop their own personal notions about ancestors and other supernatural beings and about the meaning of the rituals they undertook. Ancestors are likely to have had a pervasive presence in daily life, influencing the course of events and requiring engagement via ritual, but not necessarily to have been especially honored. The mortuary rituals can be most effectively seen as a means to ensure passage of a deceased person into the ancestral world, rather than as the worship of ancestors.

There are at least three themes in west Asian prehistoric rituals that persist over the long term. Birds of prey appear to be a key element of religious thought from the people who are likely to have worn vulture costumes at Zawi Chemi Shanidar to those who painted vultures on the walls of Çatalhöyük. Similarly, bovids appear to have had a presence in ritual activities over several thousands of years, from the time that the auroch skull was hung on a wall at Hallen Çemi to the modeling of bulls' heads in plaster at Çatalhöyük. If we assume that there were supernatural beings associated with raptors and bulls, then Boyer's arguments would suggest that such beings likely had both intuitive and nonintuitive elements to have had such long-term survival in cultural history. In both cases, the supernatural entities are likely to have had a belief-desire psychology and to have been "full access strategic agents." (Boyer 2001: 159). The third persistent theme entails the appearance of pillars within what are assumed to be domestic dwellings in PPNA settlements of the Levant and ritualistic settings in Anatolia. Whether there are significant links and religious associations remains unclear.

Cauvin's (1994) claim for a mother goddess as the prime deity of the Pre-Pottery Neolithic, one related to new concerns regarding fertility that arose with agriculture, has become less convincing during the last decade. Female figurines remain an important feature of the archaeological record but lack the priority that Cauvin proposed. It is surprising that so little of the evidence relating to ritual during the period under review can be directly linked to the changing of economies from hunting and gathering to farming. One could make rather clichéd proposals about heads being removed from people as a metaphor for heads being removed from wheat and barley, but the extreme rarity of imagery regarding reproduction and fertility is striking. The plaster statues from 'Ain Ghazal are practically asexual in character. Indeed, one of the most noticeable features is that the imagery at what are likely to be the most advanced farming settlements—Çatalhöyük and Nevali Çori—is primarily about not just wild animals, but those that are particularly dangerous.

Rather than having any specific link to changing economies, the development of religious ideas and ritual, especially those concerning mortuary practices, can be closely linked with changing patterns of social interaction that were a consequence of permanent village life, as has been so persuasively argued by Kuijt (1996, 2000, 2001). In this regard, the specific beliefs and ritual actions themselves are of secondary importance.

In summary, the anthropological theory of religion proposed by Whitehouse can enrich our interpretations of the archaeological record, but any formal testing is impossible. The whole of the period under review in this article, that from Ohalo to Çatalhöyük, most likely falls into Whitehouse's imagistic mode of religion. As there is very considerable diversity within both socioeconomic organization and ritual during this time, I find that this category is far too gross to be of substantial value. The very considerable uniformity of architecture, economy, and religious practice in the PPNB settlements of the Levant cannot be accounted for if local communities had no more than their own individual imagistic practices. Some form of shared doctrine seems most likely; but this is at least 5,000 years before the invention of writing and there is no evidence for a priestly class—unless it is represented by the plastered skulls. The site of Göbekli Tepe also questions the utility of the imagistic doctrinal model. Although this is a product of a hunter-gatherer, nonliterate economy, the extent of investment in construction suggests a degree of religious organization more typical of the doctrinal than the imagistic religious mode.

It becomes apparent that the dualistic model of imagistic versus doctrinal models of religiosity is too coarse to be of value to prehistoric archaeologists. As defined by Whitehouse, the imagistic mode would cover practically the whole of prehistory ranging from the activities of mobile hunter-gatherers to those living in substantial towns. It is evident that more attention needs to be focused on patterned variation within the imagistic mode within anthropologically documented communities before addressing how this might vary in prehistory. Nevertheless, Whitehouse's characterization of the imagistic religious mode has been recognized as useful for interpreting the archaeological data from western Asia.

Note

1. All dates in this chapter are in calendar years BCE based on the calibration of radiocarbon dates. For detailed chronology and site-specific radiocarbon dates see Mithen 2003.

References

Anderson, P. 1991. "Harvesting of Wild Cereals during the Natufian as Seen from the Experimental Cultivation and Harvest of Wild Einkorn Wheat and Microwear Analysis of Stone Tools." In *The Natufian Culture in the Levant*, edited by O. Bar-Yosef and F. R. Valla, 521–56. Ann Arbor, Mich.: International Monographs in Prehistory.

Bar-Yosef, O. 1998. "The Natufian Culture in the Levant, Theshold to the Origins of Agriculture." *Evolutionary Anthropology* 6: 159–77.

Bar-Yosef, O., and A. Belfer-Cohen. 1998. "Natufian Imagery in Perspective." *Rivista di Scienze Preistoriche* 42: 247–63.

———. 1999. "Encoding Information: Unique Natufian Objects from Hayonim Cave, Western Galilee, Israel." *Antiquity* 73: 402–10.

Bar-Yosef, O., and A. Gopher, eds. 1997. *An Early Neolithic Village in the Jordan Valley. Part I: The Archaeology of Netiv Hagdud*. Cambridge, Mass.: Peabody Museum of Archaeology and Ethnology, Harvard University.

Bar-Yosef, O., and T. Schick. 1989. "Early Neolithic Organic Remains form Nahal Hamar Cave." *National Geographic Research* 5(2): 176–90.

Bar-Yosef, O., and F. R. Valla, eds. 1991. *The Natufian Culture in the Levant*. Ann Arbor, Mich.: International Monographs in Prehistory.

Belfer-Cohen, A. 1995. "Rethinking Social Stratification in the Natufian Culture: The Evidence from Burials." In *The Archaeology of Death in the Ancient Near East*, edited by S. Campbell and A. Green, 9–16. Oxford: Oxbow Books, Monograph no. 51.

Belfer-Cohen, A., A. Schepartz, and B. Arensburg. 1991. "New Biological Data for the Natufian Populations in Israel." In *The Natufian Culture in the Levant*, edited by O. Bar-Yosef and F. R. Valla, 411–24. Ann Arbor, Mich.: International Monographs in Prehistory.

Bloch, Marc. 1992. *Prey into Hunter: The Politics of Religious Experience*. Cambridge: Cambridge University Press.

Boyer, Pascal. 1994. *The Naturalness of Religious Ideas: A Cognitive Theory of Religion*. Berkeley: University of California Press.

————. 2001. *Religion Explained.* New York: Basic Books.

Byrd, B. F., and C. M. Monahan. 1995. "Death, Mortuary Ritual and Natufian Social Structure." *Journal of Anthropological Archaeology* 14: 251–87.

Cauvin, J. 1994. *Naissance des divinités, naissance de l'agriculture, la révolution des symboles au Néolithique.* Paris: CNRS.

————. 2000. *The Birth of the Gods and the Origins of Agriculture.* Cambridge: Cambridge University Press.

Childe, V. G. 1958. *The Prehistory of European Society.* Oxford: Clarendon Press.

Crabtree, P. J., D. V. Campana, A. Belfer-Cohen, and D. E. Bar-Yosef. 1991. "First Results of the Excavations at Salibiya I, Lower Jordan Valley." In *The Natufian Culture in the Levant*, edited by O. Bar-Yosef and F. R. Valla, 161–72. Ann Arbor, Mich.: International Monographs in Prehistory.

D'Errico, F., and A. Nowell. 2000. "A New Look at the Berekhat Ram Figurine: Implications for the Origins of Symbolism." *Cambridge Archaeological Journal* 10: 123–67.

Edwards, P. 1989. "Problems of Recognizing Earliest Sedentism: The Natufian Example." *Journal of Mediterranean Archaeology* 2: 5–48.

Endicott, K. 1979. *Batek Negrito Religion.* Oxford: Clarendon Press.

Faulstich, P. 1992. "Of Earth and Dreaming: Abstraction and Naturalism in Warlpiri Art." In *Rock Art and Ethnography*, edited by M. J. Morwood and D. R. Hobbs, 19–23. Melbourne: Occasional AURA publication No. 5.

Goren, Y., N. Goring-Morris, and I. Segal. 2001. "The Technology of Skull Modelling in the Pre-Pottery Neolithic B (PPNB): Regional Variability, the Relation of Technology and Iconography and Their Archaeological Implications." *Journal of Archaeological Science* 28: 671–90.

Goring-Morris, N. 2000. "The Quick and the Dead: The Social Context of Aceramic Neolithic Mortuary Practices as Seen from Kfar HaHoresh." In *Life in Neolithic Farming Communities: Social Organization, Identity, and Differentiation*, edited by I. Kuijt, 103–26. New York: Kluwer Academic/Plenum Publishers.

Hauptmann, H. 1999. "The Urfa Region." In *Neolithic in Turkey: The Cradle of Civilization, New Discoveries*, edited by M. Özdoğan and N. Başgelen, 65–86. Istanbul: Arkeoloji ve Sanat Yayinlari.

Heun, M., R. Schafer-Pregl, D. Klawan, R. Castagna, M. Accerbi, B. Borghi, and F. Salamini. 1997. "Site of Einkorn Wheat Domestication Identified by DNA Fingerprinting." *Science* 278: 1312–14.

Hillman, G. C., and M. S. Davies. 1990. "Measured Domestication Rates in Wild Wheats and Barley under Primitive Cultivation, and their Archaeological Implications." *Journal of World Prehistory* 4: 157–222.

Hodder, I., ed. 1996. *On the Surface: Çatalhöyük 1993–95.* Cambridge, Mass.: McDonald Institute for Archaeological Research.

Hodder, I. 1999. "Symbolism at Çatalhöyük." In *World Prehistory: Studies in Memory of Grahame Clark*, edited by J. Coles, R. Bewley, and P. Mellars, 171–99. London: Proceedings of the British Academy 99.

Hodder, I., ed. 2000. *Towards a Reflexive Method in Archaeology: The Example at Çatalhöyük.* Cambridge: McDonald Institute for Archaeological Research.

Kaufman, D. 1986. "A Reconsideration of Adaptive Change in the Levantine Epipalae-olithic." In *The End of the Palaeolithic in the Old World*, edited by L. G. Straus, 117–28. Oxford: British Archaeological Reports Int. Series 284.

Kenyon, K. 1957. *Digging Up Jericho*. London: Ernest Benn Ltd.

Kenyon, K., and T. Holland. 1981. *Excavations at Jericho*. Vol. III. *The Architecture and Stratigraphy of the Tell*. London: British School of Archaeology in Jerusalem.

Kirkbride, D. 1968. "Beidha: Early Neolithic Village Life South of the Dead Sea." *Antiquity* 42: 263–74.

Kozlowski, S. K. 1989. "Nemrik 9, a PPN Site in Northern Iraq." *Paléorient* 15: 25–31.

Kuijt, I. 1996. "Negotiating Equality through Ritual: A Consideration of Late Natufian and Pre-Pottery Neolithic A Period Mortuary Practices." *Journal of Anthropological Archaeology* 15: 313–36.

———. 2000. "Keeping the Peace: Ritual Skull Caching and Community Integration in the Levantine Neolithic." In *Life in Neolithic Farming Communities: Social Organization, Identity, and Differentiation*, edited by I. Kuijt, 137–63. New York: Kluwer Academic/Plenum Publishers.

———. 2001. "Place, Death, and the Transmission of Social Memory in Early Agricultural Communities of the Near East Pre-Pottery Neolithic." In *Social Memory, Identity and Death: Anthropological Perspectives on Mortuary Rituals*, edited by M. Chesson, 80–99. Tucson, Ariz.: Archaeological Papers of the American Anthropological Association 10.

Levy, T., ed. 1995. *The Archaeology of Society in the Holy Land*. New York: Facts on File.

Lieberman, D. E. 1993. "The Rise and Fall of Seasonal Mobility among Hunter-Gatherers: The Case of the Southern Levant." *Current Anthropology* 34: 599–631.

Matthews, R. 2000. *The Early Prehistory of Mesopotamia 500,000 to 4,500 BC*. Turnhout, Belgium: Brepols Publishers.

Mellaart, J. 1967. *Çatal Hüyök: A Neolithic Town in Turkey in Anatolia*. London: Thames and Hudson.

———. 1998. "Catal Hüyök: The 1960s Seasons." In *Ancient Anatolia*, edited by R. Matthews, 35–41. London: British Institute of Archaeology at Ankara.

Mellaart, J., U. Hirsch, and B. Balpinar. 1989. *The Goddess from Anatolia*. Milan: Eskenazi.

Metcalf, P., and P. Huntington. 1991. *Celebrations of Death: The Anthropology of Mortuary Ritual*, 2d ed. Cambridge: Cambridge University Press.

Mithen, Steven. 1988. "Looking and Learning: Upper Palaeolithic Art and Information Gathering." *World Archaeology* 19: 297–327.

———. 1996a. *The Prehistory of the Mind*. London: Thames and Hudson.

———. 1996b. "Putting Anthropomorphism into Evolutionary Context (a Comment on Boyer 1996)." *Journal of the Royal Anthropological Institute* 2: 717–21.

———. 1999. "Symbolism and the Supernatural." In *The Evolution of Culture*, edited by R. Dunbar, C. Knight, and C. Power, 147–69. Edinburgh: Edinburgh University Press.

———. 2003. *After the Ice: A Global Human History 20,000–5000 BC*. London: Weidenfeld and Nicolson.

Mithen, Steven J., B. Finlayson, A. Pirie, D. Carruthers, and A. Kennedy. 2000. "New Evidence for Economic and Technological Diversity in the Pre Pottery Neolithic A: Wadi Faynan 16." *Current Anthropology* 41: 655–63.

Morphy, H. 1989. "On Representing Ancestral Beings." In *Animals into Art*, edited by H. Morphy, 144–60. London: Unwin Hyman.

Morris, I. 1991. "The Archaeology of Ancestors: The Saxe/Goldstein Hypothesis Revisited." *Cambridge Archaeological Journal* 1: 147–69.

Nadel, D. 1994. "Levantine Upper Palaeolithic—Early Epi-Palaeolithic Burial Customs: Ohalo II as a Case Study." *Paléorient* 20: 113–21.

Nadel, D., and I. Hershkovitz. 1991. "New Subsistence Data and Human Remains from the Earliest Levantine Epipalaeolithic." *Current Anthropology* 32: 631–35.

Nadel, D., and E. Werker. 1999. "The Oldest Ever Brush Hut Plant Remains from Ohalo II, Jordan Valley, Israel (19,000 BP)." *Antiquity* 73: 755–64.

Özdoğan, A. 1999. "Çayönü." In *Neolithic in Turkey: The Cradle of Civilization, New Discoveries*, edited by M. Özdoğan and N. Başgelen, 35–64. Istanbul: Arkeoloji ve Sanat Yayinlari.

Özdoğan, M., and N. Başgelen, eds. 1999. *Neolithic in Turkey: The Cradle of Civilization, New Discoveries*. Istanbul: Arkeoloji ve Sanat Yayinlari.

Renfrew, Colin. 1985. *The Archaeology of Cult*. London: Thames and Hudson.

———. 1994. "The Archaeology of Religion." In *The Ancient Mind*, edited by C. Renfew and E. B. W. Zubrow, 47–53. Cambridge: Cambridge University Press.

Rollefson, G. 1998. "'Ain Ghazal (Jordan): Ritual and Ceremony III." *Paléorient* 24: 43–58.

———. 2000. "Ritual and Social Structure at Neolithic 'Ain Ghazal." In *Life in Neolithic Farming Communities: Social Organization, Identity, and Differentiation*, edited by I. Kuijt, 165–90. New York: Kluwer Academic/Plenum Publishers.

Rollefson, G. O., and A. H. Simmons. 1987. "The Life and Death of 'Ain Ghazal." *Archaeology* (Nov./Dec. 1987): 38–45.

Rosenberg, M., and R. W. Redding. 2000. "Hallan Çemi and Early Village Organization in Eastern Anatolia." In *Life in Neolithic Farming Communities: Social Organization, Identity, and Differentiation*, edited by I. Kuijt, 39–61. New York: Kluwer Academic/Plenum Publishers.

Schmandt-Besserat, D. 1992. *Before Writing*, 2 vols. Austin: University of Texas Press.

———. 1997. "Animal Symbols at 'Ain Ghazal." *Expedition* 39: 48–58.

———. 1998. "'Ain Ghazal 'Monumental' Figures." *Bulletin of the American Schools of Oriental Research* 310: 1–17.

Schmidt, K. 1994. "Investigations in the Upper Mesopotamian Early Neolithic: Göbekli Tepe and Gücütepe." *Neo-lithics* 2/95: 9–10.

———. 1996. "The Urfa-Project 1996." *Neo-lithics* 2/96: 2–3.

———. 1998. "Beyond Daily Bread: Evidence of Early Neolithic Ritual from Göbekli Tepe." *Neo-lithics* 2/98: 1–5.

———. 1999. "Boars, Ducks and Foxes—the Urfa-Project 99." *Neo-lithics* 3/99: 12–15.

———. 2001. "Göbekli Tepe, Southeastern Turkey: A Preliminary Report on the 1995–1999 Excavations." *Paléorient* 26: 45–54.

Smith, P. 1991. "Dental Evidence for Nutritional Status in the Natufians." In *The Natufian Culture in the Levant*, edited by O. Bar-Yosef and F. R. Valla, 425–33. Ann Arbor, Mich.: International Monographs in Prehistory.

Solecki, R. L. 1977. "Predatory Bird Rituals at Zawi Chemi Shanidar." *Summer* 33: 42–77.

Stordeur, D., B. Jammous, D. Helmer, and G. Willcox. 1996. "Jerf el-Ahmar: A New Mureybetian Site (PPNA) on the Middle Euphrates." *Neo-lithics* 2/96: 1–2.

Stordeur, D., D. Helmer, and G. Willcox. 1997. "Jerf el-Ahmar, un nouveau site de l'horizon PPNA sur le moyen Euphrate Syrien." *Bulletin de la Société Préhistorique Française* 94: 282–85.

Tulving, E. 1972. "Episodic and Semantic Memory." In *Organization of Memory*, edited by E. Tulving and W. Donaldson. New York: Academic Press.

Voigt, M. M. 2000. "Çatalhöyük in Context: Ritual at Early Neolithic Sites in Central and Eastern Turkey." In *Life in Neolithic Farming Communities: Social Organization, Identity, and Differentiation*, edited by I. Kuijt, 253–93. New York: Kluwer/Plenum Publications.

Watkins, T., D. Baird, and A. Betts. 1989. "Qermez Dere and the Early Aceramic Neolithic of Northern Iraq." *Paléorient* 15: 19–24.

Whitehouse, Harvey. 2000. *Arguments and Icons: Divergent Modes of Religiosity*. Oxford: Oxford University Press.

Wright, G. A. 1978. "Social Differentiation in the Early Natufian." In *Social Archaeology, Beyond Subsistence and Dating*, edited by C. Redman et al., 201–33. London: Academic Press.

Primary Emergence of the Doctrinal Mode of Religiosity in Prehistoric Southwestern Iran　　4

KAREN JOHNSON

RECENTLY THERE HAS BEEN A FLOOD OF INTEREST and scholarship in the ories of religion from cognitive perspectives. Among these studies is Harvey Whitehouse's *Arguments and Icons: Divergent Modes of Religiosity*, which seeks, in part, a cognitive explanation for persistent dichotomies outlined in scholarship concerning religion: from Weber's world and traditional religions, to Benedict's Apollonian and Dionysian religions, to Goody's literate and nonliterate religions, among others (2000: 3). Taking together a number of the key features of all these dichotomies, Whitehouse advances a theory of divergent modes of religiosity. On the one hand, he argues there is a doctrinal mode in which religious ideas and actions are routinized, uniform, and shared among a large-scale, centralized community of participants. Whitehouse contrasts this with an imagistic mode of religiosity, in which religious ideas and actions unite small, cohesive groups through infrequent and highly emotional ritual. What makes Whitehouse's theory different from preceding dichotomous theories of religion is his argument that different modes engage different systems of memory in processes of transmission. Participants in low-frequency, high-arousal rituals (typical of the imagistic mode) tend to encode much of their revelatory religious knowledge in episodic memory (explicit mental representations resulting from an event that is personally experienced at a unique time and place). By contrast, participants in high-frequency, low-arousal rituals (typical of the doctrinal mode) tend to encode their religious knowledge in semantic memory (explicit mental representations of a general propositional and procedural nature). The social morphological trajectories that religious practices can take over time have salient effects on the kinds of memory used to store and transmit knowledge.

Whitehouse's theory has implications not only for anthropologists, but also for historians and archaeologists, and, indeed, it is to the latter two groups that

Whitehouse appeals in the final chapter of *Arguments and Icons* to test out his theory. Whitehouse identifies several historical nodes—including Mesopotamia, the Indus Valley, Mesoamerica, and the central Andes—as potential settings in which one might glimpse the materialization of doctrinal forms. Here, Whitehouse proposes that although much previous research would point to writing technologies and literacy as key elements in the independent invention of doctrinal forms of religiosity, a shift toward increasingly routinized forms of religious transmission probably played a hitherto underappreciated role in the development of large-scale, centralized religious systems. The principal aim of this chapter is to join Whitehouse in challenging hypotheses that unnecessarily privilege literacy and writing technologies in the primary development of doctrinal religious activities. The question to ask is, what other forms of communication could also qualify as a precipitating condition for the emergence of the doctrinal mode of religiosity? The strategy here is to select as a case study well before the advent of literacy and developed writing technologies and to characterize, as best possible, the nature of its religious activity and belief. This requires attention to sociopolitical institutions, as they are part of the mutually reinforcing features that set religious traditions along different trajectories (cf. Whitehouse 2001). This also requires a diachronic analysis, as transmission is a crucial element in Whitehouse's theory. To this end, I have selected to investigate religious practice and belief at archaeological sites in southwestern Iran dating to the fifth and fourth millennia BCE, since it is generally accepted that the emergence of actual pictographic script (independent of accounting signs and tokens) dates to the late fourth millennium BCE (Nissen 1986).[1]

Yet in asking one question of the data from prehistoric southwestern Iran concerning the theory of modes of religiosity, it also becomes critical to address several issues fundamental to that inquiry process. Thus, I begin this chapter by contextualizing the study of religion from the perspective of archaeological methods in order to ascertain what can and cannot reasonably be made of material evidence alone. This section also includes a consideration of the challenges associated with identifying particular modes of religiosity solely from archaeological data, a topic I return to at the end of this chapter. Once I have characterized these methodological difficulties, I turn to the description of my case study. After this, I offer a discussion that ties together the analysis of the archaeological evidence and the theory of modes of religiosity. In short, I plan to show that systems of writing were neither a necessary condition nor a precipitating factor in the independent invention of the doctrinal mode of religiosity in prehistoric southwestern Iran; rather, demands were made for the semantic encoding of religious knowledge through an increasingly complex interaction of religious practice, stylistic messaging, and sociopolitical dynamics, which in turn set the prevailing public religious activities in this region along a doctrinal trajectory. Finally, because of the intricacies of the topics at hand, I offer a section on how religious studies and cognitive theories can be synthesized in ways that frame future research on the modes theory of religiosity by using the conclusions of my case study as a springboard for ideas concerning the nature of religious images that could in turn be empirically evaluated with anthropological, historical, and archaeological data. Whitehouse's work is a substantial contribution to cognitive theories of religion as it raises new questions and provides innovative theoretical explanations, but, perhaps more importantly, it openly invites interdisciplinary research on a subject that plays a central role in so many intellectual pursuits. This chapter is offered ultimately as part of that interdisciplinary discourse.

Accessing Religious Beliefs and Activities through Archaeology

Archaeologists who aim to recover ideology or belief systems solely from material culture have often laboured in the shadow of Childe's dictum that, if early technology may be readily reconstructed from archaeological data, and reliable indicators of the ancient economy recovered by careful design, social institutions—and religious beliefs fall under this rubric—remain the most elusive.

—KNAPP 1988: 134

To be sure, there has been and continues to be ample scholarship in archaeology on the topic of religion. An unmistakable theme of this literature is the notion that extracting past beliefs from material residue alone is a perennial problem with many caveats attached. In general, these studies proceed by providing definitions for a series of relevant terms (*religion, ideology, ritual, sacred,* etc.), discussing the kinds of activities that tend to recur in religious practice, describing the material correlates of those activities most likely discernible through archaeological methods, and integrating ethnographic and ethnohistoric data where relevant. It is beyond the scope of this chapter to present a full examination of this scholarship. Instead, I concentrate on a handful of references that highlight observations crucial to an understanding of religion through archaeological data.

The nature of religious ritual as a repeated act often performed with a designated set of artifacts in a delineated area provides the basic foundation for many archaeological methods investigating religious practice. In a study of formative Oaxaca villages in Mexico, K. V. Flannery (1976) describes a "contextual analysis of ritual paraphernalia" based upon the idea that artifacts used in religious ritual should present nonrandom use and discard patterns, which upon analysis can offer insight into the beliefs that structured the ritual behavior in the first place (cf. Marcus and Flannery 1994). Studying changing patterns of public architecture and space that are frequently the venues for ritual action contributes another data set with which to evaluate religious practice and belief (Flannery and Marcus 1976a, 1976b). Following similar postulations, C. Renfrew (1994) has proposed a useful outline for identifying material indicators for ritual. In addition to the domains of ritual paraphernalia and public space, these include indications for a significant investment of wealth and resources (luxury materials); iconographical representations of deities, meaningful gestures, important symbols, and sacred animals; and the presence or tradition of associated religious texts. With regard to all of these observations, it is critical to point out that the authors advocate for a documentation process that builds converging evidence from multiple materials and contexts. Archaeological evidence is always incomplete, and, perhaps because of this, the presence of seemingly ritual material is prone to promiscuous identification as "religious." The best solution is to construct a careful case of corroborating evidence.

The building of converging evidence is especially important in studies of pre- and protohistoric religion, which are served best by attention to and analysis of the broader spectrum of social, political, and economic activities within a community (cf. Marcus and Flannery 1994). B. Knapp takes up this particular topic in his study of religious ideology in Bronze Age Cyprus (1988). Following a lucid survey of approaches to the recovery of religious beliefs through archaeological data, Knapp concludes that such ideology is best evaluated as an integral part of sociopolitical institutions and economic relations; as "elites and other special interest groups often have recourse to ideology to establish, challenge or change a specific socio-political order," so too do "power relations within society serve to establish religious authority and to legitimise specific ideological practices and insignia" (1988: 133). These observations parallel the attention Whitehouse has given to a community's sociopolitical features as mutually reinforcing factors in the divergent trajectories that religious traditions may take (Whitehouse 2001). In this context, Knapp's work—not only concentrating on ritual artifacts and spaces, but also situating such indicators within a discussion of economic differentiation and social stratification relevant to Bronze Age Cyprus—provides a methodological template for the study undertaken here.

Knapp's research and the methods outlined by K. V. Flannery, J. Marcus, and C. Renfrew are all useful in the archaeological study of religion in general, but it remains to be considered how imagistic and doctrinal modes of religiosity might be differentiated materially. According to its defining elements, the modes of religiosity theory predict that religious ideas and actions on a doctrinal trajectory will be repeated frequently and relatively faithfully among a large-scale, centralized community of participants; religious ideas on an imagistic trajectory are shared and transmitted among a small, cohesive group through infrequent and highly emotional ritual actions. Drawing upon the same kinds of archaeological indicators for religious belief and practice detailed above, it is possible to hypothesize contrasting patterns of frequency and distribution of such indicators based on the theoretical trajectories of different modes. In the case of doctrinal practices, one might expect to find in the material record comparable ritual objects, architecture, and symbols spread across large regions and in quantities that would reflect frequent ritual action over time. In the case of imagistic practices, on the other hand, one might also expect to find ritual objects, architecture, and symbols, but such items would perhaps be spatially constrained to reflect smaller groups of participants and displayed in smaller quantities, indicating infrequent ritual action over time. To be sure, when considering these predictions in practice, it will be important to take into account any biases in data recovery that might skew patterns of frequency and distribution of such ritual material. However, to return to the principle of converging evidence, whatever the interpretation offered about religious modes based on ritual indicators, it can be further evaluated within the context of sociopolitical institutions and economic activities. The more these kinds of archaeological data can be analyzed together, the better the opportunity for characterizing materially divergent modes of religiosity.

With this framework in place, I now turn to my case study of prehistoric southwestern Iran, bearing in mind both how various domains of archaeological evidence can each offer testimony to religious belief and practice and how different modes might reveal themselves in the material record. I return to this subject in the final section of this chapter where my observations from the case study provide the basis for a discussion concerning the ways in which the visual representation of religious concepts might differ between doctrinal and imagistic traditions.

Case Study: The Material Evidence for Religion in Prehistoric Southwestern Iran

The physical geography of southwestern Iran supplies a dramatic backdrop for the cultural innovations and changes taking place here over thousands of years. Multiple mountain ranges circumscribe a select number of plains areas that were the focal locations for sedentary settlements and agricultural activity. I concentrate on data from two sites in close proximity on the Susiana Plain, Choga Mish and Susa, whose interlocking occupation patterns capture the effects of shifting sociopolitical dynamics through the fifth and fourth millennia BCE (see figure 4.1). The two sites are, however, only a microcosmic glimpse, and it should be kept in mind that there is clear material evidence for long-distance trade and cross-cultural interaction with the Mesopotamian settlements to the west and other groups to the north and southeast, who are undergoing similar transformations and at the same time influencing the changes on the Susiana Plain.

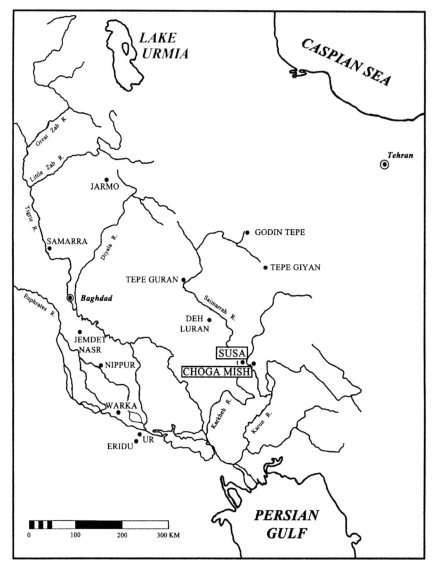

Figure 4.1.   Map showing the location of Choga Mish and Susa, along with selected other sites in southwestern Iran and southern Mesopotamia.

Of the two sites, Choga Mish has the earliest occupation beginning probably around the start of the seventh millennium BCE. Based on the presence of specific types of ceramic ware, the initial settlement was modest, but continued to expand into what was likely a complex chiefdom by the mid-fifth millennium BCE (Delougaz and Kantor 1996: 279–84). A chiefdom is characterized here as a regional entity in which the "central decision-making activity is differentiated from, though it ultimately regulates, decision-making regarding local production and local social process; but is not itself internally differentiated" (Wright 1977: 381). A spectrum of complexity can occur within these decision-making activities. Whereas a simple chiefdom has individuals drawn from a single elite subgroup exercising control, a complex chiefdom may have several ranked individuals drawn from several subgroups, who compete with each other for authority, effectively creating another level of control hierarchy. In essence, such ranked individuals are competing for larger group cohesion.

Three features of spatial organization are helpful in identifying complex chiefdoms archaeologically: a three-level settlement hierarchy marked by major centers, subcenters, and smaller settlements, along with residential and mortuary segregation (Wright 1994: 68). During the mid-fifth millennium BCE, when the maximum number of settlements on the Susiana Plain occurs (Hole 1987: 84), Choga Mish displays extensive architecture suggesting a substantial and continuous settlement covering nearly fifteen hectares, larger than any of the surrounding communities (Delougaz and Kantor 1996: 184). Additionally, reports of the architectural remains in trenches suggest that some domestic areas were larger and well planned with features for specialized functions, such as kilns and storage bins (Delougaz and Kantor 1996: 161); residential segregation may be inferred from this to some degree. Evidence for mortuary segregation is lacking at Choga Mish during this period. It may be noted, however, that other sites across western Iran at this time do demonstrate a shift from burials within domestic settings to burials within delimited cemeteries (Hole 1987: 88). Although the absence of mortuary segregation at Choga Mish may leave open a challenge to the degree of complexity for this regional chiefdom, it remains clear that Choga Mish was a major center on the Susiana Plain.

Material evidence that speaks to religious activities and beliefs at Choga Mish is much less straightforward than the evidence that informs us about its sociopolitical organization. The corpus of animal and human figurines—used as cult objects in later periods—might offer some insight. The human figurines are of several types: a slender, standing female wearing a long skirt; a face depicted on a small cylindrical piece of unbaked clay; a "thorn" figurine characterized by an elongated oval base of clay with the center stretching out to form the body and head of a human with incised facial features; and a squatting female with large breasts and buttocks. Curiously, all of the human figurines date exclusively to the end of the sixth millennium BCE. Just as Choga Mish is expanding into a regional center during the first half of the fifth millennium BCE, the iconography of the figurines appears to switch to animals. The excavators have explored the possibility that this could be an accident of recovery, but maintain that the sample sizes

from trenches should be representative, and the change from human to animal figurines is strongly suggestive of a shift in the concerns of the artisans and of cultural change at large (Delougaz and Kantor 1996: 258–60). Many of the animal
figurines depict quadrupeds, most likely sheep and oxen. Some figurines depict
birds, and there is a unique instance of a painted snake's head. A large terracotta
pendant in the shape of a bull's head is also attributed to the same period. Although this object is singular, the motif is well known: "the appearance of the bu-
cranium as a pendant, together with its prominence among the representational
motifs of the painted pottery of the Middle Susiana period [c. 5000 to 4500
BCE], suggests that it might have been an important emblem, perhaps even one
with religious connotations" (Delougaz and Kantor 1996: 255). To be sure, this
observation could also hold for the animal figurines in general, as birds, snakes,
and oxen all appear on contemporaneous painted ceramics (see figure 4.2). The
fact that such motifs are shared across different media and comprise objects with
different connotations and functions does argue for more profound meanings attached to the animal subjects by the inhabitants at Choga Mish.

Frequent skirmishes are characteristic of areas home to complex chiefdoms,
as communities vie for regional control and assert authority. In some situations, these confrontations can escalate such that there is broad political collapse and decentralization. This appears to have been the case on the Susiana
Plain in the late fifth millennium BCE. There is a substantial retrenchment of
the settlement at Choga Mish around the middle of the fifth millennium BCE,
followed by several centuries of minimal occupation. The earliest evidence for
occupation at nearby Susa can be attributed to this same period of abandonment at Choga Mish, and Susa grows continuously into the regional center by
the very end of the fifth millennium BCE. Susa's dominance of the plain is asserted, in part, by the construction of a monumental mud-brick platform on
the acropolis of the city. The remains of the platform and the buildings that
occupied it are fragmentary, but they do allow tentative reconstruction of the
complex: the platform itself rose in two tiers with each stage displaying re-
cessed corners, in effect, creating a cruciform design; atop the platform was a
complex of buildings, including, perhaps, temples, storage rooms, a residential
building, and a charnel house (Steve and Gasche 1973; Hole 1992). Adjacent
to the platform was a cemetery that has yielded numerous graves. Many of the
burials were fractional, suggesting a delayed interment of the bones after the
flesh had decomposed (Canal 1978), and many appear to have occurred simultaneously (Hole 1992). There are several interpretations surrounding the
circumstances of such a massive burial event, but for the purposes of this chapter, it is sufficient to note the monumental scale and centralized location of
these ritual practices.

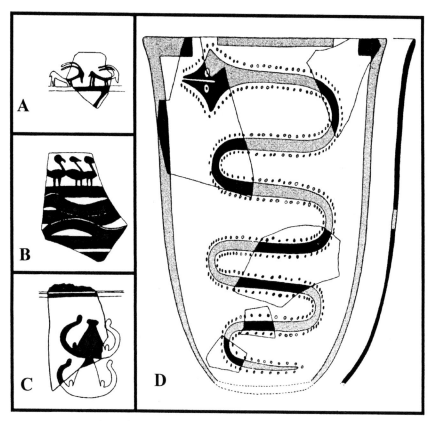

Figure 4.2.   Animal motifs on ceramics from Choga Mish, 5000–4500 BCE. Images courtesy of the Oriental Institute of the University of Chicago. Scales (A–C) approximately 1:2 and (D) approximately 1:4.

Accompanying each grave from the cemetery at Susa was a recurrent assemblage of ceramic vessels comprising three types—a drinking beaker, a serving dish, and a small jar. In total, nearly 4,000 vessels were recovered, displaying a diversity of symbolic representation that was shared among several sites on the Susiana Plain. Notable motifs include circular designs, nested cruciforms, and the representation of various animals, such as wild goats, birds, dogs, scorpions, and snakes. Only four of the vessels display anthropomorphic figures (Hole 1984). Susan Pollock (1983) conducted a stylistic analysis of Susiana ceramics in an attempt to show that a redundancy in stylistic embellishment may be indicative of an increase in the vertical articulations within a society, with the elite reinforcing their status through the use of symbolic messages. The same kind of conclusion could be reached when evaluating the Susiana material from a ritual perspective. Particular symbols predominate among the motifs applied to objects used in a burial context. This context is clear evidence for the mortuary segregation of certain individuals. It is reasonable to infer these individuals are of a higher status when considering both the proximity of the cemetery to a prominent architectural landmark at Susa and the use of ceramic vessels in large quantities, which indicates an investment of material resources and specialized craft activities for the purpose of broadcasting a social position to the larger community. The animal subjects and abstract designs are then, perhaps, components of a religious ideology being coopted by an elite group at Susa.

At the same time, the stylistic motifs from the ceramics in the grave assemblages are also those that appear to cue into beliefs and activities spread throughout the site. This is demonstrated through their display in the centralized ritual precinct and the designs on seals and seal impressions, objects that are in large part the residue of administrative activities for the management of the production, storage, and exchange of commodities such as food and textiles. The cruciform designs appearing on ceramics, seals, and seal impressions are echoed in the architectural details of the ceremonial platform at Susa; the animal motifs from the ceramics in the nearby cemetery are also witnessed on seals and seal impressions. This is strongly suggestive of both a deliberate redundancy in symbolism on the part of elites and an intentional blending of religious beliefs with political and economic institutions (cf. Wright 1994). A comparative illustration of this messaging behavior is seen in a study of seals and seal impressions from a contemporaneous site, Tepe Gawra, in Mesopotamia (Rothman 1994). Commenting generally on the administrative aspects of such objects, M. S. Rothman explains that "before the advent of writing, before even the appearance of the first state-level society, complex societies needed a technology of control. This technology was provided by . . . the seal and its impressions on clay" (1994: 104).

Rothman also notes, "to the extent that restricted goods were icons or other materials for religious ritual, their control represented oversight of formal religious practice" (1994: 104). A telling example of this particular function that designs on seals and seal impressions could serve is seen with a motif surfacing at Susa: the "master of the animals" (Amiet 1961; Le Brun 1971). This character—displayed on a handful of seals and their impressions—stands with arms akimbo, often holding snakes in each hand, and sprouting long, wild goat horns from the head (see figure 4.3). He is often regarded as a ritual figure, and the motif is not unique to Susa, but appears on seals in Mesopotamia and at other sites throughout western Iran (Porada 1995: 41). It is interesting to note that, while the design on the seal would have likely been used in the oversight of administrative and perhaps ritual activities, in some instances, seals have perforations indicating that they were perhaps worn as ornaments (cf. Porada 1995: 40). In fact, one seal impres-

Figure 4.3.   "Master of the animals" motif. Left: line drawing of seal impression from Susa, c. 4000 BCE. Image adapted from P. Amiet (1961), *La Glyptique Mésopotamienne Archaïque,* plate 6, number 118. Right: line drawing of seal impression from Choga Mish, 3500–3100 BCE. Image courtesy of the Oriental Institute of the University of Chicago. Scale approximately 1:1.

sion of the master of the animals from Susa shows the figure with a circular ornament hanging around his neck. While it is tempting to consider that this particular example of the master of the animals is shown wearing a stamp seal of the same type that was used, this reading of the very small design can only be pressed so far. What remains significant throughout all of the examples of the material presented here is evidence converging on an interpretation of social messaging spread across diverse media and incorporating religious symbols occurring at Susa.

The beginning of the fourth millennium BCE proved to be a momentous period on the Susiana Plain that was disastrous in scope with substantial conflict and population collapse (Wright et al. 1975; Wright and Johnson 1975). At Susa, the great platform was destroyed; there was a restoration of the complex, but it was followed by another destruction phase that also included the settlement (Canal 1978). As early as 3900 BCE (Johnson 1987)—or perhaps slightly later around 3700 BCE (Wright 1998; Wright and Rupley 2001)—state-level societies first begin to emerge. This judgment is based on an analysis of "multiple variable interaction," including increases in the levels of administrative and political hierarchies supported by more complex settlement organization and the presence of artifacts for record keeping; population growth based on settlement characteristics and agricultural patterns; and increases in craft production and exchange (Wright and Johnson 1975). On the Susiana Plain, it appears that Susa develops into the paramount center of the region, and renewed growth at Choga Mish signals its importance as a major center, along with the settlement at nearby Abu Fanduweh, in the state-level hierarchy controlling access to many of the surrounding smaller centers and villages (Wright and Johnson 1975: 270).

Both sites in the mid-fourth millennium BCE present evidence for religious activities and a continuation of the strategy of incorporating religious ideas into a visual rhetoric of control spanning media. At Choga Mish a monumental complex is constructed on what is referred to as the High Mound consisting of a polygonal platform, which may have been intended as the foundation for a temple, as well as surrounding buildings and ritual features (Delougaz and Kantor 1996: 27–35). While public architecture on a similar scale at Susa is unknown for this period, fragments of monumental sculpture hint that such structures did exist. Hoards of small-scale sculpture have also been recovered at Susa. Such hoards have parallels at other sites in the Near East, where they were found in temples and other locations of special significance (Pittman 1992: 50). In addition to these architectural remains and artifacts, there are again ceramics, seals, and seal impressions in large quantities with design elements displaying continuity with those seen in previous periods at both Choga Mish and Susa.

Yet, in this state-level society, there is a proliferation and elaboration of the symbolic and figural representation of enormous proportions. Writing on this phenomenon, one author explains,

> [O]ne primary purpose of the increased invention and production of visual symbols was managing social interaction, for through them it was possible to replace actual human action with its representations. Actual and ritual action, used in the past for social management, it may hypothetically but consistently be suggested, was replaced or augmented to some degree by depictions of ritual actions and relationships. That new function of social communication required both the elaboration of existing images and the creation of a substantial number of new ones, which acquired meaning through convention and homology that encompassed both human relationships and mythological and cosmological precepts (Pittman 1992: 49).

It is indeed significant that more human and ritual action is being displayed on objects that were likely to cross the paths of multiple individuals, not only within Susa, but also across the region. It is less the case that the rise of state-level organization ultimately caused an increase and elaboration of visual symbols, but rather a situation in which the various interactions coalescing into a state-level society were also factors in shaping transformations in the visual domain.

With so many different human relationships signaled by even more designs and compositions, it is difficult to draw sharp distinctions between secular and ritual motifs; it is helpful to think of the design and the object that displayed it as each having the ability to support multiple parenthetical meanings, depending on their social context. Having said this, however, there are a few representations from seal impressions at both Choga Mish and Susa that appear to highlight ritual actions and figures in particular. Two seal impressions from Choga Mish illustrate a procession of humans and animals to a temple; in both cases, the identification of the building as a temple is based on the presence of gateposts and parallels in design from other sites (Delougaz and Kantor 1996: 145) (see figure 4.4). The first shows two humans—one carrying a staff, the other a mace—flanking a lion standing on its hind legs; all three figures are next to a temple also with a niched façade. The second shows a procession of four human figures—one is next to the temple with a niched façade, and the remaining three are on the other side of the gateposts with one individual carrying a vessel—and two quadrupeds, one of which appears to be a lion. A representation of a temple is also seen on a seal impression from Susa (Pittman 1992). The scene carries a narrative of conflict and also ties the struggle for power with religious institutions: the elaborate temple displays horns that recall the exaggerated wild goat horns previously depicted on ceramics, and the figure to the far left has often been called a "priest-king," based on his frequent presence in material from Uruk in Mesopotamia. Finally, the "master of animals" figure seen at Susa at the end of the fifth millennium BCE also makes an appearance on a seal impression at Choga Mish (cf. figure 4.3). Here the figure is now holding two sets of two entwined snakes and lacks the horns springing from his head; the stance is nonetheless clearly resonant. Each of these examples demonstrates that continuity with the imagery of previous periods is sustained, even though the iconography associated with religious practice and belief is becoming more intricately woven into the hierarchies of political and economic activities.

My survey of material evidence for religious practice and belief on the Susiana Plain ends at the conclusion of the fourth millennium BCE. At this point, Choga Mish was largely abandoned and may not have been reoccupied until the beginning of the second millennium BCE, when a fortress was constructed as an outpost for trade routes to the East (Delougaz and Kantor 1996: 18–25). Occupation was sustained at Susa, but the period is difficult to interpret, in large part due to a complexity of interactions with Mesopotamia (Pittman 1992). It is worth adding that this period does offer the first examples of documents in the Proto-Elamite language, as yet undeciphered. Thus, the end of the fourth millennium BCE is an appropriate place at which to bracket off a case study intended to investigate religious ideas and activities before the emergence of writing technologies and literacy.

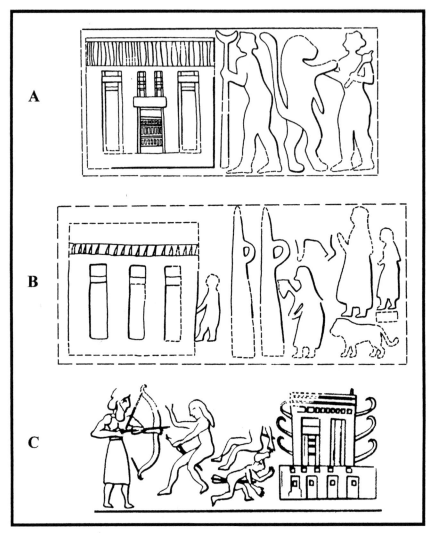

Figure 4.4.   Temple scenes. A and B: line drawings of seal impressions from Choga Mish, 3500–3100 BCE. Images courtesy of the Oriental Institute of the University of Chicago. C: line drawing of a seal impression from Susa, c. 3300 BCE. Image adapted from P. Amiet (1961), *La Glyptique Mésopotamienne Archaïque,* plate 46, number 659. Scale approximately 1:1.

Discussion

Although the main focus of this case study has been to identify material evidence for religion in a prehistoric context, I have also included evidence that details the general nature of sociopolitical organization, since the theory of modes of religiosity seeks to demonstrate how the sociopolitical features of a community are part of a mutually reinforcing system that sets religious traditions on different trajectories. Whitehouse (2001: 13) lists seven possible sociopolitical features that differ markedly in the doctrinal and imagistic modes respectively: social cohesion (diffuse/intense), leadership (dynamic/passive or absent), inclusivity-exclusivity (inclusive/exclusive), spread (rapid and efficient/slow and inefficient), scale (large-scale/small-scale), degree of uniformity (high/low), and structure (centralized/noncentralized). With respect to the sociopolitical features of Choga Mish and Susa, it appears that Whitehouse's model should predict a religious tradition that is more doctrinal in nature: the social cohesion was likely diffused across the Susiana Plain; leadership was certainly dynamic through the cycling of chiefdoms into a state-level society; the communities were arguably inclusive in the attempt to exert influence over greater areas; the spread certainly seems efficient; large-scale accurately describes the sphere of authority; the degree of uniformity is admittedly difficult to discern; and the structure is obviously centralized. Yet, systems of writing are noticeably absent.

To be sure, it is hardly clear that the evidence I have presented demonstrates a single religious tradition, and, if indeed it was a coherent doctrine, there is no way to articulate what the contents of that doctrine were. The data do, however, seem to cling together in a loosely defined set of significant symbols, figures, locations, and actions. If we entertain the possibility that this loosely defined set represents a kind of doctrine, then we must return to a question I asked at the beginning: what other forms of communication that encourage encoding in semantic memory could qualify as a precipitating condition for the emergence of the doctrinal mode of religiosity?

In light of this, one way to interpret the evidence for religion in prehistoric southwestern Iran would be as follows. The rise and organization of complex chiefdoms at Choga Mish and Susa during the fifth millennium BCE had significant effects on religious belief and practice. Religious notions became an important component of secular ideologies as a means for gaining and sustaining power and control by ruling individuals. As such, religious belief, which previously had been internally generated and transmitted through infrequent ritual, became increasingly explicit and homogeneous through stylistic messaging. The resulting images portrayed religious representations with a stronger narrative valence and reference to circulating verbal rhetoric. The centralization of ritual activity at the platform complexes and the communication of religious ideas tied to political agendas carried out in routinized economic activities contributed to both a more frequent transmission of religious belief and a greater demand for semantic encoding. The effects on religious activity generated by such sociopolitical surroundings were profound during the fourth millennium BCE when the realm of representational art became a more explicit means for managing and representing social interactions. Thus, I would assert that the doctrinal mode first emerged in southwestern Iran during the fifth millennium BCE and strengthened in form throughout the fourth. When the means for a written codification of religious belief later becomes available, it allowed for robust elaboration along a doctrinal trajectory that was long before set in motion.

If this interpretation is accepted, it supports Whitehouse's proposal in *Arguments and Icons* that writing technologies and literacy were not necessarily key elements in the independent invention of doctrinal forms of religiosity. This case study of religion in prehistoric southwestern Iran also provides a point from which current methodologies in the archaeology of religion can be refined such that it is possible to discern the kinds of trends in material culture that are characteristic of either doctrinal or imagistic modes. For example, the data and subsequent interpretation presented here do suggest that religious images and motifs associated with the doctrinal mode tend to recur across a region and over time. In addition to quantitative differences, it is also worth exploring if there are ways in which the visual representation of religious concepts might differ between doctrinal and imagistic traditions. To follow through with this is, of course, an exercise in speculation, yet I offer some thoughts in an effort to guide future research on the theory of modes of religiosity that is relevant to archaeological contexts.

The Visual Representation of Religious Concepts: A Cognitive Exploration through Divergent Modes

Much work has been done in the cognitive science of religion on the centrality and ubiquity of counterintuitive concepts in religious belief (e.g., Boyer 1994, 2001; Atran 2002). Counterintuitive concepts refer specifically to those ideas that have features that simultaneously conform to and violate our ontological expectations based on domains of intuitive knowledge. Another way to say this is that human cognitive architecture affords us the ability to have expectations and make inferences about global categories, such as natural substances, artifacts, plants, animals, and people. When a feature of one category is attributed to another—such as a tree that talks—it violates our intuitive ontological understanding. Religious concepts are, however, those ideas that are minimally counterintuitive (Boyer 1994, 2001); the notion should violate our expectations, but only slightly, since it appears that multiple violations (e.g., a rock that flies and predicts the future and is seen everywhere at all times) impose constraints on memory and transmission of the idea. While religious concepts do take on these characteristics, there is also plenty of intuitive knowledge within religious belief sets (Atran 2002); counterintuitive worlds are constructed in religious traditions, but they need not devour the entirety of the belief system, whether it is within an imagistic or doctrinal mode.

The assertion that religious representations simultaneously conform to and minimally violate intuitive knowledge may be realized, to a certain extent, in the visual realm. Thus, the presence of visual images, such as anthropomorphic characters, human-animal hybrids, animated landscapes, or creatures with human attributes and intentions, might facilitate and strengthen the identification of religious iconography. Yet, the presence of such visual images, in and of themselves, is not necessarily indicative of religious activity. Conversely, not all visual representations with a religious valence are minimally counterintuitive. For example, imagery with high emotional arousal, such as snakes or scorpions, may occur in religious contexts, often as apotropaic measures to ensure the safety of sacred precincts, yet such imagery does not violate intuitive knowledge. Or, consider the frequent presence of repetitive geometric or abstract motifs in religious contexts. One might attribute such designs simply to an aesthetic preference, a *horror vacui*, or the physical manifestation of the types of entopic phenomena (i.e., meandering lines, checkerboards, nested curves, dots, and spirals) experienced by shamans in hallucinatory states (Whitehouse 2000; Pearson 2002). In any of these scenarios it would be difficult to deny the affective influence, even if minimal, that such motifs exercise over actors and witnesses in religious activity.

If counterintuitive concepts are characteristic of religious belief, we should expect them in both imagistic and doctrinal modes. I suggest here that there are, however, subtle differences in the ways such notions are expressed and displayed. In the imagistic mode, counterintuitive ideas tend to be actualized through personal experience and are thus less frequently visually displayed. On the other hand, in the doctrinal mode, counterintuitive concepts—while they may be realized through personal experience—more readily avail themselves to visual depiction, as the ideas must be standardized to a certain degree in order to be logically integrated into a narrative that can accommodate a large-scale, anonymous community of participants. I refer back to *Arguments and Icons* to illustrate the basis for such assertions. In the passages where Whitehouse details imagery in imagistic Melanesian ritual, there are no references to counterintuitive concepts or visual depiction of them. The kind of imagery that Whitehouse recounts is completely mundane from an observer's point of view—dew, hair, wild boars—and he even describes such imagery at one point as "everyday objects" (2000: 118). Furthermore, he is explicit that religious notions and meanings for participants in a predominantly imagistic tradition are "internally generated" and "may converge on certain themes and central ideas," but present neither uniformity nor exegesis (2001: 11). Thus, if imagistic ideas are multivocal, multivalent, and glimpsed in revelatory experience within an individual's mind, it would appear impossible to identify any particular counterintuitive idea or set of ideas, much less a visual depiction of such ideas, shared within the tradition.

Nonetheless, as Whitehouse argues, rituals in the imagistic mode are loaded with sensory pageantry. They are highly emotional and can be traumatic, ecstatic, and even life threatening; their experience has profound physical and cognitive effects. What I propose here is that such ritual environments actualize ontological violations, in effect creating religious representations out of the participants themselves. For example, imagine a ritual that is so richly charged with sensory input and metaphorically evocative of the features of wild boars that the participants in the process have the revelatory experience of "transforming" into a wild boar; or perhaps individuals actually believe they have had the experience of "death" and miraculous "rebirth" through a truly life-threatening rite of terror. In predominantly doctrinal modes without such rituals, religious representations of ontological violations are less frequently, if ever, actualized through the participants themselves and become standardized through their incorporation in stories that are codified in verbal or textual rhetoric. Belonging less to the realm of subjective experience, such counterintuitive concepts more readily avail themselves to objective visual depictions that cue into oral or textual traditions.

Another way to phrase the distinction between a subjective and objective religious representation is to borrow a terminology and conceptual process of stylistic production detailed by M. W. Conkey in an account and analysis of Paleolithic art, wherein she describes how the creation of an artifact form and the application of stylistic treatment are two separate levels in the design process (1980: 233). In the case of Paleolithic art, "there is no conceptual or operational differentiation of the level of artifact from the level of decoration" (1980: 234). The design already exists within the raw material and is released from it through a substractive process; this is what Conkey refers to as a merging or nondifferentiation of levels. It is contrasted with applied art, such as that of Greek vase painting, for which the creation of the form and the design are conceptually and operationally distinct.

Following this description, I would argue that imagery found within an imagistic tradition is characterized by a nondifferentiation of levels—the religious idea and the experience merge conceptually and operationally. Visual representations associated with an imagistic tradition are the result of a substractive process of transformation, in which the design is literally drawn out or released from the material, often by the participants themselves. Imagery and visual representations associated with the doctrinal mode tend to be the result of an applied process, in which the elements of the doctrine are applied to artifacts. This differentiation of levels is necessary to some degree in the doctrinal mode for the purposes of extending a readability of the images to a wider audience of participants. The images and motifs prevalent throughout my case study presented here do accord with the notion of applied art. There is a differentiation of levels in the design process that allows the same motifs to be attached, in relatively faithful manner, to multiple types of objects and features, and the repetition of the same kinds of images and motifs acts as a stabilizing mechanism for the symbols, particularly in transmission. Understanding the visual depiction of religious concepts in these terms can potentially be another aspect of material evidence with which to evaluate the modes theory of religiosity in not only archaeological but also historical and anthropological contexts.

Summary

With respect to research on the modes theory of religiosity, I have offered here counterevidence for the proposition that literacy and writing technologies were precipitating conditions for the independent emergence of the doctrinal mode. The notions of literacy and what constitutes a writing technology are both thorny issues. I have chosen to circumvent these issues as far as possible through an investigation of religious activities and beliefs using archaeological data from two communities in southwestern Iran dating to the fifth and fourth millennia BCE. The evidence attesting to the sociopolitical morphology of these communities is more consistent with features that scaffold doctrinal religious practices. Moreover, the material that has a religious valence would appear incongruent with imagistic practices. Instead, it seems to indicate routinized exchanges of religious notions across a wide region, often in contexts that overlap with other social and economic activities. While it not possible to articulate the exact content of these religious notions, the repetition of certain images and motifs, along with their relative homogeneity and stability over time, suggests a religious tradition that employs strategies for transmission more in line with a doctrinal mode. Visual messaging of these kinds of images and motifs can place a demand on semantic encoding for the purposes of transmitting religious knowledge and can be as much a precipitating factor for the primary emergence of doctrinal forms of religiosity.

Archaeologists, in general, tread unsteady ground when it comes to evaluating religious activities and beliefs. I have suggested that it is beneficial to merge archaeological methods and interpretive processes with an understanding from scholarship on the cognitive science of religion. It provides a way of bridging mind-blind functionalist evaluations of religious behavior with a recognition that religious beliefs and practices meant something to participants. Cognitive theories do offer explanations for why certain kinds of concepts are recurrent in religious traditions and for the ways in which such concepts can come to mean something for individual participants. Narrowing in on the fact that we should expect to see counterintuitive concepts in both imagistic and doctrinal traditions, I have suggested there may be subtle differences in the ways in which such notions are located and visually expressed in either mode. Cognitive approaches to studies in the humanities and social sciences are a relatively recent development and have the potential for connecting diverse cultural contexts across time and space, while at the same time recognizing the value of human diversity. Archaeological studies can be an important component in these approaches. Undeniably, there is tremendous variability in the expression of human behaviors and activities, but understanding the cognitive constraints of the human actors themselves can help archaeologists to understand why we see patterns in material culture in the first place.

Note

1. This general date is assigned to a group of approximately 4,000 clay tablets displaying a Proto-Cuneiform script from the site of Uruk in Iraq. These documents are thought to be the oldest known examples of writing, consisting of primarily lexical lists and economic texts. The exact date of the tablets is difficult to ascertain, since they were found primarily in rubbish deposits whose stratigraphic relationship to the surrounding building levels is largely unclear (Nissen 1986: 318–20). Tablets recovered from Susa dating to the early part of the third millennium BCE were inscribed with a script that shares some elements with Proto-Cuneiform, but is properly termed Proto-Elamite in view of the Elamite language later used at Susa (Pittman 1992: 53). In both cases of these early written documents, the script is used for exclusively economic purposes; there are no known literary, religious, or historical texts from either Mesopotamia or southwestern Iran at the transition between the fourth and third millennia BCE.

References

Amiet, P. 1961. *La Glyptique Mésopotamienne Archaïque*. Paris: Éditions du Centre National de la Recherche Scientifique.

Atran, S. 2002. *In Gods We Trust: The Evolutionary Landscape of Religion*. Oxford: Oxford University Press.

Boyer, P. 1994. "Cognitive Constraints on Cultural Representations: Natural Ontologies and Religious Ideas." In *Mapping the Mind: Domain Specificity in Cognition and Culture*, edited by Lawrence A. Hirschfeld and Susan A. Gelman. Cambridge: Cambridge University Press.

———. 2001. *Religion Explained: The Evolutionary Origins of Religious Thought*. New York: Basic Books.

Canal, D. 1978. "La terrasse haute de l'acropole de Suse." *Cahiers del la Délégation Archéologique Française en Iran* 9: 11–56.

Conkey, M. W. 1980. "Context, Structure, and Efficacy in Paleolithic Art and Design." In *Symbol as Sense: New Approaches to the Analysis of Meaning*, edited by M. L. Foster and S. H. Brandes. New York: Academic Press.

Delougaz, P., and H. J. Kantor. 1996. *The First Five Seasons of Excavations, 1961–1971*, Vol. 1 of *Choga Mish*, edited by A. Alizadeh, Parts 1 and 2. Chicago: The Oriental Institute of the University of Chicago.

Flannery, K. V. 1976. "Contextual Analysis of Ritual Paraphernalia from Formative Oaxaca." In *The Early Mesoamerican Village*, edited by K. V. Flannery. New York: Academic Press.

Flannery, K. V., and J. Marcus. 1976a. "Formative Oaxaca and the Zapotec Cosmos." *American Scientist* 64(4): 374–83.

————. 1976b. "Evolution of the Public Building in Formative Oaxaca." In *Cultural Change and Continuity: Essays in Honor of James Bennett Griffin*, edited by C. E. Cleland. New York: Academic Press.

Hole, F. 1984. "Analysis of Structure and Design in Prehistoric Ceramics." *World Archaeology* 15: 326–47.

————. 1987. "Settlement and Society in the Village Period." In *The Archaeology of Western Iran: Settlement and Society from Prehistory to the Islamic Conquest*, edited by F. Hole. Washington, D.C.: Smithsonian Institution Press.

————. 1992. "The Cemetery of Susa: An Interpretation," and catalogue selections from *The Royal City of Susa: Ancient Near Eastern Treasures in the Louvre*, edited by P. O. Harper, J. Aruz, and F. Tallon. New York: The Metropolitan Museum of Art.

Johnson, G. A. 1987. "The Changing Organization of Uruk Administration on the Susiana Plain." In *The Archaeology of Western Iran: Settlement and Society from Prehistory to the Islamic Conquest*, edited by F. Hole. Washington, D.C.: Smithsonian Institution Press.

Knapp, B. 1988. "Ideology, Archaeology and Polity." *Man*, n.s., 23(1): 133–63.

Le Brun, A. 1971. "Recherches stratigraphiques à l'acropole de Suse (1969–1971)." *Cahiers de la Délégation Archéologique Française en Iran* 1: 163–216.

Marcus, J., and K. V. Flannery. 1994. "Ancient Zapotec Ritual and Religion." In *The Ancient Mind: Elements of Cognitive Religion*, edited by C. Renfrew and E. B. W. Zubrow. Cambridge: Cambridge University Press.

Nissen, H. J. 1986. "The Archaic Texts from Uruk." *World Archaeology* 17(3): 317–34.

Pearson, J. L. 2002. *Shamanism and the Ancient Mind: A Cognitive Approach to Archaeology.* Walnut Creek, Calif.: AltaMira Press.

Pittman, H. 1992. "The Late Uruk Period" and catalogue selections from *The Royal City of Susa: Ancient Near Eastern Treasures in the Louvre*, edited by, P. O. Harper, J. Aruz, and F. Tallon. New York: The Metropolitan Museum of Art.

Pollock, S. 1983. "Style and Information: An Analysis of Susiana Ceramics." *Journal of Anthropological Archaeology* 2: 354–90.

Porada, E. 1995. *Man and Images in the Ancient Near East.* Wakefield, R.I.: Moyer Bell.

Renfrew, C. 1994. "The Archaeology of Religion." In *The Ancient Mind: Elements of Cognitive Religion*, edited by C. Renfrew and E. B. W. Zubrow. Cambridge: Cambridge University Press.

Rothman, M. S. 1994. "Sealing as a Control Mechanism in Prehistory: Tepe Gawra XI, X and VIII." In *Chiefdoms and Early States in the Near East: The Organizational Dynamics of Complexity*, edited by G. Stein and M. S. Rothman. Monographs in World Archaeology No. 18. Madison, Wis.: Prehistory Press.

Steve, M.-J., and H. Gasche. 1973. *l'acropole de Suse.* Memoires de la Délégation Archéologique Française en Iran 66. Paris: Guethner.

Whitehouse, Harvey. 2000. *Arguments and Icons: Divergent Modes of Religiosity.* Cambridge: Cambridge University Press.

————. 2001. "Modes of Religiosity: Towards a Cognitive Explanation of the Sociopolitical Dynamics of Religion." Circulated preconference reading for "Modes of Religiosity: The Historical Evidence," 1–5 August 2002, The University of Vermont, Burlington, Vermont.

Wright, H. T. 1977. "Recent Research on the Origin of the State." *Annual Review of Anthropology* 6: 379–97.

———. 1994. "Prestate Political Formations." In *Chiefdoms and Early States in the Near East: The Organizational Dynamics of Complexity*, edited by G. Stein and M. S. Rothman. Monographs in World Archaeology, No. 18. Madison, Wis.: Prehistory Press.

———. 1998. "Uruk States in Southwestern Iran." In *Archaic States*, edited by G. Feinman and J. Marcus. Santa Fe, N.M.: SAR Press.

Wright, H. T., and G. A. Johnson. 1975. "Population, Exchange and Early State Formation in Southwestern Iran." *American Anthropologist* 77: 267–89.

Wright, H. T., J. A. Neely, G. A. Johnson, and J. Speth. 1975. "Early Fourth Millennium Developments in Southwestern Iran." *Iran* 13: 129–41.

Wright, H. T., and E. Rupley. 2001. "Calibrated Radiocarbon Age Determinations of Uruk-Related Assemblages." In *Uruk, Mesopotamia and Its Neighbors*, edited by M. S. Rothman. Santa Fe, N.M.: SAR Press.

GRECO-ROMAN ANTIQUITY III

Old and New in Roman Religion: A Cognitive Account

5

DOUGLAS L. GRAGG

TRADITIONAL ROMAN RELIGION has been described, paradoxically, both as conservative (e.g., Grant 1957: xiv; Rose 1959: 158; Dumézil 1970: 83–88; Turcan 2000: 1) and as highly pragmatic and open to innovation (e.g., North 1976; Turcan 2000: 12–13, 105). There is no reason to quarrel with the observations about Roman religion that underlie this dual characterization, but analyzing these paradoxical tendencies within the framework of cognitive theory involves a shift in the way this characterization is understood and expressed. As Dan Sperber (1996) has argued, a religion (or a culture in general) is not a thing in itself but is a designation for mental representations (and their public tokens and traces) that have become widely shared and persistent among individuals in a population. Consequently, it is more useful to think and speak here of the relative stability and durability of traditional religious ideas and ritual practices among many Romans and the relative attractiveness (to some of the same Romans) of new religious ideas and ritual practices, than to speak as though Roman religion were conservative and open to innovation.[1]

This distinction may seem trivial to some, but it is the very move that makes a cognitive science of culture (including religion) possible. Mental representations (unlike alleged social or cultural facts or forces) can be located in space and time (as products of neurohormonal mechanisms in the bodies of particular humans). Furthermore, they bear a relationship to common human cognitive predilections that determines the scope and duration of their differential survival in a population. This means that some representations will prove more "contagious" than others in relation to the structures of human cognition as those structures have evolved.

Working at this concrete level makes it possible to develop theories and (most importantly) predictions based on those theories that can be tested within and across populations, past and present. In this chapter I analyze the durability of traditional religion among Romans, the attractiveness of new religious options to some, and the relationship between these phenomena in terms of two cognitive theories: Harvey Whitehouse's theory of modes of religiosity and Robert N. McCauley and E. Thomas Lawson's ritual form hypothesis. This permits me to study how well the data from ancient Rome conform to the predictions of these theories and, in the process, to reach a better understanding of aspects of Roman religion.[2]

First, I offer brief sketches of salient features of traditional Roman religion and of one type of new religious option that at least some Romans found compelling— mystery cults.[3] I focus primarily on the middle and late republican periods (roughly, the last three centuries BCE) for the sake of manageability. In these sketches, I draw on Whitehouse's modes theory to help clarify what is distinctive about the religious ideas and ritual practices being described. Then I turn to the question of how one might account for the openness of some Romans to certain radically new[4] religious ideas and ritual practices, first reviewing (noncognitive) theories commonly proposed and then indicating how cognitive theory, particularly the ritual form hypothesis of McCauley and Lawson, might shed light on the issue.

Traditional Roman Religion

Any account of traditional Roman religion must proceed in medias res because evidence regarding its origins and earliest development is limited and fragmentary. If we target some moment in republican Rome of the third or second century BCE, however, we can discern a reasonably clear profile of typical practice. What we see most immediately is an elaborate set of ritual practices, touching practically every aspect of daily life in the home, on the farm, on the road, in the city, and on the battlefield. At the heart of this ritual system is sacrifice, the devotion of living things (Ogilvie 1969: 41–42) or their by-products to the gods—or, more accurately, to a particular god, goddess, or guardian spirit, according to the purpose at hand. Indeed, "every action of any importance in Rome began and ended with a sacrifice" (Turcan 2000: 103).

Sacrifice in Rome was performed according to strict rules. Even a minor infraction or mishap in performance or the discovery of an irregularity of some kind in the offering voided the sacrifice, requiring its repetition.[5] Sacrifice was a correlate of prayer, either as payment in advance in support of a petition or as payment owed in fulfillment of a vow. This transactional character of sacrifice is best summed up in the Latin expression *do ut des*, meaning "I (the worshipper) give, that you (the god) might give." Consider the prayer, recorded by the elder Cato, that accompanied the *suovetaurilia* (the offering of a pig, ram, and bull) to Mars to ensure the god's protection and assistance:

Mars Pater, I pray and beseech you to be favorable and kind to me, my house and our household; for this reason I have bidden a *suovetaurilia* to be driven around my land, ground and farm,[6] that you may prevent, ward off and avert diseases, visible and invisible, dearth and destruction, ruin and storm, and that you permit the crops, corn, vineyards and plantations to grow and flourish, and that you keep safe the shepherds and their sheep, and grant good health and strength to me, my house and our household. In respect of these things . . . be honoured by the sacrifice of the suckling victims of this *suovetaurilia*. (Cato, *On Agriculture* 141; Beard, North, and Price 1998, vol. 2: 152).

In exchange for the requested divine assistance, the sacrifice is offered for the god's benefit. The Latin expression translated by M. Beard, J. North, and S. Price as "be honoured" (*macte esto*) may also (and perhaps would better) be translated "be increased" or "be strengthened" (that is, by the sacrifice). As one modern scholar put it, "the worshipper is praying that his sacrifice may revitalise the god and so enable him to fulfill the requests that are made to him" (Ogilvie 1969: 42; cf. Scullard 1981: 23).

The fundamental context for Roman ritual practice was the home. The *paterfamilias* led his household in the regular observances by which its members sought to maintain the good will of gods and ancestral spirits and to secure their aid. Prominent among the powers honored in the domestic cult were the *lares* (spirits of the family's deceased ancestors) and the *penates* (spirits who guarded the household provisions). The *genius* (guardian spirit) of the male head of the household was also among the powers regularly invoked by the family. In addition, individual families, clans, or communities often maintained traditions of special homage to a patron deity, such as Apollo, but they were careful also to make appropriate offerings to other gods and goddesses according to their domains and to offer appeasement to any who became disgruntled.

Rituals of the domestic cult followed regular cycles, ranging from daily to annual frequency, and also marked special occasions, including high points of the life cycle—birth, passage to adulthood, marriage, and death. Each day prayers and sacrifices were offered to the household spirits upon rising, at meals, and at bedtime. At seasonal transitions and other regular intervals throughout the year and when pursuing particular projects, sacrifices were offered to various deities to ward off trouble and ensure success. The sacrifices involved in daily rituals were generally simple—burning incense, making a libation of wine, or casting a measure of grain or a portion of the family meal onto the fire of the hearth. Rituals less frequently observed, especially those celebrated jointly with other families of the clan or community, were often more elaborate, involving animal sacrifices and sometimes banquets, special attire, dancing, and athletic games.[7]

The reference to clans and communities moves us in the direction of more public expressions of Roman piety, which were, in large part, extensions of domestic practice. In the words of H. H. Scullard (1981: 17), "Many of the State cults and festivals of Rome were in a sense family cults writ large."[8] Daily rituals were performed by the vestal virgins, who tended the public "hearth," and by the *flamen Dialis* (the priest of Jupiter), who sacrificed daily to Rome's most distinguished patron deity on the Capitoline Hill. In addition, a full public ritual calendar, based largely on the cycles of nature, included ceremonies on the calends, nones, and ides of each month as well as an array of annual festivals occurring at the rate of two or more every month. Also included were a handful of festivals that were held at five-year intervals and even one, the so-called Saecular Games, that came around (in theory, at least) only once each century! Like the periodic rituals of the domestic cult, these were devoted to designated deities according to domain. In order to ensure that these rituals were performed properly—in accordance with well-tested ancestral custom (*mos maiorum*)—the senate or other state authorities entrusted their conduct to public officials and other noted citizens whom they appointed as priests of various sorts (*flamines, pontifices, augures,* etc.).[9]

Again, the rituals performed less frequently were more elaborate than those performed on a daily basis, and the pageantry attending state-sponsored ceremonies could reach impressive levels. One representative example from the many annual festivals will suffice to illustrate the contrast with the simple daily sacrifices of the vestals or of Jupiter's *flamen*.[10] Games in honor of the goddess Ceres (the *ludi Cereris* or *Cerialia*) were held in April of each year. The festivities lasted several days (April 12–19), during which chariot races were held in the Circus Maximus and grain offerings occupied altars throughout the city. The midpoint of the festival (April 15) was marked by the *Fordicidia*, the sacrifice of a pregnant cow to *Tellus* (Soil) in each of the thirty wards, or curiae, of the city. The entrails of the victims were burned in the usual fashion on the curial altars, but the thirty fetuses were handed over to the vestals for burning. On April 19 the games were brought to a close with flair. Foxes were released in the Circus Maximus with burning torches tied to their tails (Turcan 2000: 68–69; Scullard 1981: 101–3)!

Whitehouse on Modes of Religiosity

These observations about relative frequency of performance and level of pageantry in Roman ritual practice offer a point of contact with the work of Harvey Whitehouse.[11] In Whitehouse's theory, frequency of performance and level of arousing pageantry are related to the function of memory in the transmission of ritual. Two styles of transmission in particular facilitate memory, though in different ways. Frequent repetition facilitates the recording of ritual procedures and ritual meanings in what cognitive psychologists call, respectively, "implicit" and "semantic" memory systems. Highly arousing pageantry, by contrast, helps to trigger "episodic" memory.[12] The two styles of transmission are inversely correlated; the arousing effect of high levels of pageantry diminishes with increasing repetition through a process of habituation.

Ritual frequency and level of arousal are, for Whitehouse, two of the variables in a larger theory of two modes of religiosity.[13] Rituals performed frequently with low levels of arousal are characteristic of the doctrinal mode. In this mode, ritual meanings are supplied on the basis of official ritual exegesis. Dynamic and authoritative leaders impart these meanings and warn against alternative interpretations. Frequent ritual performance, with orthodox interpretation, contributes to accurate recall of doctrinal formulations (semantic memory). Ritual communities operating primarily in this mode tend to be relatively diffuse and inclusive.

By contrast, rituals performed infrequently with high levels of arousal are characteristic of the imagistic mode. The effect of the high arousal is to burn the experience into the episodic memory of participants, often with life-changing consequences. Such a ritual makes a lasting impression, and participants recall it as a singular experience (that is, not simply as a type), involving particular persons and particular events in a particular setting. Those who have such a ritual experience in common are likely to form on that basis a strongly cohesive social group, which must inevitably exclude those who have not had the experience. They are also likely, individually, to reflect deeply over time on the ordeal they experienced in order to make sense of it, a process Whitehouse (2002: 305–6) refers to as spontaneous exegetical reflection (SER). The result is a diversity of ritual interpretations rather than an orthodoxy that requires policing by authoritative leaders.

How might traditional Roman religion be located in terms of Whitehouse's theory? The range of both frequency of performance and level of pageantry we have observed in Roman ritual practice seems at first to suggest that it operated in both modes, doctrinal and imagistic, perhaps representing a blend of the two. Closer examination reveals, however, that one cannot place Roman religion unqualifiedly in either of Whitehouse's modes of religiosity. This can be demonstrated quite easily in the case of the imagistic mode; the question of doctrinal modality is more complicated.

The high level of pageantry that characterized Roman rituals performed infrequently—particularly those of the civic cult—does not appear to have produced the effects Whitehouse associates with the imagistic mode of religiosity. The festive pageantry certainly must have been dazzling and even, for many, lastingly memorable. For large, anonymous throngs of Romans, however, it would not have provided the kind of singular experience that results in a strongly cohesive and exclusive social group and that generates recurring individual SER. The heightened pageantry of annual festivals and other infrequently performed Roman civic rituals can be accounted for sufficiently in terms of its contribution—as a demonstration of wealth and civic generosity—to the honor and prestige (*gloria*) of the events' sponsors (see Orlin 1997: 66–73, 162–89). The bigger the show, the larger the crowd, the greater the glory. The fact that frequently performed rituals were not accompanied by such pageantry would also, in this case, have less to do with the cognitive dynamics of ritual than with calculations about obtaining the most *gloria* for one's expenditure (calculations governed, of course, by cognitive dynamics equally worthy of study).

If these rituals did not activate episodic memory, one might also ask how the details of performance were remembered so that replication could be achieved. Two factors make this easy to explain. First, even the most elaborate ceremonies were made up mostly of standardized components familiar from the domestic cult or from other public festivals (e.g., sacrifices, processions, games), each with its own routine protocol.[14] Second, officials performing civic rituals were able to rely on written texts or priestly dictation to ensure correct performance.[15]

If traditional Roman religion did not operate in the imagistic mode, can a case be made for doctrinal modality? A convenient way to answer this question is to address it in terms of the three features cited earlier to characterize the doctrinal mode of religiosity: (1) communion is inclusive; (2) leadership is authoritative; and (3) ritual meanings are given.[16]

1. *Inclusive communion.* One needed only to be a member of the household or a citizen of the state to belong to the ritual community. In the case of the civic cult, anonymity was certainly the rule, and we do not really know how much of the populace even attended the performances of public rituals. The desire for *gloria*, noted earlier, may suggest that one reason officials loaded many public rituals with such elaborate pageantry was to draw as large a crowd as possible! In terms of communion, then, one might argue that the data of traditional Roman religion are at least consistent with predictions associated with doctrinal modality.

2. *Authoritative leadership.* The *paterfamilias* was the unquestioned ritual authority (though not the only ritual actor) in the household, and the civic cult was led by properly appointed public officials and priests. The priests were responsible particularly for seeing that magistrates carried out public rituals according to established rules of performance. Any misstep required a restart and sometimes an additional expiatory sacrifice. At the same time (at least in the republican period, with which we are concerned), "the capacity for religious action and for religious decision-making was widely diffused among different Roman authorities (not only

priests)," with the result that "there was no single central power that controlled (or even claimed to control) Roman relations with their gods" (Beard, North, and Price 1998, vol. I: 21).[17] In terms of leadership, then, the evidence is at best a mixed bag, allowing one to place Roman religion in Whitehouse's doctrinal mode only with significant qualifications.

3. *Authoritative ritual exegesis.* It is with regard to the source of ritual meanings, however, that problems with this placement become most apparent. It is true that certain shared assumptions lay below the surface of Roman ritual practice. Among these were the ideas that divine favor cannot be taken for granted, that divine favor is nevertheless necessary for success in life, that sacrifice can elicit divine favor, and that sacrifice must be offered to the right god in the right way to be effective. These and other important ideas were often articulated through prayers and other verbalizations that accompanied ritual performances (recall Cato's prayer cited earlier). What is missing, however, is any evidence of a tradition of authoritative ritual exegesis that served as a source of ritual meanings and so informed a practice of routinized doctrinal instruction. Even the written texts mentioned earlier, on which officials performing civic rituals could rely to ensure correct performance, were only "books of religious formulae, which preserved the proper texts of prayers" or "priestly collections of rules and decisions" and not works establishing "tenets and doctrine" or explaining and interpreting rituals (Beard, North, and Price 1998, vol. I: 284).

These observations make it impossible to understand traditional Roman religion straightforwardly in terms of doctrinal modality. Two types of evidence illustrate further, however, the complexity of the issue. First, there is the recurring distinction in Roman public discourse, which picks up increasing steam in the late republican and early imperial periods, between *religio* (licit—usually Roman—practices) and *superstitio* (illicit—usually foreign—practices). Second, there is the appearance in the late republic and early empire of such works as *Divine Antiquities* by Varro (116–27 BCE), *On the Nature of the Gods* and *On Divination* by Cicero (106–43 BCE), *Metamorphoses* and *Fasti* by Ovid (43 BCE–17 CE), and *Memorable Deeds and Sayings* by Valerius Maximus (dates uncertain, but active during the reign of Tiberius). While these works do not qualify as authoritative exegesis,[18] they do represent a new interest in historical and theoretical reflection on Roman religion in (mostly Greek) philosophical, literary, and moral categories. One way to interpret these two trends would be to see them as features of a kind of protodoctrinal tendency—evoked in part by the increasing encounter with alien traditions that accompanied Roman imperial expansion—with the potential of developing into an example of full-blown doctrinal modality under the right set of pressures.

If traditional Roman religion does not fit well into either the imagistic or the doctrinal mode, does this constitute a falsification of Whitehouse's theory? An implication of the theory made fully explicit only in his most recent formulation of it (2004) suggests that this is not necessarily the case. There (especially in his chapter on the "costliness" of religion), Whitehouse clarifies that his theory is intended to explain concepts that are cognitively unnatural and, therefore, cannot be transmitted successfully without special mnemonic support. The two modes of religiosity are "attractor positions" that account for successful transmission. By contrast, concepts that are cognitively natural do not require the special mnemonic support provided by the modes of religiosity. These concepts cluster instead around what Whitehouse calls a "universal attractor position," or (following Pascal Boyer) a "cognitive optimum." In this scenario, traditional Roman religion would fall into the latter category and, therefore, outside the scope of phenomena that Whitehouse's modes theory seeks to explain.[19]

Comprised, then, of cognitively optimal concepts, traditional Roman religion proved to be remarkably stable and durable. That did not prevent some Romans, however, from becoming involved in cults of foreign origin with a very different ritual profile. Prominent among these were the cults traditionally called "mysteries," including those at Eleusis in Greece and those related to Dionysus/Bacchus, to the Anatolian Cybele, to the Egyptian Isis, and to the Persian Mithras. This is not the place for extended description of each of these cults.[20] They do not by any means follow a uniform pattern (see especially Burkert 1987), but they do share certain features that set them in sharp contrast to traditional Roman religion. It is sufficient for the present purpose to consider two of these shared features of mystery cults in relation to Whitehouse's modes theory: (1) the central place of rituals of initiation, and (2) the sense of connectedness to fellow initiates that participation in such rituals engendered.

The Ritual Profile of the Mysteries

Unlike traditional Roman religion, mystery cults offered some form of initiation in which the god or goddess accepted a postulant into his or her sphere of care and protection. The details of initiation rituals were well-kept secrets with the result that we know very little about them. Bits of evidence scattered through the literary, inscriptional, and iconographic records do make it clear, however, that these rites were full of highly arousing images and experiences calculated to make a profound and lasting impression. Experiences of alternating darkness and light, confinement and release, humiliation and praise, terror and relief, exertion and rest, and fasting and feasting are all documented. Also indicated in some cases are special uses of music and color and the presentation of startling objects. Examples from the cult of Bacchus (Dionysus) serve well to illustrate the kinds of "cognitive shock" to which initiates were typically exposed.[21]

The cult of Bacchus was already well established on Roman soil before the second century BCE, as the many knowing references in the comedies of Plautus (254–184 BCE) make clear (Beard, North, and Price 1998, vol. 1: 93). The goal of the cultist was to be possessed by the god, to "become" a Bacchus or Baccha. In early Greek Dionysism, worshippers achieved this union either through lifelong asceticism (Orphism) or through periodic exercises of ecstatic mysticism (Maenadism). The Dionysism that took root in Rome had already evolved into a mystery cult, in which the god granted to a passive postulant permanent union with himself through initiation (Turcan 1996: 295–96).

A candidate for Bacchic initiation was required to forgo sexual relations (and perhaps certain foods) for several days prior to the ceremonies. At the end of this period of abstinence, final preparations were completed, including a bath of purification, sacrifices, and an oath of secrecy and commitment. The candidate, dressed only in an animal skin and perhaps adorned with ivy or other sacred foliage and special makeup, was then led through a series of experiences about which our knowledge is scanty. Iconographic and literary evidence suggests that initiates saw evocative images and encountered various masked or hooded cult members—some of them nude—reading from scrolls, playing musical instruments, or wielding rods or whips. Almost all sources identify as a central feature of the ritual the presentation of a *liknon*, or sacred basket, which was uncovered in front of the initiate to reveal a large phallus (perhaps interpreted by many participants as a symbol of generative power). Initiates were given passwords and sacred objects as tokens of their consecration (some also received tattoos) and were welcomed to a concluding liturgy of drinking and frenzied dancing, through which their new union with Bacchus was vividly experienced.[22]

This pageantry was clearly the kind that activates episodic memory and triggers recurring SER, indicating that the cult operated in Whitehouse's imagistic mode. What we know of ancient mystery cults in general appears also to confirm Whitehouse's prediction that common experience of this kind of ritual is likely to result in a strong sense of connectedness among initiates. Walter Burkert (1987: 43–46) urges caution here; the nature and degree of community varied from one mystery cult to another. He even suggests that the very exclusiveness of these cults checked their tendency toward communal solidarity, contrasting the eagerness with which early Christian communities in various locations sought contact with one another with the relative disinterest in such contact among, say, groups of initiates of Isis. Burkert is right about this contrast, but this is just what Whitehouse's modes theory would predict. In the imagistic mode (as in mystery cults), a strong sense of connectedness arises out of (episodic) memory of the experience of vivid ritual(s) with particular coparticipants and so generally remains local. In the doctrinal mode (as in early Christianity), by contrast, (semantic) memory of authorized ideas and practices does not specify the identities of particular ritual participants. This gives rise to anonymous, idealized communities that are, as a result, interchangeable. It is true that, in some mystery cults, even local groups of initiates do not appear to have met frequently for fellowship or mutual aid. Even in these cases, however, there remained, in Burkert's words, "the memory of a sacred experience that [could] be resuscitated" in the service of some common purpose (1987: 43).

We do not know how many Romans became involved in these cults. Many (perhaps even most) of the practitioners were foreigners who brought portable versions[23] of their native cults with them when they came to Rome or to a Roman provincial outpost as slaves or as migrants in search of opportunity. Roman authorities sought at times to discourage or even forbid forms of association or extreme practices that seemed to them to undermine social order.[24] The fact that at least some Romans nevertheless became eager participants requires some explanation.

The Appeal of the Mysteries

The authors of standard handbooks on Roman religion published in the nineteenth and twentieth centuries generally accounted for the appeal of mystery cults quite confidently in terms of some inherent flaw or weakness in traditional religion. They typically contrasted the "sterile formalism," "crude materialism," and "arid legalism" of traditional religion with the "vibrancy" and "spirituality" of the cults.[25] Such assessments are rightly identified by more recent scholarship as judgments having more to do with the historians' own (typically Protestant Christian) cultural values than with historical reality (North 1976: 10–12).

Other modern scholars have emphasized the emergence of new social and political realities in the middle and late republican periods, to which traditional religion seemed unable to respond or adapt, as a way of accounting for openness to more "promising" religious options. Among the developments commonly cited in this regard are two that I mention here.

1. Critical military struggles that appeared to threaten Rome's very
    survival—particularly the Second Punic War (218–202 BCE) and the civil
    wars of the first century BCE—are said to have created a crisis of
    confidence in the efficacy of traditional religion. It was, after all, in the
    context of the taxing struggle with Hannibal that the Senate imported
    into Rome the cult of the Anatolian Cybele, the first cult of eastern

origin to be officially sanctioned (Turcan 2000: 109). It is worth noting, however, that this decision was prompted by the traditional procedure of consulting the Sibylline books. The actual transfer to Rome of the sacred stone, to which the goddess's presence was believed to be attached, and its installation—first on the Palatine and later in its own sanctuary—was also accompanied by appropriate traditional rituals (Turcan 1996: 35–37).

2. Rome's transition from city-state to multiethnic empire during this period is said to have created a crisis of identity for individual Roman citizens. Feeling increasingly alienated from the political process and nostalgic for the more participatory and communal model of the past (so the argument goes), some Romans found in the cults a renewed sense of belonging and of personal significance that traditional religion could not deliver (Turcan 1996: 17–18). This explanation remains speculative, however, because of a lack of relevant supporting evidence. One type of potential evidence would be testimonials of Roman devotees of mystery cults. Such a testimonial would be relevant evidence if it expressed enthusiasm in terms of a contrast with traditional religion, but I am not aware of any examples of this. In any case, being initiated into one or more mysteries almost never involved a rejection of traditional religion.

Scholars who argue that it was the failure of traditional religion that prompted interest in foreign cults make much of the testimony of Roman authors of the late republic, such as Varro and Cicero, and of the Augustan era (23 BCE–14 CE), such as Livy and Horace, who speak of a decline of religion in their time. These authors do paint a negative portrait of traditional religious observance during the last century of the republic: temples allowed to fall into disrepair, important public rituals neglected, the office of *flamen Dialis* allowed to go unfilled, rites of divination manipulated by cynical politicians for personal ends, and so forth. This testimony must be qualified, however, in two ways. First, these authors betray no conviction that there was some inherent flaw in traditional religion or that it was unequal to the challenge of new realities. The problem, in their view, was rather that the neglect of traditional religion had resulted in great political and social crises (North 1976: 11–12). Second, it is arguable that these authors exaggerated the neglect of religion in the interest of certain rhetorical aims. What better way, for example, for Augustan loyalists to extol the greatness of the new ruler's revival of religion than to emphasize the sorry state into which it had fallen? What simpler way to account for the national woes of the last century of the republic than to attribute them to the people's neglect of the cult of the gods that had enabled them in the past to achieve such great success? A passage from the poet Horace, published shortly after Augustus became emperor, illustrates both themes nicely:

> It's not a question of whether or not you're guilty,
>   Roman, yourself.
> The transgressions of your fathers must be paid for.
>   You must rebuild
> The broken-down temples and the toppled altars;
>   You must restore,
> Also, the fallen statues, cleaned of their grime.
>
> The only way to rule is to serve the gods.
>   All things begin
> From them; and it is only the gods who know
>   How all things end.
> Neglected, the gods brought down upon the Romans
>   All the misfortunes
> Sorrowing Italy suffers from in these days . . .
>   (*Odes* 3.6.1–8; Ferry 1997: 179).

Disruption of attention to scrupulous maintenance of the ritual calendar and to the upkeep of temples (and other public buildings) is not entirely unexpected in a time of political turmoil. Nor is political exploitation of religion surprising when factions are vying for power and resources are being redirected to military uses. The depiction of civic religion in the late republic—whether by ancient or modern authors—as one of unmitigated decline is, however, open to serious challenge.[26] To this it can be added that there is certainly no clear evidence for widespread disruption in the late republic of the domestic cult or of popular interest in civic ritual (Turcan 2000: 103–4). Traditional Roman religion was to survive, in fact, for several more centuries (though not, of course, without continuing to evolve). Many of its key features survived incognito even beyond that—in the organizational structure, ritual calendar, and popular piety of post-Constantinian Christianity.[27]

The attraction of the mysteries cannot be explained so confidently, then, in terms of the bankruptcy of traditional Roman religion. We are left with a stable and durable traditional ritual system that some Romans were drawn to supplement with initiation into one or more mysteries (and perhaps other nontraditional religious experiences as well). Because the traditional concepts and practices clustered around the cognitive optimum, their robustness is not surprising. What does still await convincing explanation is the appeal of the mysteries to some Romans in spite of this robustness of traditional religion. Can cognitive theory shed any new light on this problem?

A Cognitive Solution?

From the perspective of Whitehouse's modes theory, one might argue that there is really no problem here to solve. Just as a susceptible host may succumb to a cold virus simply by coming into contact with it, so humans may succumb to cults like the mysteries when exposed to them largely because of a susceptible cognitive architecture. Arguing this way, one might say simply that, as Rome's armies conquered new territories, more Romans came into contact with such cults, and so, an increasing number of Romans adopted them. It may be possible to say a bit more than this, however, on the basis of another cognitive theory developed by Bob McCauley and Tom Lawson.

McCauley and Lawson recently introduced a ritual form hypothesis (McCauley 2001; McCauley and Lawson 2002) based on their theory of ritual competence (Lawson and McCauley 1990, 2002). It is not necessary to review their hypothesis in detail here. Most useful for our purpose is their distinction between "special-agent" rituals, in which culturally postulated superhuman (CPS) figures are the actors, and "special-patient" rituals, in which such figures are acted upon.[28] An example of a special-agent ritual would be an initiation (as in the mystery cults) in which a CPS-agent acts to change the status of a postulant. An example of a special-patient ritual would be a sacrifice (as in traditional Roman religion) in which a worshipper offers a gift to a CPS-figure in a bid for favor or in gratitude for assistance. Special-agent rituals are performed infrequently—generally only once for each individual participant—because their effects are considered permanent. They are also typically characterized by high levels of sensory pageantry because of a sense of their religious importance (McCauley and Lawson 2002: 122–23). Special-patient rituals, by contrast, are generally repeated frequently because their effects are considered temporary. Because of this frequency of performance (and perhaps a sense of lesser importance), levels of sensory pageantry tend to be low.[29]

A striking feature of traditional Roman religion (in terms of the ritual form hypothesis) is the virtual absence of special-agent rituals. There is some evidence for an initiation rite in archaic times, but it did not survive into the republican period (Bremmer 1996), when the passage to adulthood was celebrated with no trace of CPS-agency (Ogilvie 1969: 103; Turcan 2000: 21). Dedication of temples does not appear to have been understood in terms of divine action (Orlin 1997, see especially 162–89), nor does appointment of priests.[30] One form of marriage (by *confarreatio*) does look like a special-agent ritual. It was considered indissoluble except by another powerful rite, the *diffarreatio*. Marriage by *confarreatio* was available only to the patrician class, however, and appears to have been used very rarely (Turcan 2000: 22–25). Even divination (consulting the auspices or the Sibylline books, interpreting prodigies, etc.)—a major feature of Roman religion—cannot be classified as special-agent ritual, though its purpose was to elicit divine communication. It was infinitely repeatable, and its focus lay in acts of interpretation by officials performing the ritual (Ogilvie 1969: 53–69; Turcan 2000: 85–92).

McCauley and Lawson argue that the cross-cultural evidence they examined suggests that religions without special-agent rituals are likely at some point to develop them. They cite the case of the Pomio Kivung movement of Papua New Guinea, which Whitehouse (1995) studied, as one model of how this works. In that model, splinter groups emerge on a cyclical basis and revive abandoned special-agent rituals from earlier ancestral religions or invent new ones. The splinter groups do not arise because of disillusionment with standard doctrine or ritual. On the contrary, they follow in the wake of an intensification of commitment and expectation, inspired by a fresh experience (revelation) of eschatological immediacy. These splinter groups typically "crash" and get reabsorbed by the mainstream movement, but group members return with a renewed (and contagious) energy and motivation attributable to their participation for a time in the special-agent rituals (McCauley and Lawson 2002: 192–201).

Perhaps something similar was going on in the case of Romans who sought initiation into mystery cults—although along the lines of a different model. In this case, the pattern was not one of some adherents (temporarily) radicalizing their own tradition, but of some supplementing their traditional experience through involvement in the special-agent rituals of another cult. As in the case of the splinter groups from the Pomio Kivung, there is no evidence of disillusionment with the tradition, so this suggestion need not entail the kind of negative judgment regarding the traditional rituals that we noted on the part of some earlier historians of Roman religion. It suggests only that human cognitive architecture is such that attraction to different ritual forms will follow predictable patterns. There is no reason why someone could not have been a devout participant—even a priest—in the traditional religion and also an initiate of one or more mysteries. Our evidence suggests, in fact, that this was not at all uncommon.

The fact that many Romans did not become involved in mystery cults need not count too strongly against this suggestion. After all, not getting involved does not necessarily imply not being attracted. The (provisional) idea of a protodoctrinal tendency in traditional Roman religion, which I introduced earlier, may prove useful here. Negative propaganda, issuing from officials who feared that membership in (at least some of) these cults of foreign origin might compromise loyalty to the state, may have dissuaded many from following their interest. Branding such cults as *superstitiones* would have played upon natural prejudices against alien customs. On the other hand, some Romans may not, in fact, have felt attracted at all by ritual practices that struck them as entirely too exotic or bizarre.

The reactions of others may have ranged from timid curiosity to indifference to hostility. What is important, however, is that some Romans did pursue initiation into mysteries, and the ritual form hypothesis of McCauley and Lawson may contribute to our ability to explain this without resorting to untestable forms of speculation about what sensitive Romans may have found lacking in the traditions of their ancestors.

There is much more work to be done. I believe that this preliminary study has, at the very least, illustrated the potential fruitfulness of the interdisciplinary encounter of cognitive science and the historical study of religion. More specifically, it has shown (1) that evidence from ancient Roman religion appears to support the conclusion that the theories of Whitehouse and of McCauley and Lawson are on the right track, and (2) that those theories have potentially powerful heuristic value for the historical reasoning of investigators who wish to move beyond analogies rooted in their own folk-psychological intuitions. As with all scientific theories, of course, the usefulness of the two with which we have interacted here will depend on how well they weather continuing empirical tests.

Notes

1. This conceptual shift also allows one to avoid invoking such dubious entities as "the Roman mentality and temperament" (Turcan 1996: 11), except perhaps as shorthand expressions for statistically significant distributions of particular representations.

2. There is no reason not to retain the term *Roman religion* for economy of expression, as long as one remains alert to the reification it can encourage.

3. These sketches represent, for the most part, conclusions that are broadly supported in current historical scholarship. As in any active field of research, many working results are vigorously debated. The principal purpose of this study, however, is not to resolve debated issues or advance novel reconstructions, but to consider whether and how cognitive theory might help to clarify and explain central features of Roman religion.

4. I use the expression "radically new" to limit the reference to cults, such as the mysteries, whose ritual profiles were very different from traditional Roman religion. The absorption of cults whose profiles were similar to that of Roman religion or that were easily romanized is interesting, but is less difficult to explain.

5. See, for example, Cicero, *On the Response of the Haruspices* 23; Plutarch, *Life of Coriolanus* 25.6–7.

6. Leading the animals around the perimeter of the property before they were sacrificed marked off the area for which the god's protection and assistance was being sought.

7. For details of the rituals of the domestic cult, see Turcan (2000: 14–50).

8. This is true, in many ways, even of the later cult of the emperor, who became the *paterfamilias* of the entire Roman "household" and whose *genius* was honored in both public and private worship (Turcan 2000: 136–37).

9. For details of the civic cult, see Turcan (2000: 51–85) and Scullard (1981).

10. We know little about the ritual of the quinquennial festivals and practically nothing at all about the ritual of the Saecular Games before those held by Augustus in 17 BCE. Those were indeed a spectacle the people of Rome "had never seen before and would not see again" (Turcan 2000: 84). For descriptions of Augustus' games, see Turcan (2000: 83–85) and Beard, North, and Price (1998, vol. I: 201–6).

11. The theory sketched here is set out in detail in Whitehouse (1995, 2000) and summarized in Whitehouse (2002).

12. On memory systems, see the influential studies in Winograd and Neisser (1992) and in Neisser and Hyman (2000).

13. Characteristics of the two modes are nicely represented in Whitehouse (2002: 309, figure 4).

14. McCauley and Lawson (2002: 66, 74, 153) refer to this as "compositionality."

15. See, for example, Livy 8.9, 9.46; and Pliny the Elder, *Natural History* 13.10.

16. These are not the only variables identified and discussed by Whitehouse, but they are sufficient for the present purpose.

17. This was to change with Augustus, the first Roman emperor, in whom "for the first time, Roman religion had a head" (Beard, North, and Price 1998, vol. I: 192; see their full discussion, 186–92).

18. These works stood, as Beard, North, and Price put it, "at a distance from traditional religious practice" (1998, vol. I: 153). Consider, for example, in Cicero's dialogue *On the Nature of the Gods*, how Cotta, who was a priest, insists on a sharp distinction between his personal commitment to traditional religious beliefs and observances and his interest in philosophical (even skeptical) reflection on them (3.5–6).

19. For further help in analyzing forms of religion (such as traditional Roman religion) that consist of cognitively natural concepts, one must turn to the work of other cognitive theorists, such as that of McCauley and Lawson (discussed later in this chapter) and Pascal Boyer (1994, 2001). For example, the way Romans understood relational aspects of their experience of the gods (exchange of benefits, general predictability of behavior, etc.) can be illuminated by Boyer's concept of minimally counterintuitive agents, and motivational aspects of the practice of sacrificial ritual (recurring desire for purification, meticulous concern for procedural correctness, etc.) can be related to his discussions of the instinct for contamination avoidance and the dynamics of obsessive-compulsive behavior.

20. Turcan (1996) provides a thorough survey.

21. See also chapter 6 for Roger Beck's discussion of the cult of Mithras.

22. For discussion of the evidence and of problems of interpretation, see Turcan (1996: 291–312) and Beard, North, and Price (1998, vol. I: 91–96, 161–64).

23. The portability of these originally local cults was due largely to their hellenization (Turcan 1996: 3–7).

24. One of the most notable cases was the senate's vigorous repression of the cult of Bacchus in 186 BCE. The most extensive ancient account of the incident is that of Livy (39.8–19).

25. The characterization by Grant (1957: xxxiii–xxxiv) is representative. Bendlin (2000: 116–18) cites the handbooks of Johann Adam Hartung (1836) and Georg Wissowa

(1902) as examples of a different approach to the same solution. They postulated an early dynamic form of Roman *Volksreligion* that was gradually corrupted during the republican period by a priestly agenda. Along with Bendlin's own critique of this approach, see Beard, North, and Price (1998, vol. I: 10–18).

26. These issues are discussed in more detail in Beard, North, and Price (1998, vol. I: 117–34).

27. This point has been elaborated many times. Rose (1959: 293–305) covers the bases as well as any.

28. They also identify a third form, "special-instrument" rituals, in which CPS-agency is implicated in a presupposed ritual action through which an instrument (e.g., water) is consecrated for subsequent ritual use. They group special-instrument with special-patient rituals, however, since the crux for them is whether a CPS-figure is the actor in a ritual or not.

29. The theories of Whitehouse and of McCauley and Lawson clearly overlap considerably, particularly in their common interest in the significance of performance frequency and level of arousal. One important difference is that Whitehouse's theory is designed primarily to explain successful transmission of ritual meanings—transmission whose success depends on special mnemonic support in one of two modes. McCauley and Lawson, on the other hand, are seeking primarily to explain relative frequency and pageantry (as well as other variables) in terms of ritual form. This does not mean that ritual meanings are completely irrelevant to their hypothesis, but it is clear that they are only of secondary significance (McCauley and Lawson 2002: 9–10, 36–37).

30. Possible exceptions to this in prerepublican and early republican times were the *rex sacrorum* (king of rites) and the three major *flamines* (of Jupiter, Mars, and Quirinus). Restrictions on their activities may suggest a special status resulting from a special-agent rite of consecration, but our knowledge here is very limited. At any rate, such restrictions were gradually relaxed in the later republic (Beard, North, and Price 1998, vol. I: 27–30; Ogilvie 1969: 106–11).

References

Beard, M., J. North, and S. Price. 1998. *Religions of Rome*. 2 vols. New York: Cambridge University Press.

Bendlin, A. 2000. "Looking Beyond the Civic Compromise: Religious Pluralism in Late Republican Rome." In *Religion in Archaic and Republican Rome and Italy: Evidence and Experience*, edited by E. Bispham and C. Smith. Edinburgh: Edinburgh University Press.

Boyer, P. 1994. *The Naturalness of Religious Ideas*. Berkeley: University of California Press.

———. 2001. *Religion Explained: The Evolutionary Origins of Religious Thought*. New York: Basic Books.

Bremmer, J. N. 1996. "Initiation." In *The Oxford Classical Dictionary*, edited by S. Hornblower and A. Spawforth. 3rd ed. Oxford: Oxford University Press.

Burkert, W. 1987. *Ancient Mystery Cults*. Cambridge, Mass.: Harvard University Press.

Dumézil, G. 1970. *Archaic Roman Religion*, translated by P. Krapp. 2 vols. Chicago: University of Chicago Press.

Ferry, D. 1997. *The Odes of Horace*. New York: Farrar, Straus and Giroux.

Grant, F. C., ed. 1957. *Ancient Roman Religion*. Indianapolis, Ind.: Bobbs-Merrill Company.

Lawson, E. Thomas, and Robert N. McCauley. 1990. *Rethinking Religion: Connecting Cognition and Culture*. Cambridge: Cambridge University Press.

———. 2002. "The Cognitive Representation of Religious Ritual Form: A Theory of Participants' Competence with Religious Ritual Systems." In *Current Approaches in the Cognitive Science of Religion*, edited by I. Pyysiäinen and V. Anttonen. London: Continuum.

McCauley, Robert N. 2001. "Ritual, Memory, and Emotion: Comparing Two Cognitive Hypotheses." In *Religion in Mind: Cognitive Perspectives on Religious Belief, Ritual, and Experience*, edited by J. Andresen. Cambridge: Cambridge University Press.

McCauley, Robert N., and E. Thomas Lawson. 2002. *Bringing Ritual to Mind: Psychological Foundations of Cultural Forms*. Cambridge: Cambridge University Press.

Neisser, U., and I. E. Hyman Jr., eds. 2000. *Memory Observed: Remembering in Natural Contexts*. 2d ed. New York: Worth Publishers.

North, J. A. 1976. "Conservatism and Change in Roman Religion." *Papers of the British School at Rome* 44: 1–12.

Ogilvie, R. M. 1969. *The Romans and Their Gods in the Age of Augustus*. New York: W. W. Norton and Company.

Orlin, Eric M. 1997. *Temples, Religion, and Politics in the Roman Republic*. Leiden: E. J. Brill.

Rose, H. J. 1959. *Religion in Greece and Rome*. New York: Harper and Brothers.

Scullard, H. H. 1981. *Festivals and Ceremonies of the Roman Republic*. Ithaca, N.Y.: Cornell University Press.

Sperber, Dan. 1996. *Explaining Culture: A Naturalistic Approach*. Cambridge, Mass.: Blackwell.

Turcan, R. 1996. *The Cults of the Roman Empire*, translated by A. Nevill. Cambridge, Mass.: Blackwell.

———. 2000. *The Gods of Ancient Rome: Religion in Everyday Life from Archaic to Imperial Times*, translated by A. Nevill. New York: Routledge.

Whitehouse, Harvey. 1995. *Inside the Cult: Religious Innovation and Transmission in Papua New Guinea*. Oxford: Clarendon Press.

———. 2000. *Arguments and Icons: Divergent Modes of Religiosity*. Oxford: Oxford University Press.

———. 2002. "Modes of Religiosity: Towards a Cognitive Explanation of the Sociopolitical Dynamics of Religion." *Method & Theory in the Study of Religion* 14: 293–315.

———. 2004. *Modes of Religiosity: A Cognitive Theory of Religious Transmission*. Walnut Creek, Calif.: AltaMira Press.

Winograd, E., and U. Neisser, eds. 1992. *Affect and Accuracy in Recall: Studies of "Flashbulb" Memories*. New York: Cambridge University Press.

Four Men, Two Sticks, and a Whip: Image and Doctrine in a Mithraic Ritual   6

ROGER BECK

The intent of this chapter is to explore imagistic and doctrinal tendencies in one of the ancient Greco-Roman mystery cults, concentrating on a particular ritual unique to that cult. A decade ago this ritual could not have been discussed at all; the archaeological evidence for it was still unknown and unpublished. But before we explore the ritual, we must first contextualize it with a quick overview of the cult itself.

The mystery cults were associations that offered initiation into the shared mysteries of a particular god.[1] The cult whose ritual we explore here was that of an originally Indo-Iranian god called Mithras, whom his Roman-era initiates worshipped as the sun.[2] That the god himself migrated from the East is certain; that his mysteries came with him is disputed: most scholars now hold, as do I, that the mysteries were substantially a Greco-Roman invention.[3] Today we call the cult "Mithraism"; its contemporaries called it "the mysteries of Mithras" (or "of the Persians" from its presumed alien origins).

Mithraism flourished throughout the Roman Empire (although with concentrations in the West, particularly in the city of Rome and its port, Ostia, and along the Rhine-Danube frontier) during the second, third, and fourth centuries CE. The initiates, who were exclusively male, gathered in meeting places, which for ideological reasons they called "caves" (we call them "mithraea" today): suites or single rooms in urban centres; small, free-standing buildings elsewhere; real caves where available. Mithraea were thus internally focused: a mithraeum, like a real cave and because (for reasons to be discussed later) it is itself a make-believe cave, is an inside with no outside. In this respect, it differs dramatically from the normal ancient temple with its conspicuous architectural form and striking exterior. Similarly, each group of initiates within its "cave" was self-contained and self-sufficient, looking to no higher coordinating authority. Nor does there appear to have been any cultwide, systematic, and explicitly formulated doctrine.[4] Nevertheless, from the archaeological evidence, which has revealed remarkable coherence, continuity, and integrity in the design of mithraea and in the rich and complex iconography of the extant sculptures and frescos, one may postulate the existence and transmission of certain norms that legitimized the group as initiates of Mithras in their own eyes and in the eyes of fellow Mithraists from elsewhere. These norms will have been transmitted not only in ritual forms and by the spoken word—the written word, if it ever existed as substantial sacred texts, is entirely lost—but also in visually comprehensible form as interior design and iconography.

For readers other than classicists, I should make explicit the connotations of the term *cult* in the ancient context; and particularly, I should make clear what the term does not connote. Please put aside all sociological baggage associated with sect-cult or cult-church differentiation, as well as the invidious and pejorative folk associations of the word "cult" now current. They are without meaning or utility in the ancient context. The word "cult" is classicists' shorthand for people who "pay cult to" a particular god or gods in the sense of worshipping them. It is the worship, normally by acts of sacrifice, which is properly the cult (*cultus*), not the association of worshippers. The Romans, a practical people, cultivated their gods just as, agriculturally, they cultivated their fields.

From "cult" to "culture." When we view religions as cultural systems, we should see Mithraism as a subculture of ancient paganism. That wider culture of paganism—one might as well call it that as anything else—was a loose functional coalition for the *cultus deorum*, the "cult of the gods." Within that coalition, the mystery cults, Mithraism of course included, were a peculiar subset. Christianity might also have been a member, but it adamantly refused to join, transgressing one of the coalition's fundamental principles: Don't trash my gods, and I won't trash yours; don't trash the state gods, period.

We can locate a Mithraist within three concentric cultural circles. He—and it always was a "he"—was conditioned into the general culture of Greco-Roman antiquity (experienced as a male), into that society's pagan religious culture, and into the particular religious culture of Mithraism. Since he joined the Mithras cult voluntarily and as an adult, his conditioning into this third and smallest cultural circle would have differed from his conditioning from infancy into the other two. It would have been a more conscious process of learning and experience, the latter, of course, largely acquired in the actual initiation(s) into the god's mysteries.

The Mithraic subculture was in all respects compatible in its values and world-construction with the cultures of the wider circles of paganism and of Greco-Roman society. Mithraism indeed was a conformist's religion: petty bureaucrats, soldiers, successful freedmen, slaves with talent and a measure of autonomy in the households of the great. If not a religion of the elite or the sophisticated, it was certainly not a religion of the marginal, still less of the disaffected.[5]

These considerations affect how we answer the question, to which pole, the imagistic or the doctrinal, does Mithraism tend? In particular, we should be cautious not to brigade it too easily with the imagistic cults solely on the basis of intensely memorable rites of initiation—which it certainly had—or of the autonomous cells in which it functioned. Socially, the Mithraists were well integrated into, and participated in, a dominant culture and a civilization that extended over the entire Mediterranean basin and beyond into all of Europe west of the Rhine and south of the Danube. Certainly one may profitably compare Mithraism and, for example, a Melanesian cult of initiation as forms of religion tending in some respects toward the imagistic, but to assimilate them to each other would be courting methodological disaster.

Rather than now drawing a line in the ledger and balancing off the imagistic and the doctrinal in Mithraism, I want to turn to the particular Mithraic ritual intimated in my title.

The Mainz Vessel and the Mithraic Rituals Depicted on It

The four men of my title are figures molded onto one side of a pottery vessel recovered in 1976 (but not published until 1994) from a mithraeum in Moguntiacum (Horn 1994; Beck 2000). Moguntiacum, the modern Mainz, was a legionary base on the west bank of the Rhine and the provincial capital of Upper Germany; hence, it was a town of considerable importance, thoroughly romanized, particularly into Rome's military culture.

The current estimate of the vessel's date, based on the pottery type, is c. 120–140 CE. This date is relatively early in the span of the cult's material remains, a mere thirty to fifty years after the very earliest artifacts. Consequently, the ritual actions depicted must be early too, established, in my opinion, within a half century of the cult's foundation.

The vessel is thirty-nine centimeters high. The figures representing Mithraic initiates are molded onto both sides, the four on one side balanced by three on the other. The height of the figures varies between 7.2 and 9.3 centimeters.

That the figures on both sides represent participants in Mithraic ritual has not, as far as I know, been questioned. Are they separate rituals? We do not know, but since nothing obvious suggests that they are the two parts of a single ritual, they are best treated as distinct, at least initially. Neither ritual was known to us before the vessel's discovery, which makes the find an extremely important one. In a recent article (Beck 2000), I have attempted to reconstruct and interpret the two rituals. Necessarily, my description and analysis in the present context is briefer and focused solely on what is relevant to exploring the imagistic and doctrinal tendencies at play in the rituals, especially that of the quartet of figures. I begin, however, with the ritual of the trio.

The ritual performed by the trio of figures is clearly a rite of initiation.[6] The senior officer of the local mithraeum, the so-called Father, enthroned and garbed as Mithras, whose surrogate he is, draws his loaded bow at a naked and cowering initiand, behind whom stands a mystagogue, whose open mouth and orator's gesture indicate the utterance of some sacred formula. All three figures are shown in profile (see table 6.1).[7]

The ritual exemplified by the quartet on the vessel's other side is less easy to locate. Clearly, it is a procession of sorts, and we can identify with some certainty the sacred identities of the four players. As on the first side, the figures are all shown in profile. They are processing to the left (see table 6.2).

The leading figure, wearing a breastplate, is probably an initiate of the third grade, a Miles, or "Soldier." The third figure is undoubtedly an initiate of the sixth and penultimate grade, a Heliodromus, or "Sun-Runner." In the cult's sacred economy, the Sun-Runner is to the sun as the Father is to Mithras.[8] We know for certain that this figure is a Sun-Runner because he carries a whip, which is the grade's proper signifier, the whip with which the sun god drives his team of horses across the heavens.[9]

The second and fourth figures can be identified, likewise with some certainty, by their contrasted attributes, the lowered and raised wands. They are initiates miming the pair of esoteric deities Cautes and Cautopates, who are ubiquitous in Mithraic visual representations, almost always with raised and lowered torches.[10] Their function is to signify "up" and "down," paired in spatiotemporal opposition: sunrise and sunset, moonrise and moonset, spring equinox and fall equinox, summer solstice and winter solstice, waxing moon and waning moon, ascending lunar node and descending lunar node, and so on; hence, they signify oppositions of genesis and apogenesis, growth and decay, seed time and harvest, humidity and aridity, heat and cold and, esoterically, the descent of souls into mortality and their ascent into immortality. I explain my reasons for asserting these meanings with such confidence later in the chapter.

I have named this ritual "The Procession of the Sun-Runner" since it is that officer who is clearly the most senior,[11] and he is accompanied by the other three in a file reminiscent of the procession of a Roman magistrate accompanied by his lictors and *accensus*. I suggest that this procession is an enabling ritual, perhaps for the ritual shown on the other side, which I call "The Archery of the Father." Note that the officiant of the archery is senior to the officiant of the procession; so, if

Table 6.1.

Left (facing right)	Center (facing left)	Right (facing left)
Enthroned 'Father' draws bow at . . .	Naked cowering initiand behind whom ...	Speaking mystagogue

Table 6.2.   Order in Procession Leftward

1. Soldier in breastplate	2. Cautopates with lowered wand	3. Sun-runner with whip and radiate crown	4. Cautes with raised wand

the two rituals are in fact related, the procession would be preliminary to the initiatory archery, rather than vice versa.

I further suggest that the intent of the procession is to energize the mithraeum as a sacred setting for whatever ritual follows. My warrant for this explanation/ interpretation is two passages from an essay entitled "On the Cave of the Nymphs in the Odyssey" (*De antro nympharum*) by the third-century philosopher Porphyry. Porphyry draws on much earlier sources, ultimately on information from the Mithraists themselves.

The first passage tells us why and how the mithraeum is designed as an "image of the cosmos." The Greek word is *eikôn* (our "icon"), and Porphyry uses it precisely as a modern semiotician would: the mithraeum is an icon of the cosmos because it is a cave, either in actuality or by convention, and caves—this is the main theme of Porphyry's essay—are images of the cosmos because they resemble the universe in a number of ways:

> Similarly, the Persians [i.e., the Mithraists] call the place a cave where they introduce an initiate to the mysteries, revealing to him the path by which souls descend and go back again. For Eubulus tells us that Zoroaster was the first to dedicate a natural cave in honour of Mithras, the creator and father of all. . . . This cave bore for him the image of the cosmos which Mithras had created, and the things which the cave contained, by their proportionate arrangement, provided him with symbols of the elements and climates of the cosmos (*On the Cave* 6, trans. Arethusa edition).

Paraphrased, Porphyry here tells us that the standard mithraeum, based on its presumed archetype, is designed and furnished in such a way as to replicate symbolically the cosmos and so to enable an initiatory ritual that will replicate in microcosm the macrocosmic descent and return of souls. Unless he was merely speculating or else passing on other people's misinformation,[12] Porphyry here reveals not only the symbolic intent of the mithraeum (and the principles of design by which that intent is realized), but also the ritual function to which the mithraeum's form is keyed.[13]

Now to our second passage from Porphyry's essay:

> To Mithras as his proper seat, they assigned the equinoxes. Thus he carries the knife of Aries, the sign of Mars, and is borne on the bull of Venus; Libra is also the sign of Venus, like Taurus. As creator and master of genesis, Mithras is set at the equator with the northern signs to his right and the southern signs to his left. They set Cautes to the south because of its heat and Cautopates to the north because of the coldness of its wind (*On the Cave* 24, trans. Arethusa edition).

This is a much more difficult and problematic passage than the first. It is also more patently exegetical, especially in its first half, which elaborates on a pair of attributes of Mithras as he appears in representations of his principal heroic act, the sacrificial slaying of a bull. Reference is made to the facts that Mithras is shown astride a bull and wields a knife, facts that scarcely require an explanation. Sufficient reason, surely, is that he is killing the animal in question.

It is, however, obvious enough that the logic, or rationale, that links the cosmological settings of Mithras and his two junior colleagues Cautes and Cautopates is astronomical/astrological. Not so obvious, unless one knows this idiom, is the fact that the rationale depends entirely on the system of astrological houses. If you know the system of houses, which is one of several ways of correlating the planets and the signs of the zodiac, you will get the point; if you don't, you won't.[14]

Knowledge about planetary houses is part of my working memory as a scholar of ancient astrology. It was part of Porphyry's working memory, and part of the working memory of the Mithraist who explicated the matter to Porphyry or, more likely, to Porphyry's anterior source. Clearly, in Harvey Whitehouse's terms (1995, 2000), this involves semantic memory, not episodic memory. Moreover, as a piece of knowledge, it is not esoteric. It was common to Mithraists and to anyone outside the cult who cared to master the elementary astrology involved. And, of course, it is equally accessible and transparent to me and to you (if you so wish) today.

The primary intent of the second Porphyry passage is to define in both macrocosm and microcosm the relative placements of Mithras and his two colleagues: Mithras is "enthroned" on the equator at the equinoxes; Cautopates is set on his right to the north at the summer solstice, and Cautes on his left to the south at the winter solstice. How these placements in the macrocosm are replicated in the microcosm of the mithraeum, I have demonstrated elsewhere.[15]

Here I must introduce a third passage, this one from another, much later (fifth century CE) Neoplatonist named Proclus. In his *Commentary on the Republic* (2.128.26ff., ed. Kroll 1965), Proclus criticizes an earlier (second century CE) scholar and philosopher, Numenius, on whom Porphyry also drew. Proclus censures Numenius for "cobbling together Plato, astrology, and the mysteries."[16] Now, the text of Plato that Numenius had treated so disrespectfully was a passage in the so-called Myth of Er (*Republic* 10.614) in which Plato describes two otherworldly chasms through which souls descend and ascend. Numenius (Frag. 35, ed. Des Places 1973) had identified these chasms as soul gates situated in the celestial sphere at the solstices, which is precisely where Porphyry (likewise drawing on Numenius) says that the Mithraists located not only the gates of descent and ascent, but also their two deities, Cautopates and Cautes, as the presiding powers.

Clearly, then, the mysteries to which Proclus refers are the mysteries of Mithras, a conclusion reinforced by the fact that Mithraism, more than any other mystery cult, added astrology to its cosmological mix.

But there is more: Numenius, Proclus says (commentary on *The Republic* [2.128.26ff.]), "introduces a further enormous fantasy (*teratologian*) with leapings (*pêdêseis*) of souls from the tropics to the equinoxes and returns from these back to the tropics." In the context of mystery cult initiation (*tois telestikois*), the Greek word translated here as "leapings" surely has a literal, not a metaphorical, intent. One can only infer, then, that Numenius is citing a Mithraic ritual, taking place in the microcosm of their mithraeum, in which the participants passed mimetically from tropic to equinox and back to tropic. So may we not conclude, given the identities of the three principal performers (Cautopates, Sun-Runner, Cautes = summer solstice, equinoxes, winter solstice), that the ritual procession represented on the Mainz vessel, in both form and function, is the very same ritual alluded to by Proclus?[17]

I have already suggested that the Sun-Runner's procession is an enabling ritual. Its intent, I further propose, is to activate and energize the microcosm of the mithraeum as an authentic image of the macrocosm.[18] This actualization is effected by having the sun's own surrogate, the Sun-Runner, process in mimesis of the solar journey, accompanied by a pair of colleagues representing, qua Cautes and Cautopates, the zenith and nadir of that journey, the solstices.

But to what end is the microcosm ritually energized and activated? Again, Porphyry gives us a clear answer. Whatever other function the mithraeum also served,[19] its intent was to realize a mystery of the celestial descent and return of the soul.

Next, we turn to the question germane to the present volume of studies: which mode of religiosity does this Mithraic ritual exemplify, the imagistic or the doctrinal? Would it have been "processed cognitively"[20] by episodic memory or by semantic memory? Not surprisingly, my conclusion is not to send the ritual to one pole or the other, but to suggest that it and, by analogy, cognate rituals (especially its sibling represented on the other side of the Mainz vessel) tend toward one pole or the other in different respects. As so often, a crisp and unequivocal choice would be unsustainable.

First, note that the ritual, for all we know to the contrary, is pure action without words. The same is not true of the Archery of the Father, in which the spoken word is indicated by the mystagogue's open mouth and speaker's gesture. Words may have been spoken or sung in the ritual of the procession, but if I am right about its intent, then words were not necessary; action was sufficient.

Secondly, note the economy of the images deployed: essentially, a marching file of four men, two sticks, and a whip say it all. Alone, the symbolism would be totally opaque, but taken in context and in conjunction with the various other arrangements of symbols that constituted the mysteries, the intent of the images is transparent, at least as to the identities and relationships of the four players. To make sense of the imagery of our foursome one must first supply the background of the interior of the mithraeum with its arrangement of symbols of the macrocosm. Outside that context—both the physical context of the mithraeum and the ideological context of the mysteries—the procession is pointless, hence, merely ridiculous, four men in fancy dress making fools of themselves.

My first two points send the ritual toward the imagistic pole. In so far as the imagistic mode correlates with episodic memory, the other ritual depicted on the Mainz vessel, the Archery of the Father, is even more imagistic. Clearly, it is a ritual of initiation and, thus, in principle nonrepeatable for the same subject. As for episodic memory, you will not soon forget staring at the pointy end of an arrow poised for flight on a bow drawn at you by your cult Father.

In contrast, I have suggested that the Sun-Runner's procession is a routine enabling ritual, required to activate the mithraeum as microcosm.[21] As such it belongs toward the doctrinal end of the spectrum. And, indeed, its performance, as we have seen, entails both doctrine and semantic memory.

What the Sun-Runner's procession entails is a certain cosmology. That cosmology is the model of the heavens current in Greek and, subsequently, Greco-Roman culture from the fourth century BCE onward. It was not, in fact, displaced from Western, Judeo-Christian culture—or for that matter, from Islamic, Zoroastrian, or Indian culture—until the overthrow of the model that assumes either a geocentric universe or at least a universe centered on our own sun and solar system. Indeed, in so far as positional astronomy is concerned, and with the substitution of elliptical for circular orbits, the old model is still current and valid. Scientifically, the modern astronomer holds, and the Mithraic Sun-Runner held, the same basic conception of the solstices and the equinoxes; both would give you the same answer as to the relationship between those two pairs of spatiotemporal points. The Mithraist would differ from the modern astronomer in that the former would tell you that there are soul gates at the solstices, the latter would not. Nevertheless, the two parties would agree that if, in your wisdom or your folly, you were committed to accessing those gates, it would be advisable to attempt it ritually and not à la Solar Temple or Heaven's Gate, literally and physically.[22]

In its entailments, then, the Sun-Runner's procession is massively doctrinal. Doctrine, though, is not the word I want to use, for it has—I think, but cannot argue here—crippled the study of the Mithraic Mysteries since the end of the nineteenth century. The rituals and the elaborate material apparatus of Mithraism (i.e., mithraea, sculptures, frescos, small artifacts) instantiate not a doctrine but a system of symbols, the apprehension of which by the initiate constitutes the mysteries. The mithraeum, to take that example, is a complex of symbols that realizes, for certain initiatory ends, the macrocosm in a microcosm. Other complexes of symbols serve other ends.

The Sun-Runner's procession, as represented on the Mainz vessel, presupposes the cosmology and cosmography current in antiquity throughout Mithraism's life span. Though employed to esoteric ends, there is nothing at all esoteric in the contents of Mithraic cosmology since it replicates—indeed it was intended to replicate and derives its authenticity from replicating—the common, public cosmology as regards the contents and structure of the universe. Conceptually, the ritual violated no principles of contemporaneous science.

This isomorphism of esoteric and public cosmologies has two important consequences for the modern researcher. First, the cosmology instantiated in the mithraeum and in the ritual of the Sun-Runner's procession is transparent and accessible to us precisely because it was a clone of public, scientific cosmology. Some things don't change: an equinox is an equinox is an equinox, whether for a Mithraist or for an astronomer, ancient or modern.

Secondly, the conceptual isomorphism of esoteric and public cosmologies makes tracking the cognitive process by which the Mithraic initiate apprehended the symbol complexes of mithraeum and ritual much more possible. For example, a Mithraist's cognitive apprehension of "the proper seat of Mithras at the equinoxes" is that much more imaginable to us because we know that he located "equinox" in his cognized environment exactly as did his contemporaries in the wider culture of Greco-Roman society.[23] Moreover, it is a process that we can still replicate today, subject of course to the constraint that the cognized environment we so construct is a conscious artifice. It is not our "real" world: we can't really enthrone a god at the equinoxes, and we can't realistically expect to get in or out through the solstices.[24]

Thus, although there was little explicit Mithraic doctrine in the usual sense of the word, the ritual of the Sun-Runner's procession, in its cognitive processing, appears to have been powered doctrinally by semantic memory of the generalized schema of the science of the times.[25] Mithraism functioned in the doctrinal mode not by virtue of its own doctrines but by virtue of the common learning of antiquity.

Mithraic Symbolism and "Star-Talk"

In my explication of the four figures involved in the Sun-Runner's procession, I asserted with great confidence various meanings for the esoteric deities Cautes and Cautopates with their raised and lowered torches. No, I have not stumbled unawares into the fallacy that Dan Sperber so elegantly exposed in 1975[26] and which the cultural symbolists have yet to find a way around, the fallacy that symbols convey meanings in the way that language signs convey meanings. But I do claim to have found an exception in the symbolic idiom of what I call "star-talk," the language of astronomy/astrology spoken by and through the symbols deployed across the Mithraic Mysteries.

In my current research I am exploring the semiotics and semantics of star-talk, starting with the ancients' own perception of the stars as language signs and the heavens as text. Star-talk is a peculiar language with one foot (if tongues can have feet) in the actual world of human astronomers, astrologers, and mystagogues, and the other in the constructed world of gods, angels, demons, and celestial bodies, who are themselves both language signs and speakers. Indeed, the hot star-talk issue for the ancients was the strangely modern one of language competence and language communities.[27] Obviously, it would be impossible to do justice to this language question here, so I simply give a very brief summary in point form of my claims for star-talk as a language in which symbols, such as we find deployed in the system of the Mithraic Mysteries, can and do convey meaning.

1. Star-talk is a public language having a set grammar and a set semantics transparent to all users.
2. To turn Sperber's denial into an affirmation (1975: 85), star-talk signs are "paired with their interpretations in a code structure."
3. Star-talk is a recursive language; that is, it has the limitless potential for generating new utterances within the set grammar.
4. Because it is based on the geometry of the celestial spheres, it is a richly analytical language that speaks largely of necessary relationships.

The ritual of the Sun-Runner's procession, we may say, is a "performative utterance" in star-talk. Because that language is still accessible to us (though in read-only form), we can infer certain meanings and relationships with greater certainty and precision than is possible for other systems of symbols in action. This more than offsets the disadvantage of dealing with a people and a culture long dead and gone. But one must not make overly ambitious claims. Deciphering star-talk will not yield the meaning of the Sun-Runner's procession, for language is "medium, not message."

Mithraism: Tendencies to the Doctrinal Pole, Tendencies to the Imagistic Pole

Let us return not to the particular ritual represented on the Mainz vessel, but to the Mithras cult in general. Did this religion function primarily in the doctrinal or in the imagistic mode? More precisely, in what respects did it tend to the doctrinal pole and in what respects to the imagistic pole? The obvious way to address these questions is through the variables proposed by Harvey Whitehouse. Here I use his revised list intended for a forthcoming publication. Following table 6.3, I adduce in numbered paragraphs my reasons, both evidential and deductive, for selecting the doctrinal or the imagistic mode in respect of each variable. In few cases is the choice obvious or unequivocal (see table 6.3).

Table 6.3.

Variable	Doctrinal	Imagistic	Mithraic Tendency
		Psychological Features	
1. Transmissive frequency	High	Low	Doctrinal
2. Level of arousal	Low	High	Imagistic
3. Principal memory system	Semantic schemas and implicit scripts	Episodic/flashbulb memory	Doctrinal (?)
4. Ritual meaning	Learned/acquired	Internally generated	Doctrinal (?)
5. Techniques of revelation	Rhetoric, logical integration	Iconicity, multivocality, and multivalence	Imagistic
		Sociopolitical Features	
6. Social cohesion	Diffuse	Intense	Imagistic
7. Leadership	Dynamic	Passive/absent	Doctrinal
8. Inclusivity/ exclusivity	Inclusive	Exclusive	Imagistic
9. Spread	Rapid, efficient	Slow, inefficient	Doctrinal
10. Scale	Large scale	Small scale	Imagistic
11. Degree of uniformity	High	Low	Doctrinal
12. Structure	Centralized	Noncentralized	Imagistic

1. *Transmissive frequency:* high, therefore doctrinal. (a) The principal ritual, the cult meal, was probably celebrated often, and (b) in a solar cult the solar year must surely have been recognized, especially in the context of a wider society in which annual cycles of festivals were almost universally observed. High transmissive frequency is thus highly probable a priori, although we have no hard evidence either for the specifics of a Mithraic ritual year[28] or for the frequency of the cult meal. But why join a local dining club—the cult meal was an actual, sociable meal as well a sacramental ritual—to feast with your friends and peers only once every several years? Against these presumably regular transmissions, one must set the initiations into the cult and the various grades. Given the small size of Mithraic cells, these would have been relatively infrequent, although in the one case in which we can track incoming members over a nineteen-year period,[29] there appear to have been new initiates every year, which implies at least one initiation a year, unless the newcomers had already been initiated in other mithraea elsewhere and their prior initiations were considered valid in the new cell.

2. *Level of arousal:* high, therefore imagistic. "The Archery of the Father" and the extreme rites of initiation depicted at the Capua Mithraeum[30] are clearly "high arousal"; so is the cult meal as both feast and sacrament. Sensually, Mithraism was both hot and rich.

3. *Principal memory system:* doctrinal, because the mysteries, as we have seen, are remembered by "semantic schemas" and "implicit scripts." This is generally true, despite the vivid "flashbulb memory" which those subjected to "The Archery of the Father" or the Capua initiations would surely have retained. Our choice here must also be qualified by recognizing that Mithraism's semantic schemas were conveyed, as we have also seen, not in a corpus of taught doctrine, but in a symbolic system apprehended visually and in ritual performance.

4. *Ritual meaning:* doctrinal, because "learned/acquired." Logically, the choice on this variable should align with the choice on the preceding variable. If the memory is to retain "semantic schemas and implicit scripts," then any meaning encoded in the ritual must be "learned/acquired." The same qualification also applies: the ritual meaning is conveyed and comprehended not via a corpus of taught doctrine, such as a catechism,[31] but via a symbol system apprehended visually and in ritual performance itself. Comprehension occurs at a much deeper level of consciousness than propositional knowledge. However, that is probably true of all religious ritual, so it would be better to say that in Mithraism propositional knowledge was not a necessary condition of comprehension.

5. *Techniques of revelation:* imagistic, because characterized by "iconicity, multivocality, multivalence," rather than by "rhetoric, logical integration." Here Mithraism's reliance on visually apprehended symbols rather than text drives it toward the imagistic pole. Nevertheless, note that (a) narrative, classed by Whitehouse as a doctrinal feature,[32] certainly figured in Mithraism: the scenes represented in Mithraic art tell a story, although storytelling was not their primary function; and (b) in my theory, at least, the symbols of star-talk are logically integrated and so straddle the doctrinal/imagistic divide.

6. *Social cohesion:* imagistic, because intensely "intense"! All scholars agree on this. Remember, though, that in the multiculture of the Roman Empire, the intensity of the Mithraists' in-group bonding did not preclude equally or even more intense cohesion in other social units (e.g., the imperial army).

7. *Leadership:* doctrinal, because "dynamic." Again, all scholars would agree that the Father or Fathers of a Mithraic community exercised leadership functions and enjoyed leadership status; further, that he or they would be the repository of wisdom and authenticity in the group.[33] The only qualification here—an important one—is that there was no coordinating and controlling hierarchy above the individual cell and its Father(s).

8. *Inclusivity/exclusivity:* imagistic, because "exclusive." All ancient mystery cult associations were exclusive, "members only" institutions.[34] However, this initiation-based exclusiveness should not be confused with social exclusiveness. Other than gender (men only), there was no class or status restriction on candidacy. Presumably, the candidate had to be "of good character" (i.e., morally acceptable to his peers).

9. *Spread:* doctrinal, because "rapid, efficient." However, I suspect that the rapidity and efficiency of Mithraism's spread had more to do with the ease of travel and communication in the Roman Empire than with any factor of the cult itself. In the second century CE one could travel from England to Alexandria, for example, more expeditiously and in greater security than at any other time until the nineteenth century.

10. *Scale:* imagistic, because "small scale." Mithraism, as we have seen, was a religion of small autonomous cells with no hierarchy at a higher level to command and control them. Accordingly, we should focus on scale at the local level, despite the fact that Mithraism was an empirewide phenomenon.

11. *Degree of uniformity:* doctrinal, because "high." Principally by the maintenance of its symbol system, instantiated in its rituals, in the iconography of its images, and in the design of its meeting places, Mithraism managed to retain a remarkable degree of consistency and coherence across its far-flung and autonomous cells. Unlike its coeval, Christianity, it did so apparently without coercion. That was commendable: heresy hunting is all too often the bitter fruit of religion when it begins self-consciously to strive for uniformity.

12. *Structure:* imagistic, because "noncentralized." As already noted, there was no Mithraic papacy or command central. Each community was autonomous.

Conclusion

I do not attempt to draw definite conclusions from what is obviously a first cut. However, the oscillation between the doctrinal and imagistic poles in both the psychological features (variables 1–5) and the sociopolitical features (6–12) do call for comment. What, if anything, does it indicate? In the former, I suspect the fluctuation has much to do with Mithraism's peculiar ability to transmit the functional equivalent of an elaborate doctrine through image and symbol.

As to the fluctuation across the sociopolitical features, as I suggested in my comments on variable 9, it may be that the doctrinal traits in a cult that at first blush seems intensely imagistic are largely a function of the empire's circumambient culture. In an integrated multiculture such as Rome's, it would be hard indeed for a cult, even a cult of initiation, to function entirely in the imagistic mode in respect of its sociopolitical features. The empire was not only a Roman's actual social environment; in some shape or form, it was also his or her cognized social environment. A Mithraist could no more check that cognized environment at the door of his Mithraem than can a Melanesian exchange his or her more intimate, circumscribed social universe for something more ecumenical. Indeed, it was another of Mithraism's attractive features for its conformist recruits that its mysteries fostered and amplified, rather than subverted, the cognized environment the initiate brought with him from the world outside. In the apprehension of the symbol system, the initiate could recognize and re-cognize his own world not only cosmologically but also sociopolitically.

Notes

1. In fact, the Greek word *mystéria* means "those things into which one is initiated." To say that the mystery cults were religions of initiation is thus something of a tautology. Nevertheless, it needs to be said, if only to deemphasize modern connotations of the word "mystery" or any association with the "mystical." The best general study of the mystery cults, in my view, is Walter Burkert's (1987).

2. A good general overview of Mithraism is M. Clauss (2000, English translation).

3. R. L Beck (1998a) is my scenario of the cult's foundation. For the scholarly debate on origins, see pp. 115–16.

4. Luther Martin (1994) did Mithraic scholarship a good service by directing our attention away from doctrinal or even narrative meaning in Mithraism's principal cult icon, the image of Mithras sacrificing a bull.

5. On the social profile of the Mithraists, see R. L. Gordon (1972) and W. Liebeschuetz (1994).

6. In composition (i.e. in the relationship of the three figures to each other) the scene is similar to several fresco depictions of initiation at the Capua Mithraeum (Vermaseren 1971).

7. For an illustration of both scenes, see Beck (2000: Plates 13–14, between pp. 174 and 175).

8. A reader unfamiliar with Mithraism will notice a paradox. There are contexts in which Mithras is the Sun and other contexts in which he is not, for in the latter the Sun is a separate deity who interacts with Mithras. But as Pascal Boyer (2001) has demonstrated so elegantly, working with mutually exclusive mental representations of supernatural agents is something that humans take in stride.

9. A small spike projecting from the Sun-Runner's head is all that the artist can represent of the grade's other attribute, the rayed solar crown, seen here in profile. The seven grades of Mithraism (lowest to highest) are as follows:

    1. Corax = raven (under protection of Mercury)
    2. Nymphus = male bride (under protection of Venus)
    3. Miles = soldier (under protection of Mars)
    4. Leo = lion (under protection of Jupiter)

5. Perses = Persian (under protection of the Moon)
6. Heliodromus = Sun-Runner (under protection of the Sun)
7. Pater = father (under protection of Saturn)

10. Cautopates here wears a Persian cap; Cautes does not. This distinction is obviously significant, but I can offer no functional reason relevant to the ritual itself. It may indicate some contingent fact, for example that the initiate playing Cautopates on the particular occasion commemorated also held the rank of father, one of whose identifiers is the Persian cap, or of Persian, for whom the Persian cap would be etymologically appropriate.

11. If Cautopates is played by an actual father (see preceding note), then one would have to qualify "seniority": in the context of the procession, the role of Sun-Runner is the senior role.

12. He has been accused of both. It is a melancholy fact that classical scholarship has ignored Porphyry's testimony altogether, belittled it, or misconstrued it as evidence for the doctrinal instruction of initiates rather than their initiation by ritual. On this needlessly skeptical position and my counterargument, see Beck (2000: 158–60, 178–80).

13. Though it plays no part in our discussion here, it should be borne in mind that there was another activity and another ritual to which the mithraeum's form was keyed. The mithraeum was equipped with "side benches" (as they are termed), daises on either side of a central aisle, which served as banqueting couches for the cult meal, which was not only a feast in real time, but also a replication in ritual of the feast of Mithras and the Sun god.

14. I explicate the Mithraic rationale in Beck (1976, 2000: 160n68).

15. See Beck (2000: 157–63). With some embarrassment I must admit a careless error in the key diagram (2000: 161, figure 2): from the zodiac images on the right bench Scorpius was omitted and Capricorn duplicated.

16. "Stitching (*syrraptôn*) the Platonic utterances together with astrological concerns (*tois genethlialogikois*) and these with the mysteries (*tois telestikois*)" (trans. Lamberton 1986).

17. Granted, the figures are processing rather than leaping, but the image of celestial hopscotch may be explained as Proclus's derogatory spin.

18. In terms of the "theory of religious ritual systems" proposed by E. Thomas Lawson and Robert N. McCauley (1990: 84–136), the Sun-Runner's Procession would be an "embedded" ritual implicit in, if not explicitly performed during, any ritual action that presupposes the equation "our 'cave' = the universe." The procession also serves as an "object agency filter" (Lawson and McCauley 1990: 87–113) in that it animates the bricks-and-mortar environment of the mithraeum to function as the living universe, thereby transcending the quotidian constraint that does not allow us to treat a material object as an agent. Lawson and McCauley present their theory as a tentative grammar of ritual: in those terms, the definitional ritual as utterance "mithraeum qua 'cave' is universe" would be an entailment of most, if not all, larger Mithraic rituals as utterances.

19. See note 13 above on the cult banquet.

20. The manner of "cognitive processing" is variable 3 (of 13) in the differentiation of the imagistic from the doctrinal (Whitehouse 1995: 197, table 5).

21. "Frequency of transmission" is variable 2 (see preceding note).

22. I refer, of course, to the spectacular cult murders/suicides of the 1990s. For a fuller comparison of the two cults with Mithraism, see Beck (1998a: 342–43).

23. It is still sometimes assumed that ordinary people, such as the Mithraists, were incapable of understanding the scientific cosmology of the time, with the further (false) inference that Mithraism could not therefore have been based on contemporaneous science. The fundamental error of this view is to confuse cognition with intellectual comprehension. Ordinary people can apprehend and respond appropriately to an extremely complicated and sophisticated symbol system with little or no parallel knowledge of how it coheres (or fails to cohere) epistemically.

24. Although the cultists of the Solar Temple and Heaven's Gate attempted something fairly similar.

25. See note 20 above.

26. Explored in further detail by Lawson and McCauley (1990).

27. See especially Augustine, *On Christian Teaching* (*De doctrina Christiana*) 2.21.32.78–24.37.95.

28. I summarize the meager data and the hypotheses advanced in Beck (2000: 145n2).

29. For the mithraeum at Virunum, near modern Klagenfurt, Austria, see Piccottini (1994) and Beck (1998a).

30. See note 6 above.

31. Although here, too, one must qualify: the papyrus text edited by W. M. Brashear (1992) is probably a Mithraic catechism or at least based on one. However, if it is, it represents local Mithraic practice, not the universal practice of the Mithraic "church" (there being no such thing).

32. I am not convinced that Whitehouse is right to classify narrative as a doctrinal feature. It is of the essence of narrative, as of symbols, to be multivocal and multivalent (i.e., imagistic).

33. Mithraea could, but need not necessarily (as far as we know), have more than one Father. The norm at Virunum (note 29 above), where we have the membership record over nineteen years, appears to have been two at any one time.

34. The term *association* is significant here. There were some important mysteries that did not offer continuing interactive membership and were open to all comers with few exceptions. The famous mysteries of Mother and Maiden (Demeter and Persephone) at Eleusis were open to all Greeks (unless they were guilty of some grossly polluting offence), regardless of gender or status; and "Greek" was liberally defined by language competence, not ethnicity: if you could speak it, you were in. You came, you were initiated, you went home (in Roman times, to Antioch, Milan, Carthage, wherever), and you need have no further dealings with your fellow initiates.

References

Beck, R. L. 1976. "The Seat of Mithras at the Equinoxes: Porphyry's *De antro nympharum* 24." *Journal of Mithraic Studies* I: 95–98.

———. 1998a. "The Mysteries of Mithras: A New Account of Their Genesis." *Journal of Roman Studies* 88: 115–28.

———. 1998b. "Qui Mortalitatis Causa Convenerunt: The Meeting of the Virunum Mithraists on June 26, AD 184." *Phoenix* 52: 335–44.

———. 2000. "Ritual, Myth, Doctrine, and Initiation in the Mysteries of Mithras: New Evidence from a Cult Vessel." *Journal of Roman Studies* 90: 145–80.

Boyer, P. 2001. *Religion Explained: The Evolutionary Origins of Religious Thought.* New York: Basic Books.

Brashear, W. M. 1992. *A Mithraic Catechism from Egypt (P. Berol. 21196).* Tyche Supplementband, Vienna: Verlag Adolph Holzhausens.

Burkert, W. 1987. *Ancient Mystery Cults.* Cambridge, Mass.: Harvard University Press.

Clauss, M. 2000. *The Roman Cult of Mithras,* translated by R. L. Gordon. New York: Routledge.

Des Places, Edouard. 1973. *Numenius of Apamea. Fragments.* Paris: Les Belles Lettres.

Gordon, R. L. 1972. "Mithraism and Roman Society: Social Factors in the Explanation of Religious Change in the Roman Empire." *Religion* 2: 92–121.

Hinnells, J. H., ed. 1994. *Studies in Mithraism.* Storie delle Religioni 9. Rome: Bretschneider.

Horn, H. G. 1994. "Das Mainzer Mithrasgefäss." *Mainzer archäologische Zeitschrift* 1: 21–66.

Kroll, Wilhelm. 1965. *Proclus. In Platonis rem publicam commentarii.* Amsterdam: A. M. Hakkert.

Lamberton, R. 1986. *Homer the Theologian.* Berkeley: University of California Press.

Lawson, E. Thomas, and Robert N. McCauley. 1990. *Rethinking Religion: Connecting Cognition and Culture.* Cambridge: Cambridge University Press.

Liebeschuetz, W. 1994. "The Expansion of Mithraism among the Religious Cults of the Second Century." *Hinnells* 1994: 195–216.

Martin, L. H. 1994. "Reflections on the Mithraic Tauroctony as a Cult Scene." *Hinnells* 1994: 217–24.

Piccottini, G. 1994. *Mithrastempel in Virunum.* Aus Forschung und Kunst 28. Klagenfurt: Verlag des Geschichtsvereines für Kärnten.

Porphyry. 1969. "The Cave of the Nymphs in the Odyssey." Translated by Seminar Classics 609. Department of Classics, State University of New York. Buffalo: Arethusa Monographs.

Sperber, Dan. 1975. *Rethinking Symbolism,* translated by A. L. Morton. Cambridge: Cambridge University Press.

Vermaseren, M. J. 1971. *Mithriaca I: The Mithraeum at S. Maria Capua Vetere.* Leiden: Brill.

Whitehouse, Harvey. 1995. *Inside the Cult: Religious Innovation and Transmission in Papua New Guinea.* Oxford: Oxford University Press.

———. 2000. *Arguments and Icons: Divergent Modes of Religiosity.* Oxford: Oxford University Press.

Syncretism and the Interaction of Modes of Religiosity: A Formative Perspective on Gnostic-Christian Movements in Late Antiquity

7

ANITA MARIA LEOPOLD

ARVEY WHITEHOUSE'S THEORY OF MODES of religiosity invites us to think of religion from a new angle, and it may help to clarify the much-debated category of "syncretism," a subject previously mired in historical, as well as scholarly, controversies. The notion of syncretism was invented (or rather reinvented[1]) as a polemical term in the wake of dogmatic Protestantism in the sixteenth century and used in the fight between reformed churches against dissidents.[2] From the nineteenth century on, syncretism became, in the study of religion, a pejorative designation to refer primarily to creolized Christianities or to heretical or alternative religions. Even though scholars in the study of religion are opposed to the notion's theological use, they have maintained an ambiguous attitude toward it and persistently employed syncretism as a category with reference to problems of insider-outsider positions, cultures in conflict, countercultural innovation, and the like. Because the definition of syncretism has been a hot subject of debate in the study of religion for many years, it is not an easy task to come up with any adequate definition for the term.[3] In short, however, it is a generalization about diverse elements incorporated into some target religion from an external religious or secular source or sources (see Martin and Leopold, 2004). Even though it is a general phenomenon, some religions struggle more than others to protect themselves from alien input. Hence, it may prove helpful to understand a phenomenon like syncretism in the context of divergent modes of religiosity. What is more, some of the conceptual confusion appears to be due to either antisyncretistic or prosyncretistic attitudes of the different modes.

To start with, we can observe that syncretism is a salient problem primarily for the Christian version of the doctrinal mode. For Christianity, syncretism has been a menace that the churches have tried to constrain from the beginning. In light of the widespread Christian mission, the intriguing question is whether Christian churches have promoted syncretism rather than prevented it. On the other hand, Whitehouse tells us that the imagistic mode of religiosity does not promote change, nor does it spread very easily, although there do not seem to be any restrictions against individual innovation (Whitehouse 2002). Both modes seem resistant to change, according to Whitehouse's model, but in very different ways. If we want to build a more dynamic model of historical transformation, it may help to focus on the role of syncretic processes in the interaction of the two modes of religiosity.

Syncretism and Interacting Modes of Religiosity

Whitehouse draws attention to the interaction of modes of religiosity in Christian-syncretistic movements in Melanesia and states that these movements are, on the whole, doctrinal with highly routinized religious practices (2000: 60–61). He further emphasizes that they are not merely rejecting missionary doctrine, but that they actually "map" together religion and everyday life in a more comprehensive way than did the Western missionaries (2000: 62). Whitehouse also points out how the system of sanctioning in doctrinal transmission links religious revelation to moral issues (2000: 63). This is how homogeneity, together with political stability, is secured in such large-scale Christian communities (2000: 63, 125).

No doubt the universal transmission of Christianity stimulates syncretism in the form of a recodification or reformulation of dogma in different cultural contexts. However, if we imagine that some beliefs or religious practices inside the Christian community are recast in an imagistic mode, it may very well provoke particular innovations and even the emergence of new religious forms. We may thus consider as a preliminary hypothesis that the interaction of modes provides a set of particular constructive dynamics for syncretistic processes.

The Controversies of Categories—Gnosticism

The perspective of modes in interaction is particularly significant with reference to Christian movements in antiquity. Above all, the Gnostic-Christian texts from the second and third century reveal a Christianity that shows traits of a different mode of religiosity than the orthodox Christianities. Traditionally, Gnostic religions have been defined as being predominantly syncretistic.[4] Scholars have traditionally assumed Gnosticism to be a single religious movement founded as a kind of protest or reversal theology inside Jewish or Christian circles, despite the fact that their texts vary a great deal. We know nothing, however, of a common Gnostic canon or of a Gnostic church (see Jonas 1963: 31–33, 42–47; Rudolph 1987: 53–54[5]).

Traditional views about Gnosticism have been challenged by Michael A. Williams, who criticized the category for being a modern cliché that gives the impression of a generalized historical and social unity for which there is no evidence (1996: 5). He suggests "biblical demiurgical myth" as a category for a new typology that does not obscure interesting and important things about these diverse peoples, otherwise referred to as "Sethians," "Valentinians," "Manicheans," and so forth (Williams 1996: 7). From this perspective, we must additionally question whether the writings reflect particular groups of people or groups of discourses. We must assume that what we assign to Gnostic discourse may in addition refer to a general idea or cosmology shared by divergent groups of people in the Roman-Hellenistic world.[6]

A general cliché has held that Gnosticism is a "parasitical" religion living on different "host religions" (See Williams 1996: 80–83; Rudolph 1987: 54–55; Jonas 1963: 33). In the eyes of many scholars with a Christian background, this has become a label of inauthenticity, in contrast to "prophetic" or "revealed" religions such as Judaism and Christianity. The Dutch scholar Hendrik Kraemer represented such a conviction.

The Controversies of Categories—Syncretism

While professor of the history of religions in Leiden, Kraemer was asked by the International Missionary Council to write *The Christian Message in a Non-Christian World* (1938). This book presents a very Christian and evangelistic assessment of non-Christian religions. Kraemer describes how some religions differentiate themselves from Christianity by having an "innate syncretistic apprehension" (1938: 202). To Kraemer, syncretism represents a fundamental difference between Oriental religions and Christianity. He argues that there is divergence in how syncretisms appear to the two types of religions; for the latter, they represent the rupture of authentic truth and unity, whereas for the former, they are more of "a pragmatism" leading to a synthesis (1938: 204–5). As much as I disagree with Kraemer's value-laden differentiation, there is no disputing the fact that Christianity has fought against the incorporation of alien elements more fiercely than most other religious traditions. Consequently, antisyncretism in Christianity has been taken for granted by scholars as either a sign of true revelation or one of false discrimination.

Not many since Kraemer have dared imply that there might be a fundamental difference in the mode of syncretism a propos Christian religiosity and other religiosities because of the political complexity of the term *syncretism*.[7] However, we do need to ask in an objective way whether we can find any use for characterizing religions as either prosyncretist or antisyncretist. (Or whether we really can mark out an innate difference!) Until now, views like Kraemer's have distracted attention from the social reality of the innovators of religion. The modes of religiosity theory, however, gives us an opportunity to distinguish differently between religions. At least we can now confirm that there is in fact a tendency against syncretism that is inherent to the doctrinal mode of religiosity—a "logical" result of favoring religious centralization and orthodoxy for the control of individual and unauthorized innovation (Whitehouse 2002: 297, 300, figure 2).[8] On the other hand, in order not to exaggerate the distinction between Christianity and non-Christianity, we subsequently examine the interaction of the two attractor modes.

The Gnostic-Christian Movements of the Third Century AD

In the ancient Christian movements, divergent modes may have played a part in the formation of a new trend of religiosity that was later abandoned by the official policy of the Christian church. In the case of the Gnostics, Williams stresses that the dynamic nature of the innovation process was mainly hermeneutical (1996: 76, 95). When we examine the overall use of Jewish scripture across the whole assortment of sources conventionally labelled "Gnostic," we discover that these instances of countertraditional interpretation, which have so often captivated the attention of modern scholars, tend almost always to involve passages or elements from Jewish scripture that were notoriously difficult. Some of these scriptural chestnuts had been perceived as problems generations or centuries before the beginning of the Common Era, and their difficulties had been resolved in various ways (Williams 1996: 63).

Williams's argument is important in that it refers to how people were thinking before the Christian worldview became generalized. He points out that "many of the biblical demiurgical mythologies can be viewed as attempts to reduce deviance in worldview through adaptations and accommodations of Jewish and Christian tradition to Hellenistic and Roman cosmologies" (1996: 113). The mechanisms behind the incorporation of elements of different religious origin in these Gnostic narratives are no doubt exegetical. The genre or form of these texts is at first sight doctrinal, but, upon closer examination, the Gnostic narratives display a form that Karen King has named "revelation discourse." By this concept, King refers to how these narratives inspire a process of salvation (1995: 1–3, 51–53). This view is reminiscent of the philologist Richard Reitzenstein's description of Gnostic texts as a "Lese-Mysterium" (Copenhaver 1992: li–liii; Rudolph 1987: 32–33), but with the important difference that the notion of revelation discourse leaves open the possibility of some kind of ritual activity with reference to the narratives (King 1995: 11; Thomassen 1995). However, only a few of these texts actually disclose descriptions of ritual practice (e.g., The Gospel of Philip, NHC II, 3, trans. Robinson 1978), even though most scholars today agree, on basis of the Gnostic writings and the Church Fathers' apologetic writings against them, that a special initiation intended for revelation and even salvation was required (see King 1995: 19; Thomassen 1995; Williams 1996; Rudolph 1987; Desjardins 1990). One possible answer could be that many of these groups or sects, most of Judeo-Christian origin, may have been familiar with the practice of baptism, but without the fixed liturgy that became custom in the orthodox Christian church (King 1995: 14). Another answer may be that they wished to keep the rites secret, as in any "good" mystery cult of the Roman-Hellenistic world (on the Mithraic mysteries, see chapter 6 and Martin, 2004). In any case, the lack of Gnostic texts that have ritual references may suggest that the people behind them did not follow a routinized doctrinal tradition; nor did many of the emergent Christian groups in the second century—yet.

I dare claim that the doctrinal mode of Christianity dictated by the Church Fathers was the exception rather than the rule in the formative days of Christianity. But, as they became the prime organizers of the church and the "winning team," they came to shape later scholarly views on early Christianity and the tendency to theologize the early Christian-Gnostic texts. Rather, the Gnostic or biblical demiurgical mythologies have, in spite of their variations in mythology and theology, a common core or genre that, notwithstanding a particular narrative form, tend to be more imagistic than dogmatic because of their revelatory character (see also King 1995: 39).

The Gnostic Revelation

Gnostic revelation comes in the form of knowledge of "the hidden divine father," the god, from whom all spiritual beings originated. The theme is essentially salvific with the intention to salvage each "neophyte" from "the world of Hades" (i.e., the human or material world) by recognizing each person's original spiritual and eternal being within the originator god. This knowledge is enacted in the texts as a literal ascent from the world of Hades to the spiritual realm of the Divine Father, which each individual must undergo before he or she is saved. In many of the writings, the salvific ascent goes through the spheres surrounding the planet earth, suggesting that the spiritual realm is at the borderline of the cosmos. In the same way that Roger Beck describes astrology as providing the mode of discourse for Mithraic ritual (see chapter 6), it provides that for the biblical demiurgical mythology as well. Furthermore, according to both the Gnostics and the heresiologists, the people behind the biblical demiurgical mythology may have seen themselves as part of a select group or a divine race set apart from even other fellow Christians

(Rudolph 1983: 205–7). We may therefore assume a social reality in which its Gnostic members saw themselves as belonging to small groups of like-minded initiates situated in the midst of the large-scale Christian-Hellenistic society (King 1995: 36).

It is interesting to notice that written personified revelations were in vogue in the Hellenistic world. In competition with other Christian as well as non-Christian salvation movements, these texts served the purpose of religious propaganda to recruit proselytes. While such propaganda is a form of transmission that is unquestionably doctrinal in nature, the religious mode they promoted may very well have been imagistic-like in nature, insofar as "knowledge of the hidden god" referred to the "capacity to trigger spontaneous exegetical reflection (SER)" (Whitehouse 2002: 305).

The *Gospel of Truth, Allogenes,* and *Poimandres*

We find in the following examples some hints of a possible interaction of the two modes of religiosity in the religious system of the Gnostics. The writer of the Valentinian text, the *Gospel of Truth,* after a long revelation discourse of his own revelation, states, "For the rest, then, may they know, in their places, that it is not fitting for me, having come to be in the resting-place, to speak of anything else" (*GTr.* 42.40–43.1, trans. Robinson 1978). Furthermore, he invites us to pass on "the good news" (i.e., the "gospel"; see Williams 1988: 7) of the revelation, he writes, "and blessed is the one who has opened the eyes of the blind" (*GTr.* 30.15–16); "And awaken those who wish to arise and wake up those who sleep" (*GTr.* 33.5–8). In *Allogenes,* a Sethian text, Allogenes tells us about his revelation step by step (King 1995: 1): "so [far as] I was ignorant of it, I came to kn[ow] it and I was empowered" (*Allog.* 61.2–4). In the end of the text he is urged to write down all that he has seen: "Write down [the]se things, which I will t[el]l to you an[d] which I recall to your mind for those who will become worthy after you" (*Allog.* 68.16–20). In the Hermetic text of *Poimandres,* the narrator tells of his vivid and fantastic cosmogonic vision: "Once, when thought came to me of things that are . . . an enormous being completely unbounded in size seemed to appear to me and call my name and say to me: 'What do you want to hear and see'" (*CH* 1.1, trans. Copenhaver 1992). At the end of the vision, Poimandres, the divine being, urges "the seer" to pass on his revelation: "Then he sent me forth, empowered and instructed on the nature of the universe and on the supreme vision. . . . And I began proclaiming to mankind the beauty of reverence and knowledge" (*CH* 1.27). These writings have in common the revelation and the urge to pass it on in a way that may suggest a religious form where the two modes operated together.

The Interaction of Modes in the Gnostic-Christian Movements

There are reasons to believe that the mystical revelation of the Gnostics was the product of an imagistic modality of religiosity, although it was language based and transmitted in a written form intended for a large population. Undoubtedly, the writings were composed in distinctive local communities and, for most part, were either anonymous or pseudonymous, in contrast to the Church Fathers' writings. One reason may have been that the authorship was lost or concealed in the later Coptic versions. Another reason is that a claim of authorship may not have been important. Actually, before the Christian apologetic writings, we do not know of many religious writings in which it was. The focus of Gnostic writings was the sensational news of the "holy word" spoken about a hidden god. As such, the writer was just the medium of the divinity. Consequently, these writings intended to propagate personal revelation of the word of a God calling one back to a divine origin.

In the following, I apply the modes of religiosity model as a new way of viewing the formative dynamics of Gnosticism. We may assume that the people behind the "biblical demiurgical" writings were part of Jewish-Christian circles; therefore, the Valentinian *Gospel of Truth* and the Sethian *Allogenes* are compared to the patristic writing of Irenaeus of Lyon's *Proof of the Apostolic Preaching* to accentuate the variations of religious practice and worldview represented in the texts.[9]

The Biblical Demiurgical Mythology

The *Gospel of Truth* is a typical, although extremely abstract, biblical demiurgical myth. We recognize fragments of the Gnostic mythological theme of "Sophia's fall," which is best understood as a kind of countermyth to Genesis. Through her self-willed actions, Sophia, "Wisdom," who is the youngest daughter of the divine father of the spiritual world, falls from the world of her father and accidentally gives birth to the creator god of Genesis—often referred to in the demiurgical myths as the "blind god" (Apoc. John.) (i.e., a caricature of the Jewish god Jahweh). However, the drama in the *Gospel of Truth* excludes the typical dramatis personae of the cosmogonic myth and takes up the image of human captivity in the world. We are informed that ignorance and error have caused the deficiency of the world (*GTr.* 24.21–22). Jesus is mentioned with fragmentary references to those Christian scriptures that later would become part of the New Testament (A. J. Williams 1998: 8). However, the *Gospel of Truth* basically presents a different interpretation of the Passion and is forming a whole new story. The human aspect of Jesus is gone. He is a purely divine redeemer, the fruit of knowledge that is given to the ones who seek the Father. His role as savior is an image of divine knowledge, similar to Allogenes in the Sethian text.

When Allogenes is told the way to ascent by his divine revelators, he receives a final revelation of "the Unknowable Triply-powered Spirit" that is auditory in terms of negative theology (King 1995: 1–3, 9; *Allog.* 60.37–61.3, 61.25–31, 62–67.38). Instead of the notion of resurrection of the New Testament, the *Gospel of Truth* speaks of knowledge and discovery (*GTr.* 18.24–31) and presents us with a metaphorical interpretation of the biblical narratives that converts the crucifixion into an image of knowledge. Equally, it is made clear in *Allogenes* that an inactive philosophizing about the incomprehensible leads nowhere (*Allog.* 61.25–28); rather, one is urged to "hear" through a nonverbal revelation that which is not said about the divine principles in the negative statements. Although the revelation is verbally transmitted, it is open to nonverbal imagination and multivocality (see Whitehouse 2000: 69). The same structure characterizes the *Gospel of Truth*, where different sets of images represent the hidden mystery of the name of the Father (*GTr.* 18.15, 37.35–38.20)—of which Jesus represents the visible part in the created world. It is noteworthy that Jesus is in no place a moral teacher; he is a guide who goes before and shows others the way of salvation (*GTr.* 22.20–25). There is no sin in Valentiniansm. Instead, the human situation is portrayed in terms of ignorance and predestination. Those who come to know that they are from the Father become parts of the Father (J. A. Williams 1988: 9, 169; Desjardins 1990: 1–3). Furthermore, in *Allogenes* there is no particular concern with moral issues (King 1995: 59). In both texts, the way to salvation depends on the ability to see through the false screen of the created world and to acknowledge the true spiritual world behind it. In the *Gospel of Truth*, you thereby become, through the Father's naming of the son, one of the sons of the name (*GTr.* 38.25–32).

In any event, we may conclude that the language use of the *Gospel of Truth* is metaphorical and is employed to bring about knowledge of a mystical kind. The author of the scripture warns, in particular, against those that believe that this knowledge is in the written vowels and consonants—"so that one might read them and think of something foolish, but they are letters of the truth which they alone speak who know them" (*GTr.* 23.4–23.10). The revelation of knowledge obviously transcends spoken or written language just as it did in *Allogenes,* and accordingly, both writings allude to the mystery of a transcending and salvific process for the sake of individually obtaining a divine state of being (see King 1995: 5).

The Patristic Writings

It was a common practice among the early Christians to use Jewish scriptures as their own (A. J. Williams 1988: 9, 175), and in his *Proof of the Apostolic Preaching* (trans. Quasten and Plumpe 1952), the Church Father Irenaeus offers an interpretation of Genesis with a view toward giving patristic teaching and the orthodox church divine authority. Competing Christian groups, shaped by Neoplatonic or other "mystical" religious influences, forced the Church Fathers to agree on those beliefs that eventually became those of orthodoxy (Copenhaver 1992: xxiv). In effect, the writings of Irenaeus and of the other heresiologists were formed in opposition to those they labelled heretics in their effort to form a united and universal church. Thus, the Church Fathers fashioned the didactic principles of the church that are absent in biblical demiurgical literature.

Irenaeus's writings provide an insight into the lively debate about the interpretations of Genesis that prevailed among the various orthodox and Christian-Gnostic groups to validate their beliefs. Therefore, he disputes that there is an intrinsic succession from the divine origin of Genesis down to the church (Iren. *Proof*: 30, 94). In contrast to the metaphorical language in the *Gospel of Truth*, which transforms the history of Jesus into a cosmic event of self-knowledge, Irenaeus creates a metonymic linking of the myth of Genesis to the church to give its organization and teaching divine sanction. Irenaeus states that the world is God's creation and man is the image of God (Iren. *Proof*: 10–11). The fall of man with the introduction of death happens because of man's disobedience to God (Iren. *Proof*: 15–16). Genesis becomes, thereby, an edifying story in which prohibition and the introduction of death are part of God's educational scheme for man. Jesus Christ is in the Garden of Eden as the Word and as God's cocreator (Iren. *Proof*: 5). According to Irenaeus, Jesus' passion and crucifixion metonymically relate to Adam's body, disobedience, and the origin of death (Iren. *Proof*: 31–32). Redemption, therefore, is an inversion of Adam's sin, conditioned by the actions of Jesus in the flesh (Iren. *Proof*: 34). Irenaeus uses references to the Old Testament and the prophets down to the apostles and the church to prove the coherence of God's educational plan for man in the works of Jesus (Iren. *Proof*: 98). Rhetorically, Irenaeus proves, through the metonymical linking of Genesis to the church, how the educational and ecclesiastical hierarchy is a manifestation of divine order.

The Mysterious Efficacity of Gnostic Language

The analysis so far suggests that the *Gospel of Truth* and *Allogenes* represent a mode of religiosity divergent from that exemplified by Irenaeus. I find grounds, therefore, to suggest that the Gnostic writings represented a language-based imagistic mode of religiosity associated with initiations, similar to those of contemporary mystery cults. In the Hellenistic world, and especially in Egypt, where theurgical writings were particularly popular (see Fowden 1986), religious writings were powerful not because of their doctrinal content but because of their efficacy to intervene with the divine world. Consequently, "holy scriptures" did not have to be read nor theologically understood—they worked by their presence alone. One example of the efficacy of religious writing as iconic intervention is the Orphic inscriptions on gold plates that were placed in graves along with the deceased to guide the dead safely on the fearful journey through Hades to the island of the blessed. The Orphic inscriptions obviously represented a soteriological guarantee for the deceased. We find another instance in Apuleius's *The Golden Ass*, which reports that a book, written in hieroglyphs, is shown to Lucius during his initiation into the Mysteries of Isis. It is remarkable that the author explicitly mentions that no one, not even the priest, understood a word of it (Apul. *Met.*: 11.22). This genre of writing shows, however, that initiates generally expected the language from divine sources to be incomprehensible and mysterious, but nevertheless effectual. When the Gnostics proclaimed that their writings enclosed the salvific word of a hidden god, adherers most likely would take for granted the revelatory and transcending powers of the text itself. Consequently, it probably would have taken a great deal of persuasion to convince such people to read religious texts as a doctrinal medium.

The Role of Literacy in Gnostic Mysticism

Since each word in a Gnostic scripture represented a mystery to its listeners, it is quite possible that it consequently led to multiple connotations. The act of *gnosis* may have had the capacity to trigger SER, which Whitehouse states is typical of the imagistic mode (2002: 305). The dynamics were definitely toward creative elaboration, which according to Whitehouse is an imagistic disposition, rather than the faithful repetition characteristic of the doctrinal mode of religiosity (2000: 1, 15). Irenaeus observed that "each one of them [the Valentinians], as far as he is able, thinks up every day something more novel" (Iren. *Adv. Haer.* I.18.1). Accordingly, I believe that the Gnostic texts represent an imagistic-like variable clad in the garments of a doctrinal form. By contrast, Irenaeus's writings focus on education rather than initiation and are undoubtedly doctrinal in mode.

If I am right in my assumption that Gnostic literacy signifies an imagistic-like religiosity, then literacy does not automatically indicate a doctrinal mode of religiosity. Therefore, I support Whitehouse's criticism of Jack Goody's dichotomy between literate and nonliterate societies, in which Goody describes the doctrinal mode as a product of literacy (Whitehouse 2000: 172–73).

The Enforcement of the Doctrinal Mode within the Rising Christian Church

The imagery of "the sons of the name" in the *Gospel of Truth* may suggest a religious practice that forges particular social bonds. From the heresiologists we know that the Gnostics formed elitist groups differently constituted than the Catholic communities. Tertullian accused them of disorder because they did not make a distinction between the laity and clergy (Tert. *Praescr.*: 41). This also suggests a social order closer to small-scale societies. Whitehouse characterizes orthodox Christian faith in terms of a process of accepting a common set of doctrines. He claims that "without its system of interlocking rhetoric, Christianity could not exist" and "would be a very different kind of religion" (2000: 36). The Church Fathers fought to convert all Christians to the same system of faith by strengthening doctrinal control. In this way, the ancient church finally became able to dictate what was heresy while constructing orthodoxy. If the Church Fathers had not succeeded in converting adherents to a common set of doctrines, Christians would most probably have remained diverted into small local mystery cults. As it happened, Christianity reinforced in its early days a centralized orthodoxy in its goal to unite all the Christian groups into the universal church. Thus, the role of literacy finally became redefined in terms of the doctrinal theology that we know from the Patristic writings.

Whitehouse's research is based on the situation of missionary Christianity in Papua New Guinea that was introduced to indigenous tribal communities as a totally new mode of religious transmission (2000: 34). This situation could well have been the case in the second-century Greco-Roman world. The adoption of a doctrinal mode of religiosity by the emergent Christian church seems to have established the success of Christianity in the Greco-Roman world—at least if we trust Irenaeus's educational and ecclesiastical teaching about Genesis as evidence of a new mode of religiosity. Michael Williams argues that in the early centuries of the Christian movement, orthodox Christianity, rather than the Gnostics, represented a sociopolitical deviance (1996: 105). In spite of the fact that the doctrinal mode of religiosity dominated Hellenistic Judaism and the Greek philosophical tradition, the church's system of teaching was new to most religious practitioners in the Greco-Roman world.

Memory Schemata Concerning Gnostic Revelation Discourse

If we trust the revelation discourse in both *Allogenes* and the *Gospel of Truth* to mirror an imagistic-like mode of religiosity, then we must trust narratives to evoke, under particular circumstances, religious experience with the effects of "flashbulb memory," elsewhere called "episodic memory" (Whitehouse 2000: 7–9). Normally our semantic memory is at work when we learn religious narratives. However, when it comes to techniques of revelation, Ilkka Pyysiäinen remarks that Laestadianism used rhetoric and narratives (chapter 11). He also observes how the interaction of the two memory schemata occurs in the process (chapter 11). We may assume, consequently, that both memory schemata are active in revelation discourses such as the Gnostics.

A frequent metaphor used in the biblical demiurgical mythology to symbolize the acquiring of *gnosis* is remembering. The Gnostic mystagogue is requested to remember his or her divine origin; to remember is a sign of belonging to the divine lineage. The plasticity of memory suggests, however, that remembering in the Gnostic sense could possibly have worked through the interaction of two memory systems. The narrative, thus, redirects the sense of the self-identity of the mystagogue stored in the semantic memory (i.e., from human born to divine originated), whereas the mystical act of remembering is encoded in the episodic memory, giving the mystagogue the particular and exited sensation of being divine. Finally, the exalted and even esoteric experience of belonging to a divine lineage may have evoked a social bonding similar to Whitehouse's description of imagistic small-scale societies.

The Associative Manner of Blending

Let us now return to the question about syncretism and the two modes of religiosity. In reference to Fredrich Barth's approach to analogic encoding (1975), Whitehouse describes analogic encoding as "a way to confound everyday understandings, and to emphasize the multivocal and multivalent character of revelation" (2000: 28). This largely associates analogic codes with the imagistic mode of religiosity and the use of digital codes with the doctrinal mode of religiosity (Whitehouse 2000: 88–91).

However, analogic codification is also characteristic of syncretistic blending. I would like to elaborate a little more on this by introducing Gilles Fauconnier and Mark Turner's theory about conceptual blending (2002). According to Fauconnier and Turner, conceptual blending operates largely behind the scene; it is a mental capacity that we are not consciously aware of, which operates beneath the level of "visible" language. As such language is only the tip of the iceberg of invisible meaning constructions (Fauconnier 1997: 1). Accordingly, the basic mental operation of meaning construction consists of mental spaces characterized as small conceptual packets constructed as we think and talk for purposes of local understanding and action. To blend, then, has to do with how we associate (see also chapter 11). It is an everyday action, and we all do it all the time—except blends are exceptionally striking in religion. Valentinian mythology, for example, is more or less an analogical codification of Christian beliefs in Jesus Christ as divine savior and of Neoplatonic ideas of the fall of man from his original heavenly state. Similarly, Irenaeus's Christian interpretation of Genesis, which places Jesus in the Garden of Eden as the Word of God, is also a syncretism formed by analogy. Of course, syncretistic elements can also be cast in digital codes when being used in polemical discourse, as we know from the heresiologists. We know now, however, that "syncretistic blends," contrary to Kramer's assumptions, are as ordinary as everyday blending—even inside Christianity.

Syncretistic blending presents a threat to the doctrinal modality of religiosity. According to Christian orthodoxy, it is illegitimate, and not just because of the alliance between religious elements of different origins that may go against the church policy (Leopold 2002a). In the case of ancient Christianity, the interaction of modes of religiosity by way of the recodification of Genesis and the gospels into mystical knowledge became in itself an illegitimate syncretism. As a result, it was not just the interaction of modes that caused innovation in Roman-Hellenistic religious movements, but also the confrontation of modes that fashioned the countermythology of the Gnostics and the polemics of the Church Fathers.

Splinter Groups in Ancient Christianity

Michael Williams suggests, borrowing his model from Rodney Stark and William Sims Bainbridge (1985), that the Valentinians can best be described as "church movements" drifting toward accommodation of the sociocultural environment inside the growing Christian movement (1996: 110–11): "[they] seem to have splintered off the 'front end' of the second-century CE sect-church spectrum" (1996: 112). In the case of Melanesia, Whitehouse tells us splinter groups also emerged from within the large-scale Christianized movements (2000: 155).

Typical for these splinter groups is the recodification of orthodox dogma in which the central principles of mainstream ideology are recast in terms of the imagistic modality of religiosity (Whitehouse 2000: 129). My analysis above demonstrates that language can function iconographically with reference to the "mystical" language we find in the imagery of "the Name of the Father" in the *Gospel of Truth* and in the negative theology of *Allogenes*. Furthermore, a language-based recodification grounded on unusual blending may trigger this effect. Whitehouse observes how in Melanesian movements the two modes operate together in distinct ways, concerning "not what people 'believed' but how these 'beliefs' were codified and transmitted. These domains must, therefore, be understood as aspects of a single, coherent religious tradition" (2000: 130). I argue that something similar happened inside the second-century Christian community.

Syncretism in the Ancient Church

Was Kraemer right to claim that some traditions have an inherent tendency toward syncretism? The answer must be both yes and no! Whitehouse has shown that small-scale religious communities have infrequent religious transmission. He further states that because their rituals, though infrequent, are highly emotional and encoded in long-lasting autobiographical memory, the memory failure is minimal. Accordingly, innovations inside such communities do not present a threat to the reproduction of the religious tradition as a whole (Whitehouse 2000: 102–3). Additionally, such innovations have very limited ideological consequences (Whitehouse 2000: 108–9). On the other hand, we have observed that for Christianity, cast in the doctrinal mode, innovation presents a challenge, partly because Christians were situated from the beginning in the Roman-Hellenistic context of large-scale community. Therefore, the Christian movement was more exposed to hermeneutical discordances and the consequences of SER. In fact, the goal of bringing together various religious movements in a common universal church initiated syncretistic variations that in effect necessitated prohibitions against individual innovation. In this inverse way, syncretism became innate to doctrinal Christianity.

Conclusion

We have observed that the frequency of syncretistic innovation is much higher inside large-scale societies governed by the doctrinal mode than it is in low-scale imagistic societies. This is due to the widespread transmission of religious narratives and their greater exposure to and influence on elements of different religious, cultural, and historical sources. Exposed to such various interpretations and controversies in meaning, the doctrinal mode of religiosity will indirectly generate new and interesting religious blends. This will eventually cause splinter groups or revivalist movements to come forth. Whereas the interaction of modes of religiosity probably occasioned Gnostic mysticism, the confrontation of modes within the church most probably triggered the strife against Gnosticism and shaped the antisyncretistic tendency inside the early orthodox church.

The use of Whitehouse's two modes model has given us a new perspective on such religious narratives as the Gnostic revelation discourse—the assumption that narratives may work in the same manner as other imagistic-like features and thereby provoke intense religious experience. For that reason I suggest that even a written text, such as Gnostic scriptures with their mystical language, can work similarly to imagistic strategies to effect emotional multivocal mystical experiences (SERs). Furthermore, I assume that the interaction of modes in the case of the Gnostic-Christian movements of second and third century engendered a new kind of religiosity—a language-based "mysticism" that on the whole was a syncretistic formation. However, the confrontation of modes between the Christian-Gnostic movements and the ancient Christian church (likewise syncretistic) gave rise to the incipient antisyncretistic church policy. The theory of distinct modes of religiosity has thus helped us to throw light on fundamental and distinct mechanisms for constructing religions, which are exemplified in the second-century Gnostic-Christian movements. In any case, Whitehouse's theoretical model has added some explanatory value to Williams's typology for organizing biblical demiurgical literature, as well as to my hypothesis about syncretism; the two modes of religiosity have helped me to distinguish between syncretisms without having to fall back on Kraemer's prejudiced classification of religions as those with an "innate syncretistic apprehension" versus "pure" antisyncretist religions.

Notes

1. The term *syncretism* is first known from Plutarch's treatise "On Brotherly Love" (*Peri philadelphias*), 19.

2. The humanistic theologians Erasmus of Rotterdam (1469–1536) and Georg Calixtus (1586–1656) were called "syncretists" as a term of abuse because they tried to reconcile the competing Christian parties (Engel 1976; Leopold 2002a).

3. There are several good introductions to the discussion on the definition of syncretism. I suggest Kurt Rudolph (1992: 193–213), André Droogers (1989: 7–25), Anita Leopold (2001), Luther Martin (2001), Martin and Leopold (2004), and Leopold and Jeppe Sinding Jensen (2004).

4. Religions in Brazil (e.g., Candomblé and Afro-Amerindian/American religions), Theosophy, New Age, "new religious movements," and Hellenistic religions in general are typically labelled syncretistic religions.

5. The presumption of the existence of particular Gnostic communities has partly been strengthened by the discovery in 1945 of a Gnostic library at Nag Hammadi, Egypt (Rudolph 1987: 34–44).

6. Martin characterizes the transformation of religion in the Hellenistic world as the result of a general transformation of the traditional view of cosmos through the introduction of the Ptolemaic cosmic image, which came to influence the sociopolitical world after Alexander the Great. This became a new architecture of Hellenistic cosmology that points to a coherent system of thought and suggests how divergent ideas and practices were organized by a new cosmological paradigm (1987: 3–15).

7. Complementary to the two modes of religiosity model is Timothy Light's suggestion that in all religions there are particular prominent categories that are therefore specifically protected against change and innovation. He compares how changes are judged according to how religion is acquired and comes up with an interesting suggestion of how the variation and status of syncretisms appear in different religions (Light 2000).

8. To suggest an "innate mechanism" toward syncretism in the imagistic mode of religiosity, in spite of SER—the capacity to trigger spontaneous exegetical reflection (Whitehouse 2002: 305–6)—would be to manipulate Whitehouse's theory too far.

9. Irenaeus of Lyon's *Proof of the Apostolic Preaching* and the *Gospel of Truth* are both from the mid-second century. *Allogenes* is from the third century AD. See also my semiotic analysis of Irenaeus and the *Gospel of Truth* (Leopold 2001 and 2002).

References

Barth, Frederik. 1975. *Ritual and Knowledge among the Baktaman of New Guinea.* New Haven, Conn.: Yale University Press.

Copenhaver, Brian P. 1992. *Hermetica: The Greek Corpus Hermeticum and the Latin Asclepius in a New English Translation with Notes and Introduction.* Cambridge: Cambridge University Press.

Desjardins, Michel R. 1990. *Sin in Valentinianism.* SBL Dissertation Series 108. Atlanta, Ga.: Scholars Press.

Droogers, André. 1989. "Syncretism: The Problem of the Definition, the Definition of the Problem." In *Dialogue and Syncretism: An Interdisciplinary Approach,* edited by J. D. Gort, H. M. Vroom, R. Fernout, and A. Wessels, 7–25. Grand Rapids, Mich.: Eerdmans Publishing Co.

Engel, Peter. 1976. *Die eine Wahrheit in der Gespaltenen Christenheit: Untersuchungen zur Theologie Georg Calixts.* Göttinger Theologische Arbeiten, Bd. 4. Göttingen: Vandenhoeck and Ruprecht.

Fauconnier, Gilles. 1997. *Mappings in Thought and Language.* Cambridge: Cambridge University Press.

Fauconnier, Gilles, and Mark Turner. 1996. "Blending as a Central Process of Grammar." In *Conceptual Structure, Discourse and Language,* edited by Adele E. Goldborg. Stanford, Calif.: CSLI Publications.

———. 2002. *The Way We Think: Conceptual Blending and the Mind's Hidden Complexities.* Basic Books: New York.

Fowden, Garth. 1986. *The Egyptian Hermes: A Historical Approach to the Late Pagan Mind.* Cambridge: Cambridge University Press.

Jonas, Hans. 1963. *The Gnostic Religion: The Message of the Alien God and the Beginnings of Christianity.* Boston: Beacon Press.

King, Karen. 1995. *Revelation of the Unknowable God.* Santa Rosa, Calif.: Polebridge Press.

Kraemer, Hendrik. 1938. *The Christian Message in a Non-Christian World.* New York: Harper and Brothers.

Leopold, Anita M. 2001. "The Architecture of Syncretism: A Methodological Illustration of the Dynamics of Syncretism." In *Retrofitting Syncretism?* edited by William Cassidy. *Historical Reflections / Réflexions Historiques* 27(3): 401–24.

———. 2002a. "Synkretisme: En Analyse af illegitime Blandinger og Tredje-identiteter." *Religionsvidenskablig Tidskrift* 40: 47–57.

———. 2002b. "Syncretism and Transformation in the Gospel of Truth." In *The Nag Hammadi Texts in the History of Religions,* edited by Søren Giversen, Tage Petersen, and Jørgen Podemann Sørensen, 46–53. Historisk-filosofiske Skrifter 26. Copenhagen: The Royal Danish Academy of Sciences and Letters.

Leopold, Anita M., and Jeppe Sinding Jensen, eds. 2004. *Syncretism in the Study of Religion.* London: Equinox.

Light, Timothy. 2000. "Orthosyncretism: An Account of Melding in Religion." In *Perspectives in Method and Theory in the Study of Religion,* edited by A. W. Geertz and R. T. McCutcheon, 162–86. Leiden: Brill.

Martin, Luther H. 1987. *Hellenistic Religions: An Introduction.* New York, Oxford: Oxford University Press.

———. 2001. "To Use 'Syncretism,' or Not to Use 'Syncretism'? That is the Question." In *Retrofitting Syncretism?* edited by William Cassidy. *Historical Reflections/Réflexions Historiques* 27(3): 389–400.

———. 2004. "Performativity, Narrativity, and Cognition: 'Demythologizing' the Roman Cult of Mithras." In *Rhetoric and Reality in Early Christianity*, edited by W. Braun, ch. 8. Waterloo: Wilfrid Laurier University Press.

Martin, Luther H., and Anita M. Leopold. 2004. "New Approaches to the Study of Syncretism." In *New Approaches to the Study of Religion: Comparative Approaches*, edited by Armin W. Geertz and Peter Antes. Berlin: de Gruyter.

Pyysiäinen, Ilkka. 2004. "Corrupt Doctrine and Doctrinal Revival: On the Nature and Limits of the Modes Theory," chapter 11 in this volume.

Quasten, J., and J. C. Plumpe, eds. 1952. *Irenaeus, "Proof of the Apostolic Preaching,"* translated by J. P. Smith. Ancient Christian Writers 16. New York: Paulist Press.

Robinson, J. M., ed. 1978. *The Nag Hammadi Library*. San Francisco: HarperSanFrancisco.

Rudolph, Kurt. 1987. *Gnosis: The Nature and History of Gnosticism*. San Francisco: HarperSanFrancisco.

———. 1992. "Synkretismus: Vom Theologischen Sheltwort zum Religionswissenshaftlichen Begriff." In *Geschichte and Probleme der Religionswissenschaft*, 193–213. Leiden: Brill.

Stark, Rodney, and William Sims Bainbridge. 1985. *The Future of Religion: Secularization, Revival and Cult Formation*. Berkeley: University of California Press.

Thomassen, Einar. 1995. "Logos apo sigês proelthôn. (Ignatius, *Mag.* 8:2)." In *Texts and Contexts: Biblical Texts in their Textual and Situational Contexts. Essays in Honor of Lars Hartman*, edited by Tord Fornberg and David Hellholm, 847–67. Oslo: Scandinavian University Press.

Whitehouse, Harvey. 2000. *Arguments and Icons: Divergent Modes of Religiosity*. Oxford: Oxford University Press.

———. 2002. "Modes of Religiosity: Towards a Cognitive Explanation of the Sociopolitical Dynamics of Religion." *Method and Theory in the Study of Religion* 14-3/4: 293–315.

Williams, A. Jacqueline. 1988. "Biblical Interpretation." In *The Gnostic Gospel of Truth from Nag Hammadi*. SBL Dissertation Series 79. Atlanta, Ga.: Scholars Press.

Williams, A. Michael. 1996. *Rethinking "Gnosticism": An Argument for Dismantling a Dubious Category*. Princeton, N.J.: Princeton University Press.

CHRISTIAN TRADITIONS   IV

Testing the Two Modes Theory: Christian Practice in the Later Middle Ages

8

ANNE L. CLARK

HAVING ARTICULATED THE THEORY of two modes of religiosity, Harvey Whitehouse has invited historians of various religious traditions to address its relevance in understanding the materials from the traditions they study. Such a program situates the theory and this "testing" in an empirical context. Grounding these basic patterns within the nature of the human organism—in this case, in the types of memory activated—further connects this theory to empirical research. This latter aspect of the theory (i.e., its cognitive basis) is not something that I address in this chapter. Instead, I offer my reflections on some aspects of medieval Christianity that I think are relevant to the categories employed in the two modes theory. But before doing that, I start with confessing my reservations based on the presentation of the theory itself.

Whereas the articulation of the imagistic mode is based on significant field work in and examination of the extensive ethnographic work about Papua New Guinea, the characterization of the doctrinal mode is based on generalizations about Christian ritual, sometimes cast as hypothetical experiences ("An Anglican layman asked to recall the chain of events at a Sunday service five years ago" [Whitehouse 2000: 9]). When the doctrinal mode is more extensively discussed, evidence is largely from polemical contexts in which there have been attempts to impose often radical religious change upon particular communities.[1] There is no discussion of evidence for the doctrinal mode as it is exists in long-term, stable communities of people committed to its teachings, rituals, and social organization. What is necessary is attention to the experience of ritual in such doctrinal communities. It is not self-evident that participants cannot remember particular past experiences of a frequently experienced ritual. It is not self-evident that repeated rituals are boring. Whereas there is great willingness to assume that participants in imagistic rituals engage in deep reflection on the meanings of their experience, there is no willingness to grant an interior or imaginative life on the part of the participants in frequent rituals. Instead, there is the assumption that they are simply absorbing the teachings announced by the authoritative specialist and/or that they are bored. These assumptions need to be supported. Thus, although there is a stated desideratum for archaeology and ancient history to illuminate the emergence of the doctrinal mode (Whitehouse 2002: 311), for me there is also the desideratum for history and anthropology to illuminate the contours of ritual experience deemed doctrinal and to consider whether the sociopolitical features of the doctrinal mode do in fact cluster in the proposed way.

The assertion of the imagistic mode as the most archaic form of religious experience also raises questions for me as a historian. What kind of evidence would need to survive for there to be doctrinal practices coexisting with those so-called most ancient imagistic forms? What about women repetitively singing the same songs for generations as they do their everyday work, songs and gestures of work that encode their daughters' willingness to marry, have children, and bury the dead, that keep the world in place? Do these ritualized words and gestures that create meaning and reproduce the community (literally and symbolically) make a mark on the archaeological record or the ethnographer's perception? The linkage of the most ancient with the most violent—and often exclusively male—rituals makes me leery of a theory that perhaps has a very narrow sense of what counts as religious ritual. Ritualized behavior that men, women, and children routinely engage in, that shares features of both modes—frequent performance, low arousal, use of semantic and corporeal scripts—behavior that doesn't rely on or produce dynamic leaders, but rather reproduces the small-scale, decentralized community, seemed invisible in the modes theory. My initial reaction as a historian (about survival of evidence), however, is somewhat misdirected. There is acknowledgement of routinized ritual in nondoctrinal societies; in fact, it is recognized as existing in every society. It's just that it is considered irrelevant to the forging of the "in-group and thus of 'humanity'"(Whitehouse 2000: 184). That kind of ritual is just not sacred enough! But a theory that discards the possibility that such ritualized behavior is constitutive of profound meaning and social grouping seems to be searching for the big (in this case, nonverbal) myths in imagistic religion, while ignoring the ongoing mundane work of reproducing the world—its conceptual, as well as social, reality. This focus then on the rare, dramatic rituals seems parallel to looking for theology (authoritative ontological assertions, even if only relevant to part of the community) instead of examining religion (the complex ways in which a community reproduces itself in relation to its definitions of humanness and, perhaps, supernatural forces). It also makes me wonder if the introduction of the doctrinal mode into a previously imagistic society really needs either the introduction of literacy or the exposure to a full-blown doctrinal cult if there is in fact already an ongoing doctrinal-like experience of repetitive ritual verbalizing and/or corporealizing of community and individual identity (Whitehouse 2000: 161).

With these reservations in mind, I turn now to what I have found most intriguing about the two-modes theory. When reading *Arguments and Icons: Divergent Modes of Religiosity* (Whitehouse 2000) and "Modes of Religiosity: A Cognitive Explanation of the Sociopolitical Dynamics of Religion" (Whitehouse 2002), I was always most drawn to the discussions about the interaction of the two modes within a single religious tradition, such as the characterization of the Paliau movement and the imagistic splinter cults as separate domains of operation that must be understood as aspects of "an intricate and coherent religious tradition" (Whitehouse 2000: 294–95, 306). As a historian of medieval Christianity, I am particularly struck by the characterization of monasteries as the bastion of doctrinal religiosity in the Middle Ages and by the view that inadequately doctrinized lay communities will resort to the imagistic mode to motivate their allegiance to routinized rituals (Whitehouse 2002: 310). Let me turn first to the issue of monastic life.

It is undeniably the case that there was higher literacy and greater religious learning among monastics than the general population of the later Middle Ages. However, it is also undeniable that there was quite a range of competencies among monastics, and it should not be assumed that all monks and nuns were learned in religious matters. But having said that, monastic life offers a real test for the doctrinal mode because of the way in which daily existence was structured by the very repetitive ritual of the divine office, a wordy service if ever there was one. In theory, the twenty-four-hour day of a monk or nun was punctuated by as many as seven or eight ritual events, including services that interrupted the sleep and required gathering in the church for communal prayer. The services themselves consisted largely of chanting the psalms, as well as other antiphons and hymns, brief readings, and at least weekly sermons. Mass, itself a highly routinized ritual, was also integrated into the office on Saturdays, Sundays, and major holy days (sometimes more frequently, depending on the community). The core texts of the divine office—the 150 psalms—were repeated once a week; the antiphons and hymns were likewise very frequently repeated, and the other readings rotated on an annual basis, some even to be recited by heart.[2] Thus, the words heard in ritual context became very familiar, and the ritual space and movements likewise were routinized. There was little that an outsider might consider high arousal about these rituals, and monastic texts urge attentiveness in these settings.

With this high transmissive frequency, low level of arousal, and use of semantic schemas, one would expect the ritual meaning to be learned by absorbing the pronouncements of a logically integrated oration by an authoritative leader.

Monastic communities definitely had authoritative hierarchy that was displayed and reproduced in ritual: the abbot or abbess, to whom the other monastics owed obedience, preached or had an authoritative role in the liturgy. (This was more complicated in women's communities than in men's because women's liturgical roles were radically curtailed in this period.) But, in any case, the role of oratory was not primary in these services. Rather, the fixed texts of the psalms, hymns, prayers, and readings dominated the services. With such repetition and low arousal, what about the tedium effect? There is indeed evidence of concern that monastics remain attentive and engaged in this round of liturgical services,[3] but is that sufficient evidence to deem the regimen boring? Although the outside observer may see nothing dramatic, traumatic, violent, or even life-threatening (the characteristics that seem to make ritual engaging in the modes theory), the divine office was a potentially emotional experience. In addition to the fact that the primary verbal discourse—the Psalms—were expressions of sorrow, joy, fear, or despair, they were chanted in musical settings that were keyed to creating particular emotions.[4] The familiarity of text enabled greater imaginative freedom during singing, while not necessarily detracting from the emotional tug of the chant's mode. The style of reading taught in the monasteries, a meditative practice that encouraged free association rather than linear reading from start to finish, as well as emotional stimulation rather than detached comprehension,[5] also would have contributed to the monastic's imaginative experience while chanting. The architecture and ornamentation of the church through which the monastic walked to reach his or her place in choir offered not simply iconography to be decoded intellectually but stimuli for that most complex and monastic emotion—fear (Carruthers 1998: 261–66). But the experience did not become a completely interiorized one—the singing itself was communal, thus requiring some attention to the exteriorizing of one's voice into the communal voice, an experience that mirrored the larger monastic program of the dissolution of ego into the communal identity.

Furthermore, the routinized liturgical life of the monastic communities was sometimes the setting for what participants claimed to be visionary or other modes of revelatory experience.[6] For example, Elisabeth of Schönau, a twelfth-century nun who had lived in a Benedictine monastic community since the age of twelve, narrated a series of visionary experiences that were firmly rooted in the liturgical calendar. Her descriptions of her revelations usually begin with an explicit reference to the feast day (most days of the year were dedicated to a particular saint or event of sacred history), to the service during which she had the experience, and often even to the psalm, antiphon, hymn, or biblical reading taking place at the moment she was ecstatically transported to another world, knocked down by supernatural force, struck dumb, greeted by an angel, or tormented by a demon. What she saw or heard in her ecstasies was often triggered by the whole complex of liturgical stimuli: music, words, gestures, images in books or the church, smells, tastes. And at some point, she was able to render her experience orally, in words comprehensible to others. However prosaic and predictable the stimulus and response may seem to us, Elisabeth and her contemporaries interpreted it as divine revelation (Clark 1992: 68–100).

In a wonderfully suggestive and astute characterization, rare and climactic rituals are said to "evoke abundant inferences, producing a sense of multivalence and multivocality of religious imagery, experienced as personal and unmediated inspiration" (Whitehouse 2000: 306). But why is this only possible with rare and climactic rituals? The imagery deployed in Christian ritual is very multivalent, at least as experienced by Elisabeth. In the context of a Christmas Eve ritual ("While we were celebrating the vigil of the birth of the Lord, around the hour of the divine sacrifice, I came into a trance"), Elisabeth states that she saw a vision of a virgin sitting in the sun. When she describes this vision to her brother Ekbert, who served as her secretary and scribe, she asserts that the virgin was a symbol of the "humanity of Christ." He questioned her vision, pointing out the oddity of the humanity of Christ being symbolized by a female image. After another vision, Elisabeth explains to her brother that the female virgin also symbolizes the Virgin Mary, the mother of Christ (Roth 1884: 60–61; Elisabeth of Schönau 2000: 123–25). The Christmas ritual celebrating the incarnation, the birth of Jesus from a woman whose flesh is believed to be the only source of his flesh, was the liturgical setting for Elisabeth's experience that she exegeted as affirming a female symbol for the humanity of Christ. Her brother, seeking greater rational coherence as well as neater gender boundaries, questioned her revelation, and she piled yet more exegesis on top, not negating, not explaining, not rationalizing the first assertion, but affirming the capaciousness of the symbols to hold it all.

A century later, Gertrude of Helfta, who at age five entered a monastery and began the monastic routine of the divine office, also narrated a series of extraordinary experiences. As with Elisabeth, Gertrude's experiences were grounded in the routine of monastic ritual, usually taking place in the context of specific communal rituals. The texts later created to record Gertrude's interpretation of her experience attest to her complex and sometimes ambivalent relationship to the repertoire of symbols, beliefs, prayers, and readings available to her in the context of the ritual and intellectual life at Helfta (Bynum 1982: 170–262; Clark 2000: 37–56). For example, the regular celebrations of the Mass are the occasion for numerous experiences of what she described as melting into Christ, turning the same "color" as him, or simply seeing and conversing with him. On the Feast of the Assumption, one of the feast days dedicated to the Virgin Mary, she participated in a ritual in which the preacher (probably a Dominican friar, a member of an order most committed to doctrinal preaching) effusively praised the Virgin Mary. Gertrude expressed her distaste for the style of piety and could not summon the appropriate warmth to imitate it (Gertrude of Helfta 1968: 112; 1993: 186). This setting of routinized ritual with authoritative preaching and personal annoyance at the preaching was then the context for an extraordinary experience of what Gertrude said was a vision of Jesus, the true object of her desire. This testimony is unusual in the experiences narrated by Gertrude for its reflection on the specific preaching that she heard; more commonly, her visions and auditions are more directly related to the hymns or prayers or Eucharistic liturgy.

The visionary texts associated with Elisabeth of Schönau and Gertrude of Helfta suggest how the highly routinized, verbally expressive, low-arousal ritual life of monastic liturgy could have been encountered as engaging, emotionally powerful practices that offered the possibility of (even stimulated) extraordinary cognitive experience.[7] While it may be objected that Elisabeth and Gertrude were exceptional, there is no evidence that anyone thought their experiences were incompatible with or threatening to the ongoing practice of monastic ritual.[8] In fact, by the fourteenth century, Christina Ebner, a nun at Engelthal, was puzzled by one of her fellow nuns who did not have visions and ecstasies (Bynum 1987: 83–84; Garber 2003: 127). Also, the testimonies of Elisabeth, Gertrude, and Christina Ebner point to another salient aspect of these claims about ecstatic experience: for each of these nuns, ecstasy took place within a community who witnessed it and to varying degrees could participate in it.[9] It was not the sole prerogative of the extraordinary religious virtuoso; it was outside the normal realm of the mind and the senses, but it was something that the normal routinized prayer life could lead to. In fact, in writing a rule for anchoresses (professed religious women who lived alone or in very small communities), Aelred of Rievaulx, a twelfth-century Cistercian monk, could give detailed instructions about how to have ecstatic, visionary experiences. With adequate ascetic and intellectual preparation (that is, observing the monastic practices of fasting, sexual renunciation, minimized sleep, silence and minimal contact with others, manual labor, scriptural reading, and the divine office), the anchoress was to enter into an ecstatic state, triggered by her meditation on and visualization of the events in the life of Jesus. This ecstatic state involves bodily activity (e.g., throwing herself on the ground, weeping, singing, kissing, groaning, licking the dust), as well as intense emotional experience (Aelred of Rievaulx 1971: 662–73; 1971b: 79–102). Aelred seems to have envisioned this as a routine part of the anchoretic life. It could not be done without the supporting physical and mental conditioning provided by the monastic life, but anyone appropriately engaged in that life should seek—and achieve—regular ecstatic, visionary experience.

So, were medieval monasteries islands of doctrinal religion? Semantic schemas abounded, authoritative interpretations were available, hierarchy was enforced, policing of orthodoxy was more possible than in the world outside the monastery walls. Yet the highly routinized ritual of the divine office offered its congregants opportunities for intense, emotional, visionary experience that became the foundation for personal, spontaneous (and later deliberative) exegesis that may or may not have accorded with the prevailing orthodoxy. These visionaries didn't form splinter groups; nor were they simply using visionary claims as the legitimation for articulating their views.[10] They were not rejecting deadening doctrinal religion; they were using their complex ritual life to stretch its emotional, cognitive possibilities, possibilities that were inherent in the repeated rituals and—some would argue—represented the very purpose of the ritual.[11]

And what was going on outside those monasteries, among the lay people? The two-modes model characterizes these as follows: "It is precisely within those populations that lack access to the authoritative corpus of religious teachings, and so cannot be adequately motivated by these teachings, that we find the greatest profusion of imagistic practices" (Whitehouse 2000: 310). The lay people of the later Middle Ages did not command a sophisticated knowledge of Christian theology, or often not as sophisticated as the preachers they might hear, not nearly as sophisticated as the professional theologians who taught in the universities, and not in the same universe as the modern scholars who look at religion primarily in terms of doctrinal synthesis and are gratified by their own ability to make logical connections between disparate beliefs and practices that may never have been linked by medieval people.[12] But did medieval people get bored with their rituals through lack of theological understanding? Why has doctrinal grasp of what is theoretically possible to communicate in words become the litmus test for whether a repetitive ritual works for an individual? The modes theory assumes that the transmission of religious knowledge and the formation of identity as member of a religious community take place primarily through the communication of the most basic beliefs of the tradition, that is, the transmission across generations of a stable and comprehensible creed. I would like to suggest that formation of religious identity can take place in a different way. To illustrate this, I want to focus on a very powerful part of late medieval Christian tradition, the cult of the Virgin Mary.[13]

Devotion to the Virgin Mary had been a part of Christian life for centuries, although many scholars point to very significant new developments from the mid-eleventh to fifteenth centuries. In this period, which also witnessed a significant rise in literacy, the development of new religious orders dedicated to teaching the laity, and the development of a class of professional philosophers and theologians who ultimately became organized into universities, devotion to the Virgin Mary took on much more emotional expressions than can be seen in the early Middle Ages.[14] Effusions of love, dedication, and praise overtook the more staid, theologically centered hymns and prayers of the early Middle Ages. Devotion to the Virgin Mary was expressed in major feasts celebrated publicly (there were four annual feasts dedicated to the Virgin) and in private domestic practices. The public festivals were celebrated with Mass in a language that lay people did not generally comprehend. Yet, there were sometimes components of these rituals that must have created some kind of meaning for the illiterate (i.e., non-Latin-comprehending) laity. For example, in parts of Germany, the Feast of the Assumption was celebrated with a ritual of blessing of herbs. The plants, loose or in bundles, were to be carried by the people into the church and placed on the altar. They were then blessed, with specific reference being made either to the celebration of Mary's assumption or to Mary's intercession in the blessing. The blessed herbs were then taken home to be used as protection against all manner of harm (Franz 1909, vol. 1: 398–413). As one prayer from a fourteenth-century manuscript beseeches the Lord:

> [T]hrough the assumption of the most holy virgin Mary, pour out the blessing of your strength upon these herbs, so that all who carry these herbs with them may not be condemned by judgment or fire or water, nor feel the wound of iron, nor ever suffer infamy, envy, mockery, opprobrium, magic, accusations, wrath, subjugation, the diverse machinations of anyone, jealousies, illusions, trickeries, or sadness. And if a pregnant woman has the herbs with her at the time of birth, may she be freed and not die, and in whatever home they are found, may it endure neither scandal nor danger" (Franz 1909, vol. 1: 409–10).

In this prayer, we can see how the annual commemoration of Mary's triumph over death and bodily corruption was used as a means for ensuring supernatural protection of the bodies and emotions of the local community.

At first glance, this might seem a classic example of the assertion that "No Christian ritual, no painting, no hymn, no statue, no altar, no posture in the church—in fact, no aspect of Christian culture in general—can be adequately understood without reference to a body of ideas codified in language" (Whitehouse 2000: 35). I exemplified this point myself by suggesting a rational connection between the theology of the Assumption and the ritual of blessing herbs. And it makes a lot of sense to me that some version of this rational connection may have provided clerical justification for the ceremony. But whether or not such a logical connection was part of the experience of the lay people gathering the plants, bringing them to church, and then bringing them home as protective devices is very much open to question. And this seems to me crucial if, ultimately, the theory is about how religious identity and community are formed (rather than about whether religious specialists are able to create elaborate theologies). Instead of projecting the theological connections in all their gratifying elaboration, I would feel pretty confident in suggesting that people knew this was a feast dedicated to the Virgin Mary, knew that they gathered herbs that were now something more than mere herbs, and perhaps had a lingering sense of protection in their homes that was linked to the Virgin Mary. Nothing ecstatic here, and nothing particularly doctrinal.

A little more doctrine, perhaps, invested the blessing performed in a twelfth-century German ritual at the bed of a woman endangered in the act of childbirth with the following rubrics and prayers. The officiant, presumably a cleric,[15] was to thrice touch the woman's belly at her navel, then her right side, then her left side, each time reciting a prayer to God the Father. Then, he was to recite, "Hannah brought forth Samuel; Elizabeth brought forth John; Anne brought forth Mary; Mary brought forth Christ. Infant, whether you be male or female, dead or alive, come forth; the Savior calls you into the light" (Franz 1909, vol. 2: 198). If there was one doctrinal association with the Virgin Mary, it was that she was the mother of Jesus. A prayer invoking her name in a childbearing, yet life-threatening, situation might have triggered that minimal doctrinal association. But outweighing lengthy associations with the foundational stories of the faith would be the more immediate dynamics of fear and pain, and perhaps hope for safety brought by the ritual act. One clerical observer of lay piety suggests how the pronouncement of Mary's name in the context of ritual, even Latin ritual, might have functioned. Hélinand of Froidmont (who died after 1229) declared,

> When the sweetest name of Mary is heard in church, immediately the stony hearts of the laity are shaken as if struck by a certain hammer of piety. They lift their hands and eyes to heaven and they beseech help from Mary; and like ships in danger, they frequently look to the star that they know (Hélinand of Froidmont 1855: 649).

This mode of listening and being stimulated to devotion—triggered by the sound of a word rather than the particular theological details being expressed—could be the means of participating in a formal liturgy as well as in the more urgent prayers intoned at bedside during childbirth. Words are significant in these rituals, but those words did not always function as we see them, knit together in the textualized versions accessible to us when considering past societies.[16]

Certainly lay people were being taught to venerate the Virgin Mary: by the late twelfth century, regional church synods began to mandate that the Hail Mary (a brief prayer addressing the Virgin) be recited as a standard prayer, along with Pater Noster and the creed.[17] These efforts on the part of the clerical hierarchy conform to a picture of doctrinal evangelization, although there were more appealing motives for lay people to learn the prayer than simply obeying the local priest who received a mandate to teach it. Hundreds of stories portraying Mary as a supernatural figure who would protect those devoted to her circulated in oral and written form.

These miracles of the Virgin,[18] as they are known, supported the various devotional practices dedicated to Mary: singing particular songs, saying particular prayers, kneeling or standing at particular shrines, and affirming the physical presence of Mary as localized and truly present in the thousands of paintings and sculptures newly created in this period.[19]

Consider the popular story told by Caesarius of Heisterbach, writing in the second half of the twelfth century, about Beatrice, a nun who was sacristan of her convent and fervent in her devotion to Mary. Driven by lust to leave the convent, Beatrice first went to the altar of the Virgin and laid the keys upon it, acknowledging her inability to withstand her temptation. She leaves, is corrupted, and becomes a prostitute. Fifteen years later, she returns to the convent in secular dress, only to discover that the Virgin Mary has taken her place and no one even knew she had left (Caesarius of Heisterbach 1851: 42–43).

Although it is possible to tease out theological subtleties and variations in these stories, they all share a common purpose: to encourage a relationship with Mary, a relationship understood to be reciprocal and one in which strong emotions were to be cultivated. Poignant stories personalizing belief are recognized as part of the doctrinal mode, but this assumes that transmission is tantamount to the author's or preacher's intention in telling a story in a particular way. Yet, sometimes the miracles of the Virgin seemed to defy even the basic teachings of the church, suggesting that doctrine was secondary to the emotional relationship between the all-powerful mother and the individuals who loved her. The symbol of Mary was in fact capable of ambiguous, sometimes divergent, emotional and intellectual appropriations.

A glimpse of how the encouragement of Marian devotion may have been appropriated is offered by a vita of Umiliana dei Cerchi, a Florentine woman who became a Franciscan tertiary after the death of her husband. The vita was written shortly after her death in 1246 by Vito of Cortona, a Franciscan friar. Umiliana is said to have owned a painted panel of the Blessed Virgin that she kept in her cell and revered by adorning it with crystal and amber seals (Vito of Cortona 1685: 395). When her young daughter died in her presence, Umiliana prostrated herself in front of the image and tearfully begged Mary to restore her daughter. After Umiliana made this prayer and blessed her daughter with the sign of the cross, "a wonderful and beautiful child stepped out from that panel, went to where the girl lay, and blessed her. At this, her daughter arose restored and the child disappeared" (Vito of Cortona 1685: 396). For the author of this text, the painting of the Virgin is not only the focus of prayer, but it is also the site where the Virgin and her son enter into the world of their needy devotees. The description of Umiliana's death also highlights aspects of her devotion: "Out of reverence for our Lady, Umiliana humbly requested of the Lord that she might die on a Saturday," Saturday being the day on which the Virgin was especially commemorated. According to Vito, her request was fulfilled. As she lay on her deathbed, she saw the devil standing by. "And she threatened him with her words and her hands, driving him back and saying, 'Leave quickly, wretch, because my Lady is with me and she will immediately smash and destroy your sly machinations.'" Mary's role here is not simply as a general guardian for all who serve her, but she is also on call for the most dangerous moment of life, the moment of death.

As Umiliana cried out against the devil, her female companion ran to the painting of Mary, which is now described as also having some of the Virgin's hair. She took from there two blessed candles, which she lit, holding them in the form of a cross. She also brought a panel on which there was an image of Our Lady and the crucified Christ, and she placed this image on Umiliana's chest. With the candles she illuminated Umiliana, and she burned incense and sprinkled holy water over Umiliana's head. After this, Umiliana again admonished the devil, who then left her in peace. She then opened her eyes and saw the painting on her chest, wrapped it in a silk cloth, and repositioned it on her chest. She rested quietly and then died at the hour in which she was accustomed to receive the Lord's body (Vito of Cortona 1685: 399).

As is always the case with hagiographical documents, it is difficult to determine exactly the historicity of events narrated since the primary purpose of these documents is to attest to the sanctity of the person described. Furthermore, these texts were also often written to present holy lives for imitation. Thus, although we cannot read the vita of Umiliana as unimpeachable testimony of historical fact, we can read it as articulating a pattern of piety that a Franciscan friar deemed exemplary, at least for women (see Coakley 1994: 91–110). The contours of this pattern were shaped by the presence of a physical object, a painting of Mary, which served as focus of prayer, as site of divine contact with this world, and as portable talisman to be put on the body. The death scene is striking for its lack of miracles and its unusual detail. Clerics and their sacraments are notably absent, surprising especially since the vita attests to the frequent presence of a Brother Michael, who was Umiliana's confessor (Vito of Cortona 1685: 389, 391, 392, 393, 395, 398). Instead, Umiliana's companion, probably Gisla, who is named in the prologue of the text as Umiliana's guardian during her illness (Vito of Cortona 1685: 385), turned to what appears to be a veritable shrine in the cell. The painting of Mary was also the repository of Marian relics; candles, incense, and holy water were kept there, as was another painting, that of Mary and the dead or dying Christ. The companion used these objects to fortify Umiliana in her struggle with the devil. The image of Mary with her dying loved one was placed on the chest of her other dying loved one, and the ritual succeeded in preparing Umiliana who died in peace. The life that was led in the physical presence of Mary ended with physical contact between painting and body. Instead of receiving the body of Christ from the hands of a priest, Umiliana received the image of Mary and Christ on her body at the hands of woman and awaited the reception of her soul into the hands of Mary.

The paintings in this story do not simply serve the purposes usually envisioned by theologians or scholars of religion: as didactic reminders or even stimulants of devotion.[20] The images structure the contours of the relationship between Umiliana and Mary and literally are the media of their interaction (cf. Camille 1989: 220–41; Belting 1994: 300). The vita of Umiliana testifies to how late medieval Christians were encouraged to understand the presence of Mary localized and embodied in images that were increasingly available in churches, on street corners, and even in their own homes. The images—while certainly capable of doctrinal content—did not, could not, dictate the ways in which they would be appropriated. Theological authorities did try to shape this appropriation. The author of this vita was one of them, but note what he tried to shape: an emotional relationship with a supernatural power localized in a woman's bedroom, a relationship that didn't fit into or reject the clerically controlled ritual life of Eucharist and last rites.

There are certainly other aspects of medieval Christian practice relevant to the two-modes theory. For example, the role of violence (in visionary experience, iconography, and Marian devotion) could complicate each of the sections above. Furthermore, the types of memory practices that were part of monastic education could raise the issue of the historicity and constructedness of memory functions. Without developing these latter points, I turn to some concluding observations. As I mentioned at the outset, I was particularly intrigued by the reflections on the relationship between the two modes of religiosity. Here is one of the most striking assertions:

> Doctrinal and imagistic modes of religiosity are not types of religion but organizing principles for religious experience and action. It is very common for both modes of religiosity to be present within a single religious tradition. *This does not, however, result in a simple fusion of the two modes. Invariably, those aspects of a religious tradition associated with doctrinal and imagistic modes respectively, remain distinct from the viewpoints of both participants and observers* (Whitehouse 2000: 309, emphasis added).

I do not think that this claim adequately characterizes ritual life and religious practice as represented in medieval Christian texts. It is not just that doctrinal and imagistic practices coexisted in medieval Christianity, something that is accounted for by the two-modes theory. Rather, it is that there were practices that do not fit either category and that share characteristics of both. Repetitive, verbalized ritual was sometimes the stimulus for ecstatic, visionary, intensely emotional experience that often provided the materials for spontaneous and long-term personal exegesis. Repetitive rituals in an unknown language could be the setting for an experience of emotion directed to a supernatural power or for charging mundane elements with supernatural power. Representational images could "teach" doctrine (or at least that is what their apologists hoped), or they could be the media of direct personal connection to another reality. Medieval people could see them as doctrine or they could see them moving, weeping, raising their dead. This is not independent coexistence of the two modes, fusion of the two modes, or resorting of the unlearned to imagistic practices to juice up their boring rituals. Rather, it is a limitation of the two-modes theory to account for typical kinds of ritual experience in medieval Christianity. I am not going to suggest that these practices are examples of yet a third mode of religiosity, because that would hold the two modes in place as a valid way of describing other religious cultures, something about which I have already noted my suspicions.

Also, since much of the material I have presented about medieval Christianity suggests that gender is very important in the structuring of religious identity, I would urge further reflection on gender as part of the refinement of any theory of religion. Historians and anthropologists are not alone in considering gender; cognitive science and the theorizing of how the brain encodes and reactivates memory do allow for a model that acknowledges sex difference (e.g., Canli et al. 2002). Whether such research in cognitive science would allow a more nuanced view of modes of religiosity, I cannot say—I am quite willing to look elsewhere to explain gender roles. However, given the vast evidence of gender difference within religious communities, I think that a theory aimed at connecting some of the most salient aspects of religion (e.g., communal organization and forms of transmission) ignores gender at its peril. Even if neural science and the analysis of memory functions do not offer a robust basis for nuancing the modes theory to account for gender difference, the rich records of religious artifacts as well as the living communities of religious adherents do.

Notes

1. The new patterns of religious life strenuously imposed on the people of Papua New Guinea by Anglican missionaries (Whitehouse 2000: 34–53) and imposed on European Catholics by Protestant (and I might add Catholic Counter-Reformation) activists (150–59), offer fascinating evidence about religious change, resistance, the lack of appeal of particular styles of ritual to people unfamiliar with them, and the emphasis on verbal expression among some sixteenth-century Protestants. It should be remembered that this evidence, however, is largely polemical (that is, drawn from the materials reflecting the

ambitions, beliefs, and frustrations of the missionaries) and does not offer the same kind of evidence as would analysis of communities committed to the practice of doctrinal religion.

2. The basic structure of the monastic divine office was outlined in the sixth-century rule of Benedict of Nursia. See Benedict of Nursia (1981: 50–65, chs. 8–19). Various modifications within this basic framework were made over time.

3. Benedict hints at the possibility of tedium in the divine office. He requires monks to stand "with respect and awe" (*cum honore et timore*) during the reading of the Gospel (Benedict of Nursia 1981: 54–55, ch.11). He describes monks as tepid, as possibly manifesting "sluggish devotion" (*inertem devotionis suae servitium*) in contrast to earlier desert ascetics who could energetically say many more psalms a day than they (62–63, ch. 18), but this is part of his consistent sense of the greater religious athleticism of the "holy fathers." He mandates punishment for monks who are late in coming to the liturgy (45–55, ch. 11; 90–93, ch. 43), or who make mistakes in performing it (94–95, ch. 45). To maintain proper interior disposition, he mandates standing while chanting "so that our minds will be in harmony with our voices" (*ut mens nostra concordet voci nostrae*; 65–65, ch.19) and that prayer should always be brief (64–65, ch. 20). Many monastic legislators discuss *acedia* or *accedia*, sometimes translated as "sloth" or "tedium," defined most influentially by John Cassian (1894: 266) as "weariness or distress of heart . . . akin to dejection." Usually this term refers to something much larger than, though potentially including, tedium experienced in ritual; it usually refers to weariness with the ascetic or monastic life.

4. "Tone" was the basic melodic formula with which the psalm was chanted. It was keyed to one of eight "modes" or basic melodic sequences of the antiphons that were part of the particular service. (*Mode* is the technical term for this musical sequence, not to be confused with the word as used in "modes of religiosity.") For a brief discussion of modes, see Cynthia J. Cyrus (1999). For a discussion of the monastic divine office that emphasizes its mystical possibilities, see Richard L. Crocker (2000: 128–47).

5. The classic discussion of monastic reading is Jean Leclercq (1961: 87–96). For how reading itself was to involve bodily affliction and emotional wounding, see Mary Carruthers (1997: 1–33), who demonstrates that medieval memory techniques invested even what we call "rote learning" with "gut reaction." For the connection between mortification of the body, study, and ecstatic experience, see below the comments on Aelred of Rievaulx.

6. I use the term *revelatory experience* here to generalize about a variety of phenomena described in medieval texts. The terms used in the texts include "rapture" (*raptio; raptus sum*), "ecstasy" (*extasis*), "vision" (*visio*), being "lifted out of the self" or "out of the mind" (*in mentis excessu*), or simply "I saw" (*vidi*), or "I heard" (*audi*) or "I felt" (*sensi*), or something "appeared to me" (*apparuit michi*). These phrases always express that what happened was not an ordinary sensory or cognitive experience. For the person described in the text, the experience is inevitably revelatory, and the text itself is the product of a process of exegesis, often created in some type of collaboration between the visionary and a scribe or a supporting community. There were Christian theorists of such experiences (e.g., Augustine, Gregory the Great, Richard of St. Victor), although people claiming to have revelatory experience were not necessarily familiar with such theories.

7. These texts raise other issues relevant to the modes theory, particularly the connection between literacy and doctrinal religion. The significant increase in literacy in mid-twelfth century Western Europe (see Stock 1983) is the context in which women emerge on the literary scene as authors of religious literature (other than isolated earlier examples of women writing hagiographical texts). It is striking that women's emergence in literary activity is very closely tied with the production of visionary texts (Clark 1999: 51; Dinzel-bacher 1985: 152–78). Thus, literacy in medieval Christianity (which was definitely gendered; women were not educated to be religious teachers and authors) was in a very powerful way linked to visionary experience, which was itself strongly linked to the repetitive rituals of monastic life.

8. This is different from saying there was no evidence of objection to the content of particular visions or to Elisabeth's or Gertrude's interpretations of their experience. Elisabeth was keenly aware of the possibility that someone might object to her (that is, an unworthy woman) as recipient of such revelations, and she also worried about reactions to the specific content of her visions. But even these concerns are not about the nature of visionary experience per se.

9. For the relationship between the visionary and community, see Anne L. Clark (1999: 44–48; 2000: 47–55).

10. Some version of this argument—that women's claim of visionary experience is a literary motif used to authorize their words—is often implicit or explicit in commentary about medieval visionary texts. For the inadequacy of this view, see Clark, "Introduction," in Elisabeth of Schönau (2000: 27–32).

11. I tend to think of the ecstatic practices of medieval Christians in this way, acknowledging that "the very purpose of the ritual" is a problematic phrase implying a single intentionality in the construction of a ritual process, which I do not accept. Rather, I am suggesting that rituals enabled the possibility for the person to feel transported out of normal consciousness.

12. I must be guilty of this somewhere in this chapter; it is probably a big part of what I typically do. The danger of it becomes apparent to me when the belief system (created by the scholar ingenuously connecting the dots) is then made synonymous with religion.

13. Much of the material discussed below is examined in greater detail in Clark (2004).

14. For discussion of Marian devotion as the site of mapping new emotional and imaginative terrain in the history of Western culture, see Rachel Fulton (2002).

15. The Latin formula with its biblical references and transmission in a liturgical manuscript is strong evidence that the blessing was composed and used by clerics. Often such formulae are found in books that make no distinction between bedside rites and church services. This practice of bedside ritual officiated by the clergy waned after the thirteenth century. See Adolph Franz (1909, vol. 2: 197–98).

16. This raises a major issue. How can we know about the ritual experience of others, particularly those in past societies? For a thorough critique of reading narrative descriptions of ritual at face value, see Philipe Buc (2001). His critique applies to other cultures beyond early medieval Europe. In my characterization of the blessing of the herbs and the

bedside childbirth ritual (which are based on prescriptive ritual rubrics rather than ostensibly descriptive narratives), I tried for an interpretive minimalism. In part, this minimalism is in reaction to what I see as an overly theologized characterization of Christianity in the two-modes theory. But my comments on Umiliana and the role of icons (below) are based on a narrative text.

17. For example, see the canons of the following regional councils: Paris in 1198 (C. 10, in Mansi 1960–61, vol. 22: col. 681); Coventry in 1237 (Mansi 1960–61, vol. 23: 432); Salisbury in 1217 (Mansi 1960–61, vol. 22: 1107–8), Beziers in 1246 (Mansi 1960–61, vol. 23: 693); Albi in 1254 (Mansi 1960–61, vol. 23: 837); Le Mans in 1247 (Mansi 1960–61, vol. 23: 756); Norwich in 1257 (Mansi 1960–61, vol. 23: 966–67), Liège in 1287 (Mansi 1960–61, vol. 24: 889), Bergen in 1320, Drontheim in 1351, and Skalholt in 1354 (Beissel 1909: 230).

18. For an introduction to this vast literature, see Guy Philippart (1996). For the range of stories, see the description of Cambridge, Sidney Sussex College MS 95, a late fifteenth-century compilation of 500 miracle stories, in M. R. James (1895: 76–109).

19. For the "newly visual culture" that emerged in the thirteenth century with thousands of representations of the Virgin Mary, see Michael Camille (1989: 224–25).

20. The extensive literature on medieval theology about images usually highlights the view of Gregory the Great on images as the books of the illiterate. Because of theologians' concern with images as doctrinally didactic, there was concern for orthodoxy in images. See, e.g., Camille (1989: 231–32) and Larissa Taylor (1977: 111–12).

References

Aelred of Rievaul. 1971. "De institutione inclusarum." In *Aelredi Rievallensis opera omnia.* "Corpus Christianorum, continuatio mediaevalis" I, edited by A. Hoste and C. H. Talbot. Turnhout: Brepols.

———. 1971b. A Rule of Life for a Recluse. In *Treatises and Pastoral Prayer.* Cistercian Fathers Series 2. Kalamazoo, Mich.: Cistercian Publications.

Beissel, Stephen. 1909. *Geschichte der Verehrung Marias in Deutschland während des Mittelalters.* Freiburg: Herderliche.

Belting, Hans. 1994. *Likeness and Presence: A History of the Image before the Era of Art,* translated by Edmund Jephcott. Chicago: University of Chicago Press.

Benedict of Nursia. 1981. In *RB 1980: The Rule of St. Benedict in Latin and English with Notes and Thematic Index,* edited by Timothy Fry. Collegeville, Minn.: Liturgical Press

Buc, Philipe. 2001. *The Dangers of Ritual: Between Early Medieval Texts and Social Scientific Theory.* Princeton, N.J.: Princeton University Press.

Bynum, Caroline Walker. 1982. "Women Mystics in the Thirteenth Century: The Case of Helfta." In *Jesus as Mother: Studies in the Spirituality of the High Middle Ages.* Berkeley: University of California Press.

———. 1987. *Holy Feast and Holy Fast: The Religious Significance of Food to Medieval Women.* Berkeley: University of California Press.

Caesarius of Heisterbach. 1851. *Dialogus miraculorum,* edited by Joseph Strange. Cologne: H. Lempertz and Comp.

Camille, Michael. 1989. *The Gothic Idol: Ideology and Image-Making in Medieval Art.* Cambridge: Cambridge University Press.

Canli, Turhan, John E. Desmond, Zuo Zhao, and John D. E. Gabrieli. 2002. "Sex Differences in the Neural Basis of Emotional Memories." *Proceedings of the National Academy of Sciences* 99: 10, 789–94.

Carruthers, Mary. 1997. "Reading with Attitude, Remembering the Book." In *The Book and the Body,* edited by Dolores Frese and Katherine O'Brien O'Keefe, 1–33. Notre Dame, Ind.: University of Notre Dame Press.

———. 1998. *The Craft of Thought: Meditation, Rhetoric, and the Making of Images, 400–1200.* Cambridge: Cambridge University Press.

Cassian, John. 1894. *The Institutes of the Coenobia,* translated by Edgar C. S. Gibson. Vol. II. *Nicene and Post-Nicene Fathers, Second Series.* New York: Christian Literature Company.

Clark, Anne L. 1992. *Elisabeth of Schönau: A Twelfth-Century Visionary.* Philadelphia: University of Pennsylvania Press.

———. 1999. "Holy Woman or Unworthy Vessel? The Representations of Elisabeth of Schönau." In *Gendered Voices: Medieval Saints and Their Interpreters,* edited by Catherine Mooney, 35–51, 202–7. Philadelphia: University of Pennsylvania Press.

———. 2000. "An Ambiguous Triangle: Jesus, Mary, and Gertrude of Helfta." *Maria: A Journal of Marian Studies* 1: 37–56.

———. 2004. "The Cult of the Virgin Mary and Technologies of Christian Formation in the Later Middle Ages." In *Educating People of Faith: Exploring the History of Jewish and Christian Communities,* edited by John Van Engen. Grand Rapids, Mich.: Eerdmans Publishers.

Coakley, John 1994. "Friars, Sanctity, and Gender: Mendicant Encounters with Saints, 1250–1325." In *Medieval Masculinities: Regarding Men in the Middle Ages,* edited by Clare A. Lees, 91–110. Minneapolis: University of Minnesota Press.

Crocker, Richard L. 2000. *An Introduction to Gregorian Chant.* New Haven, Conn.: Yale University Press.

Cyrus, Cynthia J. 1999. "Music: Introduction to Church Modes." In *ORB: The Online Reference Book for Medieval Studies,* available at www.vanderbilt.edu/~cyrus/ORB/orbmode.htm.

Dinzelbacher, Peter. 1985. "Die 'Vita et Revelationes' der Wiener Begine Agnes Blannbekin (+1315) im Rahmen der Viten-und Offenbarungsliteratur Ihrer Zeit." In *Frauenmystik im Mittelalter,* edited by Peter Dinzelbacher and Dieter R. Bauer, 152–78. Stuttgart: Schwabenverlag AG.

Elisabeth of Schönau. 2000. *The Complete Works,* translated by Anne L. Clark. New York: Paulist Press.

Franz, Adolph. 1909. *Die Kirchlichen Benediktionen im Mittelalter,* 2 vols. Freiburg: Herdersche Verlagshandlung.

Fulton, Rachel. 2002. *From Judgment to Passion: Devotion to Christ and Mary, 800–1200.* New York: Columbia University Press.

Garber, Rebecca L. R. 2003. *Feminine Figurae: Representations of Gender in Religious Texts by Medieval German Women Writers 1100–1375.* New York and London: Routledge.

Gertrude of Helfta. 1968. *Legatus memorialis abundantiae divinae pietatis.* Vol. 3 of *Oeuvres spirituelles de Gertrude d'Helfta,* edited by Pierre Doyère et al. *Sources Chrétiennes* Vol 143. Paris: Éditions du Cerf.

————. 1993. *The Herald of Divine Love*, translated by Margaret Winkworth. New York: Paulist Press.

Hélinand of Froidmont. 1855. Sermo XXI: In Assumptione B. Mariae, II, "Sermones." In *Patrologia Latina, the Full Database*, edited by J. P. Migne, vol. 212, col. 646–52, Alexandria, Va.: Chadwyck-Healey, Inc., 1996.

James, M. R. 1895. *A Descriptive Catalogue of the Manuscripts in the Library of Sidney Sussex College, Cambridge*. Cambridge: Cambridge University Press.

Leclercq, Jean. 1961. *The Love of Learning and the Desire for God: A Study of Monastic Culture*, translated by Catharine Misrahi. New York: Fordham University Press.

Mansi, J. D. 1960–1961. *Sacrorum conciliorum nova et amplissima collectio* 54, vols. 1757–98, 1901–27, reprint ed. Graz: Akademische Druck-u. Verlagsanstalt.

Philippart, Guy. 1996. "Le récit miraculaire marial dans l'Occident médiéval." In *Marie: le culte de la Vierge dans la société médiévale*, edited by Dominique Iogna-Prat, Eric Palazzo, and Daniel Russo. Paris: Beauchesne.

Roth, F. W. E. 1884. *Die Visionen der hl. Elisabeth und die Schriften der Aebte Ekbert und Emecho von Schönau*. Brünn: Verlag der Studien aus dem Benedictiner-und Cistercienser-Orden.

Stock, Brian. 1983. *The Implications of Literacy: Written Language and Models of Interpretation in the Eleventh and Twelfth Centuries*. Princeton, N.J.: Princeton University Press.

Taylor, Larissa. 1977. *Soldiers of Christ: Preaching in Late Medieval and Reformation France*. New York: Oxford University Press.

Vito of Cortona. 1685. *Vita b. aemilianae seu humilianae*. In *Acta Sanctorum Maii IV*, edited by Godesfridus Henschenius et al. Antwerp: Société des Bollandistes.

Whitehouse, Harvey. 2000. *Arguments and Icons: Divergent Modes of Religiosity*. Oxford: Oxford University Press.

————. 2002. "Modes of Religiosity: A Cognitive Explanation of the Sociopolitical Dynamics of Religion." *Method & Theory in the Study of Religion* 14: 293–315.

Modes of Religiosity and Changes in Popular Religious Practices at the Time of the Reformation

9

TED VIAL

THE REFORMATION ERA PROVIDES plenty of data to test Harvey White-house's modes of religiosity theory. The Reformation was as much a change in ritual behavior and social behavior as it was a change in theology. But more than grist for the theory mill that any religious group would provide, the Reformation plays a pivotal role in the modes theory itself. Whitehouse argues that "the European Reformation indirectly provided the models for many subsequent varieties of missionary Christianity, and thus may help to explain the peculiar patterns of interaction between doctrinal and imagistic modes of religiosity in certain regions of Melanesia" (2000: 150). The Reformation data, in addition to testing the theory's applicability, is itself part of the theory because it may be the historical source of the doctrinal mode of religiosity that interacted (courtesy of Christian missionaries) with the imagistic religions of Papua New Guinea where Whitehouse first observed the phenomena that gave rise to his theory.

It is doubly important, then, to get the story right when it comes to Reformation era Europe. We are fortunate that historians have recently turned their attention to very detailed and specific accounts of the daily lives of many kinds of people in the sixteenth century. Most of these focus on very limited areas because Europe was such a patchwork of various political arrangements and economic situations. I rely on a couple of these studies to construct a story, one that seems to offer support for Whitehouse's modes theory, but which raises several difficult questions.

The Story

The story of religious behavior in the sixteenth century seems to offer support for the modes theory, but it also raises tough questions. It is not hard to make almost any data fit a theory, but not much is gained by that exercise. Although we do not really need a theory with predictive power when studying history, we can expect a good theory to throw light on poorly understood or documented areas. The modes of religiosity theory has the potential to help explain religious behavior in sixteenth-century Europe, but to do so it will have to be pushed farther. The important part of this chapter, then, is not so much the story and how it fits White-house's theory, but the questions raised by the data that must be confronted if the theory is to be useful to historians. These questions come in the final section.

Max Weber described the Reformation as a tearing down of the monastery walls. This is literally true, as princes and cities happily secularized church prop-erty and appropriated the proceeds for their own purposes and as Luther tried to find new jobs for monks and marry off the nuns (he himself married one). But Weber had something more in mind, too. Medieval Catholicism can be seen as a two-tiered system in which monasteries and convents approximated as closely as possible the Christian ideal, while the laity practiced a less rigorous version deemed sufficient for salvation (even if it earned time in purgatory). The number of people who could literally sell all they have and give it to the poor, as Jesus rec-ommends in the Gospel of Luke, or who could live celibately, as Paul recom-mends, is probably fairly small in any society or era, and it is difficult to imagine the society that would survive long if the number increased greatly. Monks and nuns lived an ascetic life apart from the world, designed to reduce the temptation and occasion of sin to a minimum, thus giving humans their best chance at the sinless state necessary for entrance into heaven. The idea that medieval religion was a two-tiered system has been discredited in recent secondary literature, but if one is operating with the modes theory and focusing on monasteries versus village and city religious life, rather than a class theory or a popular versus elite distinction, this is not a bad model.

As Weber argued, when Protestants tore down monastery walls, they removed more than a physical barrier. The Protestant ethic is, in his famous phrase, a "this-worldly asceticism" (1958: 170). People's callings are to work in the world, not apart from it. Expectations for religious belief and practice are raised in the priest-hood of all believers. This is not a bad model of the story I want to tell, which is a story of what historians refer to as the reform of culture rather than a story of the Reformation itself. This is not a story of Protestant versus Catholic, for the reform of culture was attempted as much by the Catholic Church following the Council of Trent as it was by the Protestant churches. And this attempt to reform culture does seem awfully doctrinal, to use that word in the sense that it is used in the modes theory.

Medieval Europe can be envisioned as a set of overarching pan-European strata, of greater size than a modern nation, with a fairly unified set of beliefs and a common language (Gellner 1983: 9–14). The monastic system formed one of these strata, with, of course, large variation from order to order and cloister to cloister. These monasteries were by and large highly regulated, having invented the concept of the hour so that the monks and nuns could chant scripture, pray, write, and work on a rigorously set schedule. These monasteries were a crucial component in the educational system of the other pan-European strata, the nobility, providing a large percentage of university professors, who formulated a complex scholastic theology, and a great number of court tutors.

Beneath these overarching strata were a series of local communities of a much smaller size than a modern nation. In the past their languages have been denigrated as dialects, which only means that not many people spoke them, and that, from village to village or city to city, people might have trouble understanding one another. Ernest Gellner proposes that in such localities the references and allusions made, the very gestures and facial expressions, would be so particular that even speakers of similar dialects would find themselves at sea in a neighboring region (1983: 12). The priests serving each community were largely local boys, with little or no more formal education than their parishioners. Their main function was to provide the sacraments. While there is clearly less emphasis on doctrine at this local level than in a university or most monasteries, we will have to return later to ask just how doctrinal or imagistic this local level of late medieval Catholicism was.

How did life at this local level change in the wake of the Reformation, during the so-called reform of culture? Because of the very local character of much of medieval life, it can quickly become futile to speak in generalities. I take great comfort in the following admission of Robert Scribner, the pioneer of social historical studies of popular religion at the time of the Reformation. He writes, "No one can claim to speak of the Reformation in relation to the 'religion of the people' without confessing to wide seas of ignorance concealing vast tracts of unexplored territory" (1993: 241). Fortunately, a fine set of studies of local practice, removed from the confessional battles that drove Reformation scholarship for so long, has begun to appear. These studies examine precisely what religious life was like in specific times and places for all classes of people.

Before looking at some examples of daily life during the reform of culture, we should set out a formal list of the characteristics we are looking for that will allow us to classify religious systems as doctrinal. Whitehouse lists a cluster of eight features we expect to see in the doctrinal mode (2002: 296–303).

1. *Repetition of doctrine.* The ideas transmitted in the doctrinal mode tend to be a logically coherent, orally transmittable, rhetorically persuasive body of teachings.

2. *Clearly marked leaders.* These leaders emerge based on their rhetorical ability to cast doctrines persuasively and relevantly.
3. *Orthodoxy checks.* Arranged by leaders to keep the doctrines stable, these checks also enhance the leaders' authority since they prevent alternate visions from gaining status, giving the leaders a monopoly on access to divine truth.
4. *A rigorous schedule of ritual occasions.* This was established to enforce the frequent rehearsal of this body of doctrine as required by the complexity of the body of doctrine defining group membership that must be remembered and transmitted. Information repeated in this way is stored in semantic memory (as opposed to episodic memory).
5. *Low spontaneous exegetical reflection.* Because the scripted rituals stored in semantic memory that are the occasions for the rehearsal of doctrine can be performed on autopilot, there is little occasion for people to feel the need to produce their own interpretations of rituals. In many cases, sixteenth-century religion being a great one, the leadership provides authorized exegeses of rituals.
6. *Hierarchical and centralized leadership.* This was set up to enforce orthodoxy.
7. *An imagined community.* Groups whose religion is predominantly doctrinal often form such communities, which can include people far beyond one's face-to-face acquaintances because membership in the group is defined by possession of this scripted memory, which can be orally rehearsed and easily transmitted.
8. *Proselytization.* The ease and desire to spread this set of beliefs.

The religion of the Reformation and afterwards seems to fit this cluster of characteristics. Johann of Saxony (a Protestant territory, home turf of Luther), in 1529, promulgated a catechism in his region with the following introduction:

> Dear God, help us! What misery I have seen! The common man, especially in the villages, knows absolutely nothing about Christian doctrine, and unfortunately, many pastors are practically unfit and incompetent to teach. Nonetheless, they are called Christians, have been baptized, and enjoy the holy sacraments even though they can recite neither the Lord's Prayer, the Apostles' Creed, nor the Ten Commandments. They live just like animals and unreasoning sows (Quoted in Karant-Nunn 1997: 67).

The early Protestant churches developed a three-pronged approach to the problems outlined by Johann: (1) regular visitations to every church, (2) creation of superintendencies to continue the work of itinerant inspectors, and (3) catechisms (Karant-Nunn 1997: 67). It is this approach that appears so doctrinal to Whitehouse.

1. *Visitations.* In 1528 Luther drew up instructions for a visitation to each community and church in Saxony. The results of this visitation surprised and horrified him. This visitation became the model for similar processes in almost all Protestant territories. Visitors wanted to know who did and did not attend church, who took communion, and who visited local wise women and men, as well as the level of moral conduct in each parish (who was committing adultery, etc.). Visitors met separately with the pastor and with his congregation, so that each could speak freely about the other. Much of our information about popular religious life comes from the records of these visitations.

2. *Superintendents.* In many regions this visitation became a regular, sometimes annual event. This required a new bureaucracy and the creation of the post of superintendent to oversee the visitors, collect information, and make reports to the secular authorities on what punitive steps should be taken. The information sought in visitations set ever higher and more detailed standards. The Prince of Nassau Saarbrücken wanted very specific information about religious practices: Was a hymn sung after collect and epistle? If a hymn was sung after the sermon, was it long or short? Was every word in the liturgy used in collective confession? Was the Lord's Prayer recited out loud or silently? Was it said while kneeling? Did the pastor preach the catechism on Sunday midday? Did he grasp the bread and wine and elevate them as he said the words of institution? Were the Eucharistic hosts large or small, whole or broken (Karant-Nunn 1997: 121)?

3. *Catechisms.* The Reformation produced a spate of catechisms from every church and sect. I offer just one brief example of the increasing expectations that led to their production. Recall the state of catechumens reported by Johann of Saxony in the introduction to his catechism. Johann would have been pleased had his subjects been able to recite the Lord's Prayer, the Apostles' Creed, and the Ten Commandments. By 1569 Martin Chemnitz called for confirmands to recite Luther's catechism from memory and then be quizzed by the minister (Karant-Nunn 1997: 68). This set a very high bar for knowing and being able to recite a complex set of doctrines.

Furthermore, Protestant pastors were no longer locals from the same economic class as the villagers. They were overwhelmingly drawn from the growing bourgeois class, and a far higher percentage of them had attended university than their Catholic predecessors.

The efforts of all denominations, largely through the process of visitation, aimed at more than doctrinal purity. It also took aim at the medieval folk ritual practices, which we might, at first glance, deem imagistic.

Let's look first at the ritual of baptism. The medieval Catholic rite spent a fair amount of time on exorcism. Ritual objects to protect the child against Satan included salt, spittle, oil, chrism, candles, and a special baptismal gown (Karant-Nunn 1997: 51). Protestant changes to this ritual are instructive. Luther wrote, in 1523, a "Little Book of Baptism," a liturgy for ministers for performing this ceremony. Although he did not forbid the use of these ritual objects because he did not want to offend those who in his view have weak consciences, he deemphasized them, arguing that all that is needed to frighten demons is to listen to God's word. In 1526 he revised this liturgy, omitting all mention of weak consciences and drastically reducing the part of the ceremony devoted to diabolical presence and magical aids against it. Bucer, the famous Strasbourg reformer, also got rid of such practices, writing, "Such magic tricks ill become intelligent and rational Christians, who ought to pay heed to the word of their Lord and follow it alone" (Karant-Nunn 1997: 54). He instructed ministers to speak loudly and clearly for all to hear, to direct their explanations of the ceremony not only to family and Godparents, but to the whole congregation. The result was a service just as long as the Catholic one, but one in which explanations and exhortations took the place of repeated exorcisms (Karant-Nunn 1997: 55). Surely this is an example of a doctrinal mode seeking to displace an imagistic one. I return to this question later.

Civil authorities, with the encouragement of religious leaders, began cracking down on the festivities surrounding baptism, especially the lavish parties, the practice of delaying baptism to allow friends and relatives time to travel to the party, and the giving of expensive gifts (Karant-Nunn 1997: 64). Protestants also cracked down on "magical" practices associated with the Eucharist. The Fourth Lateran Council in 1215 had decreed that all able-bodied Catholics must take communion at least once a year. As the doctrine of transubstantiation became codified and the awesome nature of the host became more inflated, the rites of preparation for receiving communion became more onerous. As a consequence, most laity opted to receive communion the minimum number of times allowable, just once a year, usually at Easter. But the benefits of merely seeing the consecrated host grew to fill the gap. In a 1375 sermon Bishop Brinton of Exeter taught that observers of the host would not suffer hunger, lose their eyesight, or be struck by sudden death (Rubin 1991: 63). By the late Middle Ages the host was most commonly experienced by most Christians as an object viewed from afar, always under the control of the clergy (Zika 1988: 31).

This awesome power of the host resulted in the growing importance of Corpus Christi festivals. In 1389 Pope Urban VI raised this feast to the status of the other four major feasts: Christmas, Easter, Pentecost, and Assumption. The celebration of this feast centered on a procession through town. The center of the procession was the host in a monstrance. Various confraternities grew up to sponsor these feasts, and they were often joined in this by the guilds. These groups jockeyed for a place of honor in the procession (Zika 1988: 38, 42). One's proximity to the center of the procession, where the host, carried by priests, rode under a canopy carried by local dignitaries, signaled one's importance. Thus, the relative positions of various social groups in relation to the host in the center of the procession mapped out the social hierarchies of the town for all to see.

In a 1518 sermon Luther argued against what he saw as the magical quality of the host. "You will receive as much as you believe you receive" (quoted in Muir 1997: 172). This clearly shifts the importance of the ceremony from an objective quality of the ritual object to the internal state of the participant, an internal state that is linked up with a set of beliefs. In a 1523 tract titled "On Adoring the Sacrament," Luther argued that the whole point of the sacrament is to lead participants to God's Word. Since adoration is a spiritual state, it need not be reflected in gestures, and bowing before the altar was no longer required (Karant-Nunn 1997: 115).

The 1528 visitation convinced Luther that the Word of God would not take root through mere preaching—it would require support of the secular authorities. Luther also realized that Protestant ministers would have to take every opportunity to indoctrinate their charges. Communion thus became an opportunity to instruct as much as a chance to relieve burdened consciences and was never allowed without such instruction in doctrine and the meaning of the ritual. It was the one chance to preach to many who otherwise avoided catechisms or going to church (Karant-Nunn 1997: 97).

A church ordinance promulgated in Lindau in 1573 directed pastors administering the sacrament to sick or dying parishioners that they must first preach to them and that the sermon was to be directed not at the sick or dying person but to the family and friends in attendance. The following prayer comes from an ecclesiastical ordinance for deathbed rites in Augsburg in 1555:

> It is a special work of God's love, dear Christians, toward us poor, sinful humans that God presents to us, in addition to his dear and holy Word, daily examples of sick and dying people, in order thereby to keep us in a state of repentance and not to let us quickly and in large numbers to be ripped away in his fury, as every day we so richly deserve (Karant-Nunn 1997: 153).

Medieval Catholic Eucharistic practices seem magical compared to the sixteenth-century Protestant emphasis on the Word. They emphasize the objective power found in ritual objects, whereas Protestants took pains to highlight that the efficacy of sacraments depended entirely on a subjective state of belief (belief linked to certain specific doctrines). Are they therefore more imagistic than sixteenth-century religious practices? Again, this is a question we will need to take up.

Medieval Christians also made great use of sacramentals (holy water, candles, etc.). They were popular objects for use in apotropaic magic (Muir 1997: 157). In post-Zwingli Zurich the baptism liturgy had to call for the sexton to pour out publicly the baptismal water on the church steps following the ceremony so that people could not use it for magical purposes.

Medieval weddings included the *Ansingwein*, in which the priest entered the wedding-night bedchamber to exorcize the bed, followed by a raucous and often bawdy party during which wedding guests sang suggestive songs. Protestants disapproved of the tradition and banned the minister's presence (Muir 1997: 38).

In Strasbourg, a city of 20,000, there were roughly 150 pastors whose activities were directed by a church assembly. Residents could choose from about fifty church services a week in the nine parish churches. The church assembly coordinated their themes so that each week the pastors sent one idea into almost every home (Abray 1985: 80).

Every Sunday there was a special service for the youth of the city, drilling them in the fundamentals of the faith. The church ordinance of 1534 states that each child must know the articles of faith, the Lord's Prayer, and the Ten Commandments. Parents and guardians were legally obligated to have their children attend these services (Abray 1985: 167).

By the 1570s complaints of lay ignorance in Strasbourg had dropped off. The standards had dropped some; parishioners weren't expected to master the subtleties of the Eucharistic debate, but they did need to know the Apostles' Creed, the Ten Commandments, and the Lord's Prayer. Abray states that effort at indoctrination in Strasbourg was largely a success (Abray 1985: 170).

The reform of culture has been described by Peter Burke as the triumph of Lent over Carnival. It expected peasants to act like monks and nuns. And it extended beyond what we delineate as religious behavior (Muir 1997: 118). Norbert Elias has identified the sixteenth century as the period when human behavior of all classes began to be shaped by the ritualized social graces of the court (Muir 1997: 117). The Stoic golden mean, which had been preserved in monasteries, for example under the influence of Bernard of Clairvaux, and from there had in turn influenced the education of the aristocratic classes, was taken up or imposed on all classes (Muir 1997: 119). When Erasmus, the great Catholic humanist, wrote "Manners for Children" (1530), it became a bestseller (Muir 1997: 120).

The Jesuit order was founded to a great extent to remissionize territory lost to the Protestants. The Jesuits were the educational elite of the Catholic Church. Their curriculum included instruction on manners, ballet, and acting, on the theory that playing a role teaches one to dominate passions and present a suitable face in public (Muir 1997: 123).

The Council of Trent was careful to maintain sharp theological differences from the Protestants, but otherwise called for reforms along much the same lines: improved moral standards and better-trained clergy preaching more and better sermons. Although there were sharp theological differences between Catholic and Protestant, both traditions were very doctrinal (in Whitehouse's sense) in the wake of the Reformation.

If we return to Whitehouse's eight criteria listed above that mark the doctrinal mode, I think we can easily see all of them in the changing religious practices of both Protestants and Catholics in the sixteenth century. Protestants and Catholics were both purveyors of logically coherent persuasive bodies of teachings; both had clearly marked leaders and systems for checking on the orthodoxy of their adherents; both stressed frequent repetition of rituals during which doctrine was rehearsed and authorized exegeses of the rituals provided; both made efforts to transmit these bodies of beliefs far and wide. This, of course, is the root of Whitehouse's claim: that the Reformation provided the paradigm of doctrinal practice that was exported by both Protestant and Catholic missionaries to Papua New Guinea.

The success of this reform of culture has been called into question. Gerald Strauss argues that the reform of culture had little impact on the lives of people (1975). His evidence comes largely from visitation reports in the countryside. If one construes Protestantism as a desacralizing or disenchantment of the world (another famous Weberian hypothesis), Scribner also argues that it did not succeed. He chronicles the many magical Protestant folk practices that continued on into the nineteenth and twentieth centuries in Europe (1989). On the other hand Abray argues that, in Strasbourg at least, it was a success (1985: 209). What is not debatable is that the post-Reformation religious and secular elites tried to impose a mode of religion that fits Whitehouse's description of the doctrinal mode uncannily.

Issues

I think the issues this data raises for Whitehouse's modes theory can be clustered into two general categories. The first is what I think of as an unfortunate set of baggage that accompanies with the terms *imagistic* and *doctrinal*. The second is the need for refined models of interaction of the two modes.

1. Chapter 7 of *Arguments and Icons: Divergent Modes of Religiosity* is titled "Entangled Histories," and I suspect that the entanglement runs deeper than Whitehouse suspects. It is not just that the Reformation produced high-octane doctrinal religious groups that began a missionary effort eventually stretching to Papua New Guinea. The Reformation already stands at the base of how we imagine religion.

In other words, when I wrote that post-Reformation religion fits Whitehouse's doctrinal mode uncannily, this is no coincidence. I think this is apparent in the very choice of terms. Let's begin with doctrinal. Clearly Protestantism has all the eight characteristics of the doctrinal mode. Justification by faith is at the core—you will be saved by your belief, not your ritual actions. Furthermore, in the priesthood of all believers, everyone is a theologian. The Catholicism of the Council of Trent is no less doctrinal. But is pre-Reformation Catholicism less doctrinal, even at the local level? The reform of culture is an attempt, in part, to replace magical rituals with theologically sanctioned ones. But my sense is that apotropaic uses of ritual objects are not, in fact, imagistic, even if they are magical. That a priest should exorcize the wedding bed, that a host can make a field fertile, that a page of the Bible hung over the stable can protect the cattle from disease, that a Bible opened to the page where Christ cured an epileptic and turned face down on the chest of a palsy victim could act as a cure (examples from Scribner 1989), these strike us as not doctrinal because they are superstitious compared with the erudite debates about the real presence of Christ in the host between Lutherans, Catholics, Calvinists, and Zwinglians. But on second glance these superstitions seem to fit most of the criteria of the doctrinal mode. They were often repeated, orally transmittable (when asked by a Calvinist visitor why he kept going to a "cunning woman," Hans Pemmerler responded that when he's sick, he goes to the doctor), and widespread. Though there was no church or overarching institution to coordinate and patrol these practices, they were most often administered by the priest (the local representative of a very hierarchical and centralized set of relationships) with the tacit approval of the church and were patrolled and enforced at the local level (priests who balked at serving as the officiant at these ceremonies were often forced from their posts or even killed because the people in their charge perceived these practices as necessary). In other words, I am suggesting first that medieval popular religion may fit the doctrinal mode very easily, and second I am suggesting that the very term *doctrinal*, while defined neutrally by Whitehouse, carries with it baggage that leads us to contrast implicit definitions of what looks a lot like Calvinist dogma and miscategorize religious behavior that may in fact fit the mold.

The term *imagistic* is even more problematic. I think it is entangled with the term *icon* in a way that leads to difficulty. Surely Protestants are doctrinal since they kicked off their movement with acts of iconoclasm. But would not rushing into a cathedral and slashing a picture of the Virgin Mary be an experience stored in episodic memory? I suspect it was quite a flashbulb moment. At a more important level, Peter Matheson has recently made a very provocative argument that the Reformation should be understood not so much as a stripping of the altars (to use Eamon Duffy's memorable phrase) but as a change in metaphor. Iconoclasm is eclipsed by what he calls the Reformation's "iconopoaic energies . . . its creativity in producing new allegories and metaphors for the divine and human which, by their novel connections and collocations, bedded together the hitherto incompatible and subverted one cosmos while paving the way for another" (Matheson 2000: 6). In too easily buying the argument that the Reformers replaced sensual superstitions with intellectual beliefs, we may be allowing their theoretical framework to skew our own view of them as data. It's not that Zwingli's Eucharist is more doctrinal than the Catholics'—"what excites wonder and awe now is the free forgiveness of sins," not the transformation of elements. "Biblical images are being reworked here, released and unleashed to emphasize gratuity, access, intimacy. From this perspective the Reformation can be seen as an infinitely varied, but coherent and extended, metaphor for the bountifulness of God's grace" (Matheson 2000: 7–8).

Whitehouse cites Patrick Collinson's idea that the Secondary Reformation (when some Lutheran territories went Calvinistic) was not just iconoclastic but iconophobic (2000: 155). And immediately Whitehouse writes, "Not surprisingly, the most virulent anti-imagistic Protestant traditions have always been subject to the 'tedium effect.'" Notice how imagistic is contrasted with iconoclastic. But the list of characteristics of the imagistic mode he provides nowhere includes presence or absence of visual images. There are plenty of other ways to produce "vivid and enduring episodic memories" (Whitehouse 2002: 304). Iconoclasm need not be doctrinal. Again, an interpretation of the iconoclasm of the reformers themselves has slipped subconsciously into our category.

2. These reflections, couched in terms of semantics, but really about theory, I think, lead me to my second set of concerns, which are my deepest concerns. The beauty of the modes theory stems in part from its ability to account so well for the data in Papua New Guinea. It looks something like this: the doctrinal mode spreads effectively in Papua New Guinea, but it suffers from the tedium effect. In other words, it does one of the two things a religious system must do quite well—it provides for the memory of the beliefs that defines the group. But it does not do the second critical thing as well—motivate people to want to remember and practice. For this it relies on periodic imagistic splinter groups that reenergize their adherents. When these splinter groups (like the one at Dadul described by Whitehouse) are reabsorbed into the mainstream, they are emotionally committed to the doctrines and motivated to remember and spread them. This works well in Papua New Guinea in part because people still have vague memories of earlier imagistic practices that predate the doctrinal religious system (Whitehouse 2000: 128).

The Reformation data suggest that the doctrinal mode will always be parasitic on the imagistic mode for motivation and that the way that these two modes interact in the Pomio Kivung is one possible pattern of the interaction of the modes, but not the only one. It is not the one that applies to most of Christian Europe in the sixteenth century. The fact that this pattern of interaction comes first chronologically in the formation of the theory dangerously gives it theoretical priority.

First there is the problem of grain of analysis that is not present as markedly in Dadul: Do we consider Christianity the religion and ask what movements within it cluster in the imagistic basin and which cluster in the doctrinal basin? Or do we pick Protestantism versus Catholicism, or Lutheranism versus Calvinism, or Lutherans and Reformed versus Anabaptists? Do we pick splinter groups in general versus mainstream traditions? Splinter groups from Christianity? From Protestantism? From Anabaptists (for example, the splinter movement in Münster that resembles in many ways the splinter group in Dadul)? Is the growing nondenominational megachurch movement in the contemporary United States part of mainstream Christianity, or is it independent?

More importantly, whenever Whitehouse turns to Christianity, the language gets more vague, the use of terms looser. Two examples: "Christianities have tended to incorporate, if not an imagistic domain of operation, more sensually and emotionally evocative forms of routinized worship (for instance, as in Pentecostalism)" (Whitehouse 2000: 148). How much more? Is "more sensually and emotionally evocative" imagistic or not? How much pageantry (to borrow Robert N. McCauley and E. Thomas Lawson's phrase) do you need before something is a good candidate for storage in episodic memory? Here the use of terms becomes critical. A Catholic mass is more sensual, perhaps, than one in Zurich, but it's repeated more often, has the oversight of a centralized hierarchical leadership, offers a standard exegesis to fill the vacuum left by lack of spontaneous exegetical reflection, and so forth.

Second: "In general, the spread of Reformation ideas seems to have conformed to a pattern in which newly established doctrinal orthodoxies came to be sporadically disrupted by the innovation of localized imagistic cults" (Whitehouse 2000: 156). It is not clear here if Whitehouse means splinter groups, like the one at Münster, or local "magical" practices that proved resistant to the reform of culture, as we have seen from the records left by visitations. If the latter, we can no longer avoid the question of whether or not these local systems are imagistic. Superstitious, magical, to be sure. But the belief that a host can aid fertility is as much a belief as that Christ is present in spirit but not in the flesh in the host. It has theories to explain it and is reiterated in regular rituals. The liturgy of pre-Reformation religion was very regular, arranged on an annual cycle. The Corpus Christi processions were wild, but annual. However, Christmas and Easter, too, occur only once a year, and they are part of a doctrinal mode since they rely on more frequently rehearsed ideas. The same could be said of Corpus Christi, as well as of partaking of the Eucharist once a year at Easter. To what extent does it make sense to speak of medieval Catholicism as "more imagistic"? At the very least, there is nothing to rival the rites of terror in Papua New Guinea. I am less concerned here with the problem of how to categorize Catholicism (it is clearly doctrinal) than with carefully delineating patterns of interaction of the two modes.

It seems to me that all three of the religious systems we have discussed are best classified as doctrinal: pre-Reformation Catholicism and post-Reformation Catholicism and Protestant Christianities are widespread and long lasting. And this is as true of the folk religions as it is of the elite formulations. But they do not relate to the imagistic mode in the same way (with the exception of post-Reformation Catholicism and Protestantism, which probably are similar in this respect). What are these patterns of interaction between the two modes? I am asking for something along the lines, structurally, of what one finds in McCauley and Lawson's latest book: models of dynamic interactions of variables that produce different effects (for McCauley and Lawson the logically possible kinds of ritual systems and their dynamics).

The model found in Papua New Guinea is that members of the highly doctrinal Pomio Kivung had memories of precontact imagistic practices that they could fall back on to alleviate tedium. That's one plausible model of interaction, but it's not the European one in the sixteenth century. It is clear that because of the tedium effect, the doctrinal mode must "tank up," either slowly and steadily or sporadically, with imagistic techniques that foster emotion and motivation. Formation and reabsorption of splinter groups is one pattern. A second is splinter groups that are not reabsorbed but create an apparently hostile religious system that reinspires commitment to the original one among the people that remain (this would be the case in Münster, on the one hand, and with the reaction of Trent and the founding of the Jesuits to counteract Protestantism as a whole, on the other). A third model is revivalism, which sometimes is seen as a threat to the established group (pattern 2), but sometimes is welcomed and encouraged by the mainstream (here America provides great examples, such as Jonathan Edwards and the Great Awakening or the tent revivals of Methodism). A fourth model would be the one of pietism, which, while sometimes falling under suspicion, was profoundly part of the mainstream religious experience in Germany in the eighteenth and nineteenth centuries. A fifth model would be one of equilibrium (medieval Catholicism seems to be a good example of this)—a system that does not spin off splinter groups or fluctuate back and forth but manages to draw on enough imagistic techniques to keep people engaged. And here there are surely submodels (again, drawing just from Catholicism, the authorization of new religious orders is one type, the pageantry of Mass another).

Is it useful to create so many models? Yes, it is, for two reasons: first, it prevents the Dadul prototype from forcing us into misreadings of other patterns, as I think Whitehouse comes close to doing when he discusses the sixteenth century.

Second, I suspect (but much more data is required) that these patterns are real and could be shown to follow predictable trajectories. If that turns out to be the case, then Whitehouse's theory will be tremendously useful to historians of Christianity because, if enough information exists to classify a religious system correctly, then empirically verifiable trajectories for each model of interaction could help fill in the inevitable gaps of information left by history.

References

Abray, Lorna Jane. 1985. *The People's Reformation: Magistrates, Clergy, and Commons in Strasbourg, 1500–1598.* Ithaca, N.Y.: Cornell University Press.

Gellner, Ernest. 1983. *Nations and Nationalism.* Ithaca, N.Y.: Cornell University Press.

Karant-Nunn, Susan C. 1997. *The Reformation of Ritual: An Interpretation of Early Modern Germany.* London: Routledge.

Matheson, Peter. 2000. *The Imaginative World of the Reformation.* Edinburgh: T and T Clark.

Muir, Edward. 1997. *Ritual in Early Modern Europe.* Cambridge: Cambridge University Press.

Rubin, Miri. 1991. *Corpus Christi: The Eucharist in Late Medieval Culture.* Cambridge: Cambridge University Press.

Scribner, Robert W. 1990. "The Impact of the Reformation on Daily Life." In *Mensch und Object im Mittelalter und in der frühen Neuzeit,* edited by G. Jaritz, 315–42. Wein: Verlag der Österreichischen Akademie der Wissenschaften.

———. 1993. "The Reformation of the Common People." In *Die Reformation in Deutschland und Europa: Interpretationen und Debatten,* edited by H. R. Guggisberg, G. G. Krodel, H. Füglister. Gütersloh: Gütersloh Verlagshaus.

Strauss, Gerald. 1975. "Success and Failure in the German Reformation." *Past and Present* 67: 30–63.

Weber, Max. 1958. *The Protestant Ethic and the Spirit of Capitalism,* translated by Talcott Parsons. New York: Charles Scribner's Sons.

Whitehouse, Harvey. 2000. *Arguments and Icons: Divergent Modes of Religiosity.* Oxford: Oxford University Press.

———. 2002. "Modes of Religiosity: Towards a Cognitive Explanation of the Sociopolitical Dynamics of Religion." *Method and Theory in the Study of Religion* 14–3/4: 293–315.

Zika, Charles Zika, 1988. "Hosts, Processions and Pilgrimages: Controlling the Sacred in Fifteenth-Century Germany." *Past and Present* 118: 25–64.

Modes of Religiosity and Types of Conversion 10
in Medieval Europe and Modern Africa

ULRICH BERNER

R ELIGIOUS STUDIES HAS NEGLECTED the concept of "religiosity," a term that, in some respects, may be preferable even to the basic notion of "religion," the problems of which having been discussed extensively since the 1960s (cf. Berner 2003). The talk about modes of religiosity theory introduced by Harvey Whitehouse (2000: 9–12) sounds particularly interesting and promising, although we might discuss whether these modes should be ascribed primarily not to religious movements or other kinds of social institutions but to individual human beings. The notion of religiosity, it might be argued, normally refers to individuals, to human beings who are considered to be religious. Taking this usage as the starting point, "religiosity" could also be defined in a totally different way—for instance, fundamentalism and scepticism could be described as different modes of religiosity (cf. Berner 2002: 55).

This chapter focuses on the distinction between Whitehouse's doctrinal and the imagistic modes of religiosity as well as on the related and underlying distinction between the semantic and the episodic memory. The central question is whether Whitehouse's modes theory provides useful conceptual tools for the historian of religions. This chapter does not discuss whether the theory claims to be, or is, one of religion, but it does argue that the set of concepts provided by this theory has a great heuristic value for historical research in religious studies. Providing new conceptual tools for the study of religion certainly contributes to the construction of a basis for theorizing about religion.

However, deviating from Whitehouse's theory, which is restricted to social morphology, this chapter applies the distinction between the two modes of religiosity on two levels that might be called macro- and microanalysis, respectively: to religious movements or institutions, on the one hand, but also to religious individuals, on the other. Limiting the scope of application to systems or traditions would incur the danger of reifying abstract concepts—speaking about religions as if they had intentions and acted like human beings.

This shift in the theoretical approach implies also a slight modification of the basic definitions. A doctrinal mode is understood as being based on arguments, emphasizing rational explanation and justification of beliefs about God or the gods; an imagistic mode is understood as being based on experiences, emphasizing irrational means of communication with God or the gods, as, for instance, visions and dreams, the normative implications derive not from their argumentative, but from their iconic, power. These modes relate to the semantic or to the episodic memory respectively, in basic consonance with Whitehouse's modes theory. Language, however, plays an elementary role in both these modes, although to different degrees, since truth can be regarded as codified in texts, traditions, or both, or as embodied in persons, groups, or both. Accordingly, interpretation of and obedience to the accepted truth differ, emphasizing either verbal exegesis and repetitive ritual or dramatic exegesis and climactic ritual.

On the level of microanalysis it should be possible to distinguish between and identify different inclinations or dispositions in religious individuals—whether they lean more toward the doctrinal or more toward the imagistic mode of religiosity and, thus, depend more on the semantic or the episodic memory in their religious lives. This chapter maintains that such a difference in the religious inclination or disposition, which Whitehouse's modes theory does not suggest, explains the different degrees of attraction that the different modes have for individual human beings: not every adherent of a doctrinal mode group will be ready—at least not to the same extent—to join an imagistic mode group if and when such a group arises as a new religious movement. An example from ancient Greece can be found in Euripides's "Bacchae." The poet describes different reactions to the new religious movement brought by the adherents of the ecstatic cult of Dionysus: Teiresias, the seer, adjusts immediately to the demands of the new cult and does not mind behaving irrationally, whereas Pentheus, the king, sticks to his one-sided rational religiosity and tries desperately to suppress the new ecstatic cult.

There may also be, perhaps rare, cases of a balance between the two modes within one religious individual. An example from medieval Europe might be Raimundus Lullus, who was leading a secular life when he suddenly experienced visions and apparitions that changed his life totally. His conversion to a religious life, however, resulted in the conviction that it was his task to develop a totally rational demonstration of the Christian doctrine in order to convert the nonbelievers.[1] Another example from the European religious history might be Girolamo Savonarola, preacher and theologian in fifteenth-century Florence: on the one hand he was a powerful visionary and prophet, moving and changing political conditions; on the other hand he was a well-educated philosopher and theologian, reflecting rationally about the justification of his religious experiences.[2]

On the level of macroanalysis, looking at religious movements and institutions, it is perhaps more difficult to find the different modes in isolation—as they have been observed and described in Whitehouse's *Inside the Cult: Religious Innovation and Transmission in Papua New Guinea* (1995: 194–99). History will, in most cases, as the modes theory itself has already suggested, show a balance more or less successfully working between the two modes. In medieval Christianity, for instance, the Catholic Church offered and propagated different kinds of rituals: on the one hand, for instance, mass as a highly routinized kind of worship, on the other hand, for instance, pilgrimage as an infrequent and exceptional event in the religious life of the individual. Repetitive worship, and a highly routinized form of religious life as practiced in a medieval monastery could also be a framework for the emergence and development of ecstatic experiences. The most famous example, probably, is Hildegard of Bingen, mystic and/or prophetess in a monastery of the twelfth century. Comparable examples are Elisabeth of Schönau and Gertrude of Helfta, as presented in Anne Clark's chapter.[3] As Clark has rightly stated, it is not self-evident that routinized and repetitive worship is boring and cannot lead to emotional experiences, although it has to be admitted that these examples are exceptional.

There may also be, perhaps rare, cases of a balance between the two modes within one ritual system. Greek tragedy of the fifth century might be a case in point. On the one hand it was highly routinized and repetitive, since it was fully integrated into the religious calendar of the local community; on the other hand it implied elements of creativity leading to unpredictable results. There was an ongoing competition between the poets, and poets also had great freedom, each time, to give a new version of the old myths, thus counteracting against the "tedium effect" as the inherent problem of the doctrinal mode. The strong competition between the poets is mirrored by Aristophanes' Greek comedy, "The Frogs."

Historical research, therefore, will be primarily interested in investigating the complex relationship and interplay between the two modes of religiosity, as it is also emphasized by Anne Clark and John Peel.[4] Defining and isolating these different modes on a conceptual level, however, remains a necessary precondition for such investigations. A good starting point might be the theme of conversion, for it seems reasonable to assume a connection between modes of religiosity and types of conversion. Leaving the religious tradition in which one has grown up and joining a different tradition or leaving a well-established religious group with highly routinized rituals in order to join a new religious movement—these different types of conversion could be explained partly by assuming that the tradition or movement that is chosen has a greater appeal because its mode of religiosity is experienced either as perfectly developed or as totally different.

Concerning the second case, plenty of examples could be drawn from early-twentieth-century Africa, where the mission churches saw many members leave and join the Aladura churches (in West Africa) or the Zionist churches (in South Africa). The mission churches, of course, had laid great emphasis on correct doctrine and had offered rituals routinized according to European standards, thereby creating the "tedium effect" for a part of their membership (cf. Ayegboyin and Ishola 1997: 31). In West Africa as well as in South Africa in the twentieth century, many African prophets founded new religious movements, in the beginning centered on charismatic leadership, which was often based on visionary experiences, certainly belonging to the imagistic mode of religiosity (cf. Chidester 2000: 412–33). Baptism for adults played an important role in these movements, offering an opportunity for spiritual experiences to be kept by the episodic memory, as had been the case in the early church before infant baptism was introduced.[5]

Those new religious movements, however, in the long run developed their own hierarchies, routinized rituals, and means of establishing their doctrine—it seems impossible for a movement to survive without integrating the other, doctrinal mode of religiosity. Doctrinal, it should be added, is not to be identified with "conceptual." For doctrines can also be couched in narrative form—it would be sufficient for interpreting images and icons to have stories that transmit doctrine in narratives. The Mithraic mysteries, perhaps, were of such a kind of balance, leaning more toward the imagistic mode of religiosity, but not being totally without doctrines since there was probably a set of narratives in the background. It is, however, not known to which degree of consistency Mithraic theology was developed or whether it was centralized at all. In any case, Mithraic ritual, as Roger Beck has argued (chapter 6), comprises aspects of both modes of religiosity.[6]

The significance of the narrative element in religion has often been underestimated and neglected. It had been emphasized by one proponent of the analytical philosophy of religion (Braithwaite 1978; cf. Berner 1997: 161–62). Tom Sjöblom has rightly drawn attention to the significance of narratives in religion.[7] This observation, however, does not make it necessary to construct a third mode of religiosity, linked to the autobiographical memory. The autobiographical memory could either be identified with the episodic memory, or it could be constructed as drawing on both basic kinds of memory. In any case, it is also possible to take the narrative element as a means of mediating between the two basic modes proposed by Whitehouse—transmitting doctrine by appealing to the episodic memory.

Plenty of examples could be drawn from medieval Christian literature, beginning with Alkuin in the ninth century—hagiographical narratives side by side with purely doctrinal texts. Petrus Alfonsi, a convert from Judaism to Christianity, was a medieval author of the twelfth century productive in different fields of literature. He is compared later in this chapter with Hermann of Scheda, another Jewish convert of the twelfth century. The chapter then presents two religious movements from modern West Africa, focusing on Joseph Babalola, prophet of Christ Apostolic Church, Nigeria, and Joeseph Oschoffa, founder of Celestial Church of Christ, Nigeria.

At the beginning of the twelfth century, a Spanish Jew, named Moses, converted to Christianity and made his career in medieval Europe, travelling from Spain to France and later to England. He is known by his Christian name, Petrus Alfonsi. His pride in his Talmudic scholarship and his accurate description of Islamic doctrines and laws give the impression that he was well acquainted with the doctrinal mode of religiosity (Dialog, prooemium; titulus quintus). The question arises whether he converted to Christianity because he was longing for a different mode of religiosity. This, it seems, was not the case. On the contrary, his contention was that he found the doctrines of Christianity to be more rationally constructed and more consistent, including the dogma of Trinity—normally the greatest obstacle from a Jewish point of view.

Some of his former fellow Jews accused him of simply having followed his ambition to make a career in a Christian environment—this would have been a very "rational choice," indeed, although a nonreligious one. Whatever his final motivation was (cf. Cohen 1987: 27f), he is an interesting figure because he wrote a fictitious dialogue between a Jew and a Christian, named Moses and Petrus, obviously his old and his new identities (cf. Ricklin 1999: 147–49)—the preface to this dialogue includes a brief account of his conversion and baptism.

In this account his baptism is mentioned in order to explain his new Christian name, Petrus Alfonsi (the name Alfonsi refers to King Alfons, who participated in the ritual). So it might be expected that the experience of baptism would be important for him as an event to be kept by the episodic memory, indicating an acquaintance with the imagistic mode of religiosity. The first name Petrus, however, does not refer to a person participating in the ritual, such as, for example, the acting bishop, who is also mentioned by name; the name Petrus refers to one of the saints of the day of his baptism, Peter and Paul. So the event of his baptism is remembered mainly by reference to the ritual calendar of the year, and the choice of Peter as his first name could even indicate a preference for a specific theological program that is associated not with the apostle Paul, another of the saints of the day of his baptism, but primarily with Peter, the disciple of Jesus himself (cf. Ricklin 1999: 155).

The whole dialogue avoids emotional polemics and emphasizes rational arguments, trying to demonstrate the superiority of the Christian doctrine. This Jewish convert to Christianity seems to have been a very rational person, moving from one tradition to another, within the framework of the doctrinal mode—an example of a rather one-sided religious disposition.[8] The question arises whether Petrus Alfonsi ever experienced the "tedium effect," which is, according to the modes theory, an inherent problem of the doctrinal mode. An interesting point is that he seems to have been aware of this problem: he composed another book, the *Disciplina Clericalis*, in the prologue to which he addressed this problem explicitly.

In the prologue to the *Disciplina Clericalis*, Petrus Alfonsi reflects on the fragility of human nature, which is always in danger of growing bored with religious indoctrination.[9] That is, he says, why human beings need a cautious and special kind of treatment in this area, in order to keep in their memory what they have learned.[10] This is the reason, Petrus Alfonsi declares, he decided to collect and translate from the Arabic a lot of proverbs, short stories, fables, and similes, in order to make it easier for people to recall and remember what they always tend to forget. The materials contained in his book, he says openly, are taken from different cultural and religious backgrounds—Jewish, Pagan, and Islamic.

The examples of a "disciplined" life provided by Petrus Alfonsi, it might be argued, appeal primarily to the episodic memory, not to the semantic one, although they are encoded in language. In the beginning he declares formally his obedience to the doctrines of the Catholic Church. He indicates his conviction, however, that every human being leading a disciplined philosophical life will reach his or her destination, the kingdom of heaven. Doctrine apparently is not relevant on this level where he provides materials for the episodic memory of his audience, thus taking care of and moving toward the imagistic mode of religiosity. By the way, the *Disciplina Clericalis* proved useful as a collection of stories and, in this respect, had a considerable impact on European theology and literature (cf. Tolan 1993: 136–58).

A different case is Hermann of Scheda, a German Jew who converted to Christianity later in the twelfth century. His original Jewish name had been Juda. Many years after his conversion he wrote an autobiography giving an account of this decisive period in his life.[11] In contrast to Petrus Alfonsi, he does not talk so much about doctrines but describes in great detail his encounter with individual Christians, recalling and remembering past situations and episodes of his life. It was by pure chance—if not providence—that he had come into close contact with Christians: as a young man he had lent money to a Christian bishop, and he was sent by his family to the bishop's site in order to make sure that the money was refunded. This business affair took a rather long time, which gave him the opportunity to learn about the Christian religion. Step by step, he was drawn closer to Christianity, not however through the superior rationality of its doctrines, but mainly through the behavior of individual Christians who showed an unexpected kindness toward him. He remembers, for instance, that he was quite surprised and astonished when a servant of the bishop passed the best food to him—to a Jew who had expected that all Christians would regard him as an enemy (*Opusculum* 5). Such are the episodes he recalls in the account of his conversion. Experiences of human relationship and friendship like this episode, it seems, were far more important in the long process leading to his formal conversion than arguments exchanged in the discussions he had with learned Christian theologians.[12] The kind and nonoppressive attitude of his host, the Christian bishop, is explicitly designated an "exemplum" which ought to be followed by all Christians. On the whole, Hermann of Scheda says, examples are a better means of teaching than words (*Opusculum* 5).

The long process of his move toward conversion finally led to Hermann's baptism, which he describes in great detail and in a very specific way. He remembers, again, not the ritual as such, but his very personal and traumatic experience of the ritual:

> I stepped into the waves of the life-giving font. Immersed in it once, toward the east, I believed that that one immersion sufficed for the renewal of the ancient state. But the clerics standing around the baptistry shouted that I ought to be immersed more times. Having already just left the font, I could not hear their voices distinctly, nor, since water was running down the hairs of my head, could I see clearly the gestures that they were making to me (*Opusculum* 19, trans. Morrison 1992).

The knowledge of the Christian doctrine of baptism and of the correct ritual obviously is interwoven with his memory of personal experiences—an episode in his life ever to be remembered as such. Additionally, it might be said, the whole framework of his conversion narrative is leaning toward the imagistic mode of religiosity: he begins his account by recalling a dream that he had as a young boy, a vision he could not understand at that time but was later able to interpret as pointing to his future conversion. This inclination toward the imagistic mode of religiosity also comes to the surface when he recalls his prayers during a phase of terrible uncertainty about which religion he should adhere to: he remembers having asked God to reveal his will through inspiration, dreams, visions or, at best, through visible signs (*Opusculum* 6). Periods of intensive fasting and vigils, waiting for a divine inspiration or miracle, and the preparation for an ordeal as a means to bring about the break through[13] all point to a preference for the imagistic mode of religiosity.[14]

The set of concepts provided by the modes of religiosity theory has proved useful in interpreting these medieval sources: the application of these concepts helps in analyzing and describing different types of conversion. Both these cases of conversion show a close relationship and interplay between the two basic modes, but also different ways of relating them.

Petrus Alfonsi's religiosity seems to be dominated by the doctrinal mode, as the short and rational account he gives of his baptism indicates. His rationality even goes as far as discovering the inherent problem of this mode, the "tedium effect." Therefore, he embarks on a project meant to strengthen the complementary, imagistic mode by providing pieces of biographical narratives appealing to the episodic memory.

In contrast, Hermann of Scheda seems in his religious life to have depended on the episodic memory as the detailed and emotional account he gives of his baptism indicates, his religiosity on the whole being more open toward the imagistic mode. However, doctrinal religiosity also played a role in his life. This is obvious not so much in the summary he gives of his dialogue with Rupert of Deutz—this rational disputation was a failure[15]—but in that later he made his career in a monastery and was ordained a priest. Thus, it should be assumed that he identified with a religious institution of a highly routinized structure. However, the special spirituality of the religious order he joined should be taken into consideration: it was the Premonstratensian order, which had been founded recently in the twelfth century. So one could say he joined a new religious movement that had been institutionalised just a short time ago. Before his conversion, Hermann, with his mentor bishop, had visited a Premonstratensian monastery, and he later writes that he had been deeply impressed by the communal spirituality he encountered there, although, at that time, he had not yet been able to discern the full significance of this new form of communality (*Opusculum* 6).

Neither case can be said to have had sociopolitical effects in a strict sense. Neither Petrus Alfonsi nor Hermann of Scheda started a religious movement or obtained a position from which he could move sociopolitical conditions, as, for instance, Girolamo Savonarola was able to do, at least for a short period of time. The next two cases, taken from the modern African context, are different in this respect: conversion experiences in both these cases had a sociomorphological impact. Thus, they are more in line with Whitehouse's research interest and closer to the research on which the modes theory was based.[16]

The history of Christ Apostolic Church in Nigeria can be traced back finally to the Diamond Society, which was originally a prayer group founded within St. Saviour's Anglican Church at Ijebu-Ode in 1918. It was initiated by the visionary experience of one member of this parish, who had a series of dreams in which he saw two groups of church members, one of them in the light, the other in total darkness, representing the praying and the nonpraying Christians. When in 1918 an influenza epidemic broke out, causing the closure of the Anglican church at Ijebu, the prayer group emphasized the idea of divine healing, that is, healing through prayer alone. This shift of emphasis was reinforced by Sophia Odunlami, who joined the group after having had visionary experiences herself, pointing directly to reliance on God and healing through prayer (cf. Omoyajowo 1998: 56–57). After the epidemic was over, this group remained a movement within the Anglican Church for some time, separating from it again because of doctrinal incompatibility—because of its "sole reliance on prayers for healing and excessive reliance on dreams and visions for guidance" (Omoyajowo 1998: 62).

The Diamond Society then affiliated with the Faith Tabernacle Church of Philadelphia for some time, separating from it because of doctrinal incompatibility again—because of its "quest for more spiritual power and deeper spiritual experiences" (Omoyajowo 1998: 81). One of the leading figures in the further development of the Faith Tabernacle Church in Nigeria was Joseph Babalola, who is known as an Aladura prophet.[17]

Babalola had been brought up an Anglican. In 1928 he experienced his prophetic call: he heard a strange voice and after a period of fasting had a vision in which he encountered "the voice"; he obtained also some items as visible symbols of his prophetic ministry (cf. Omoyajowo 1998: 88–91). When he began to preach in a village, prophesying a catastrophic event for the near future, and when this prophesy could be regarded as fulfilled in some sense, he was able to found his first prayer group. According to reliable sources, he was baptised into the Nigerian Faith Tabernacle Church in 1929, thereby converting from a mission church to an Aladura church.[18]

Already a member of this Aladura church, Babalola was responsible for the Oke-Oye Revival in 1930, started by a demonstration of his power of divine healing. The movement resulting from this revival was named "The African Apostolic Church" because of its resemblance to the life and doctrine of the early apostles. It met with some hostility and even persecution from the side of the mission churches and the colonial authorities (cf. Omoyajowo 1998: 104–13). After undergoing another affiliation and separation, this religious movement, at least the main part of it, finally developed into the "Christ Apostolic Church, Nigeria," registered in 1943. The church's first president was Isaac B. Akinyele, an influential Yoruba politician who was responsible for the doctrinal side, authoring a series of theological treatises (cf. Omoyajowo 1998: 69–74, 188–209), while Babalola represented the prophetic element in the church until his death in 1959.

In the further development of the Christ Apostolic Church, efforts were made to prevent the prophetic charisma from leaving the institution. In the 1970s several charismatic movements emerged within this church, founded by individual church members who had had visionary experiences; these movements were organized as interdenominational "ministries" within the church (cf. Omoyajowo 1998: 132–33). In spite of these organizational efforts, the church suffered a serious crisis later when the blind prophet Obadare, founder and leader of one of these ministries, became too powerful and was accused of causing a split in the church (cf. Omoyajowo 1998: 145–76).

The Celestial Church of Christ was founded by Joseph Oschoffa in Porto Novo, Dahomey (Benin), in 1947. Oschoffa was of Yoruba origin and moved back to Nigeria in 1977. His life story is recorded in the church constitution of 1980. He was brought up as a member of the Methodist Church. For a short period of time he was even living in a Methodist mission house. However, Oschoffa used to give the impression that he was an illiterate having been chosen by God.

His life story, called "Foundation History," as recorded in the church's constitution, contains an account of his traumatic visionary experience, which resulted in a complete change of his life: "On the 23rd of May 1947, the day of the eclipse of the sun, as I was praying in the forest on this trip, I heard a voice and could not open my eyes" (Celestial Church of Christ [Nigeria Diocese] Constitution 1980: 5). He saw a white monkey with winged hands and feet, a bird like a peacock, and a short snake. When he heard this voice, he remembers, "I felt quite different from my normal self. . . . I then noticed that there was a complete change in me" (Constitution 1980: 5; cf. Adogame 1999: 24). After a period of seclusion in the forest, he started his prophetic activities by demonstrating his power of divine healing (Constitution 1980: 7). Later on the same year he experienced another vision, seeing a strong ray of light and a winged being flying toward him, revealing to him his mission of preaching and exhortation, concerning those Christians who "seek after fetish priests and other powers of darkness for all kinds of assistance" (Constitution 1980: 7).

The rumour of his healing miracles, including the report about a deceased person brought back to life, attracted lots of people from different religious backgrounds to his residence at Porto Novo, which caused problems for him in the beginning. The name of the emerging movement, "Celestial Church of Christ," was derived from another vision experienced by one of his adherents. The word "church," according to Adogame, was probably a later addition (1999: 25). The original French name had been "Le Christianisme Celeste."

The movement was brought to Nigeria by a small group of fishermen settling at Makoko near Lagos for business reasons, not because of missionary motivations. When some local people, mostly of Yoruba origin, had been attracted, Oschoffa, after some hesitation, started to pay visits to this Nigerian group. The rumor of new healing miracles spread and attracted more people, resulting in a new social composition of the membership of the Makoko group. Two of the early converts were to become of special importance for the development of this new Aladura church: Alexander Bada, a member of the African Church, who converted in 1951–1952, succeeded the founder in 1985, when Oschoffa died; Samuel Ajanlekoko, a Catholic, became the Diocesan head of the Celestial Church in Nigeria. He was drawn to Oschoffa's movement by his wife, who found a solution to her existential problems there. The personal encounter with Oschoffa in 1951 brought about a total change in his life, including his conversion from the Catholic Church to this new Aladura church; it was an episode in his life he was able to recall in an interview more than forty years after the event (cf. Adogame 1999: 30f).

For some time the Celestial Church remained a small local group at Lagos, spreading slowly. It witnessed a phenomenal growth later on, after Oschoffa had moved to Nigeria in 1977. Under the leadership of A. Bada, the Celestial Church developed even further, operating worldwide (cf. Adogame 2000b). Since the beginning of this development, the Celestial Church has met serious opposition and hostility from the mission churches and has been regarded as syncretistic for its emphasis on visible symbols, material objects, such as candles and "green water," and excessive rituals, apparently based on traditional Yoruba culture (cf. Adogame 2000a).

In the organization of the Celestial Church, efforts were made to keep the prophetic spirit in the institution: a double line was constructed in the hierarchy— a prophetic line as a counterbalance to the administrational line of elders or leaders, respectively (cf. Adogame 1999: 94–98). On top of the hierarchy, both the prophetic and the administrative lines converged in the absolute charismatic power of the founder, Oschoffa. In spite of this carefully organized balance, the church suffered a serious crisis after the founder's death, when his chosen candidate, Bada, took over and met some opposition (cf. Adogame 1999: 72–73).

At first sight, both these Aladura churches seem to represent the doctrinal mode of religiosity, at least regarding the final stage of institutional development. This applies particularly to the Celestial Church of Christ as a worldwide operating institution. The efforts of this church to be registered as a member of the World Council of Churches in Geneva also point in this direction (cf. Adogame 2000b: 37–38). However, the Celestial Church of Christ is known for its emotionally stimulating rituals and its excessive use of material items and visible symbols. The constitution of this church, it should be added, does not contain a system, but only a very elementary set of doctrines and norms, such as renunciation of idolatry and abstinence from alcohol, its emphasis apparently being on the detailed accounting of revelatory episodes from the church's foundation history, which resulted in its hierarchy, the structure of which is detailed toward the end of the constitution. The miracles and revelations narrated therein place the emphasis on nonroutinizable and nonpredictable events.

Therefore, it seems reasonable to look for further elements of the imagistic mode that might have played a role in the history of these churches. The modes theory has already suggested that great religious traditions comprise both modes of religiosity. The interplay and balance of these modes, it could reasonably be argued, contributed to the successful development of movements like these two Aladura churches. This explanation also applies well to the success of Neo-Pentecostal movements in modern Africa, as John Peel has already suggested.[19]

Regarding the history of the Christ Apostolic Church, one might assume that the initial prayer group, focusing on divine healing and seceding from the Anglican Church mainly for this reason, was dominated by the imagistic mode. This may also apply to Babalola's first prayer group and to the early Makoko group of the Celestial Church at Lagos. Another case in point certainly is the Oke-Oye Revival started by the prophet Babalola. As Peel has already suggested, the very term *revival* indicates the presence of the imagistic mode.

Once these movements have developed into hierarchically organized churches, it seems clear they will emphasize the correctness of doctrine to maintain their identity. In both cases, however, it must be remembered that efforts have been made to avoid an imbalanced, one-sided mode of religiosity that overemphasizes doctrine either by providing a prophetic line in the hierarchy, as in the case of the Celestial Church of Christ, or by organizing interdenominational ministries within the church, as in the case of Christ Apostolic Church.

An element of the imagistic mode might be seen, first of all, in the initial visionary experience of the prophet or founder of such a movement: a spiritual experience, dominated by icons, not by arguments, resulting in a total change of life ever to be remembered in the episodic memory.[20] Encoded in an autobiographical account, these experiences have become the model for a set of conversion narratives, which constitutes a great part of the doctrinal body. Doctrine in a strict sense is of secondary importance for a great part of the membership. The converts who join the movement or church after experiencing a crisis and a solution through divine healing will, in their later religious life, depend primarily on their episodic memory, in which the event of healing and conversion, as well as the dramatic ritual of baptism as the concluding phase, is stored forever.

One could assume the imagistic mode of religiosity dominates this type of conversion from a mission church to an Aladura church, at least when viewed from the convert's point of view. What the ritual expert may experience as routine, the client who undergoes the ritual experiences as an exceptional event. Thus, another possibility for observing the interaction of the two modes seems to emerge, corresponding to the different perspectives of the persons involved in the complex situation of religious interaction. This would apply also to another example from

Yoruba culture presented by John Peel: the Ifa oracle could be regarded as doctrinal on the one side and as imagistic on the other side of the interaction.[21]

Regarding the Aladura churches, several approaches are obviously needed to explain the emergence, rise, and decline of such movements. For instance, the themes of "colonialism and anticolonialism," "charisma and routinization," and "cultural identity and syncretism" have to be considered in this context. The distinction between different modes of religiosity, if applied additionally, adds another dimension to the theoretical explanation. Further investigations into the social morphology of these movements, applying Whitehouse's theory in a strict sense, might also yield rewards.

Notes

1. See Raimundus Lullus's autobiography, *Vita Coaetanea*, 1–7.

2. See Savonarola's treatise, "De veritate prophetica," written shortly before his execution.

3. See Anne Clark's contribution to this volume (chapter 8).

4. See Clark's contribution to this volume (chapter 8) and Peel's contribution to volume 2 of this series (2004).

5. See, for instance, Cyprian's account of his conversion to Christianity (*Ad Donatum* 4ff). Concerning baptism in the South African Zionist churches, see Inus Daneel (1984) and Allan Anderson (2000: 156–59).

6. See Roger Beck's contribution to this volume (chapter 6). A more radical interpretation in terms of the imagistic mode has been given by Luther H. Martin (2004).

7. See Sjöblom, forthcoming, *Historical Reflections/Réflexions Historique*.

8. A similar case of rational conversion is described in *Exemplar Humanae Vitae*, the autobiography of Uriel da Costa, a Portuguese Jew of the seventeenth century who had been brought up a Catholic, converted to Judaism when he found inconsistencies in Christianity, and later left Judaism after again finding inconsistencies.

9. "Fragilem eciam hominis esse consideraui complexionem: que ne tedium incurrat, quasi prouehendo paucis et paucis instruenda est."

10. A similar argument is given by Odo, bishop of Cambrai, in the twelfth century, at the beginning of his "Disputatio contra Judaeum": he decided to use the form of dialogue, based on a real encounter with a Jew, assuming this would make it easier for the reader or listener to keep the respective doctrines—concerning the coming of Christ—in memory (Migne 1996: vol. 160, 1103).

11. The authenticity of this autobiography has been denied by Avrom Saltman (1988: 31), who argues that it is a work of fiction. This critical interpretation has been opposed by Aviad Kleinberg (1992: 346), who is sure it can be proved that the text is "not necessarily a fabrication"; he sees even "strong arguments for its authenticity."

12. Rupert of Deutz, a theologian well known for his interest in dialogue with the Jews, is mentioned in Hermann's autobiography (*Opusculum* 3–4; cf. Roos 2002: 38–40).

13. He was prevented from realizing the ordeal because the bishop stepped in (*Opusculum* 5).

14. Saltmann (1988: 45) has rightly stated that the "general message" of the *Opusculum* is "anti-intellectual."

15. Reinhold Seeberg (1891: 15) has rightly stressed already: "Die Unterredung mit Rupert dürfte Juda eher zurück als vorwärts gebracht haben."

16. The following account is not based on the author's own fieldwork but on the work of two of his former Ph.D. students, Akin Omoyajowo Jr. and Afe Adogame, respectively.

17. Compare with David Olayiwola (1995) and Ulrich Berner (2000: 274–75). Another Aladura prophet, who might be of interest in this context because of his scriptural visions, is Josiah Oshitelu (cf. Probst 1989: 482–88).

18. Compare with Justus Akinwale Omoyajowo (1998: 91–99). According to Deji Ayegboyin and S. Ademola Ishola (1997: 73), Babalola was excommunicated from the Anglican Church "for his operation of the gift of prophecy, insistence on prayer to heal and profuse use of water."

19. See Peel's contribution to volume 2 of this series (2004). Asonzeh Ukah will give empirical evidence in his thesis on the Redeemed Christian Church of God (Diss. Phil., Bayreuth 2003).

20. A comparable case from South Africa would be the spiritual experience of Josiah Shembe, founder of the Ama Nazareth Baptist Church. For his autobiographical account, see Robert Papini (1999).

21. See Peel (2004).

References

Adogame, Afeosemime. 1999. *Church of Christ: The Politics of Cultural Identity in a West African Prophetic Charismatic Movement*. Frankfurt am Main: Peter Lang.

———. 2000a. "Doing Things with Water: Water as a Symbol of Life and Power in the Celestial Church of Christ." *Studies in World Christianity* 6: 59–77.

———. 2000b. "Mission from Africa—The Case of the Celestial Church of Christ in Europe." *Zeitschrift für Missionsund Religionswissenschaft* 84: 29–44.

Anderson, Allan. 2000. *Zion and Pentecost: The Spirituality and Experience of Pentecostal and Zionist/Apostolic Churches in South Africa*. Pretoria: University of South Africa Press.

Ayegboyin, Deji, and S. Ademola Ishola. 1997. *African Indigenous Churches: An Historical Perspective*. Lagos: Greater Heights Publications.

Berner, Ulrich. 1997. "Religionswissenschaft und Religionsphilosophie." *Zeitschrift für Religionswissenschaft* 5: 149–78.

———. 2000. "Reflections upon the Concept of 'New Religious Movement.'" *Method and Theory in the Study of Religion* 12: 267–76.

———. 2002. "War das frühe Christentum eine Religion?" *Zeitschrift für Neues Testament* 7: 54–60.

———. 2003. "Christentum (Historische Einleitung)." In *Handbuch Religionswissenschaft*, edited by J. Figl, 411–19. Innsbruck/Göttingen: Tyrolia/Vandenhoeck & Ruprecht.

———. 2004. "Moderner und antiker Religionsbegriff." In *Neues Testament und antike Kultur*, edited by Kurt Erlemann. Neukirchen: Neukirchener Verlag.

Braithwaite, R. 1978. "An Empiricist's View of the Nature of Religious Belief." In *The Philosophy of Religion*, edited by Basil Mitchell, 72–91. Oxford: Oxford University Press.

Chidester, David. 2000. *Christianity: A Global History*. San Francisco: HarperSanFrancisco.

Cohen, Jeremy. 1987. "The Mentality of the Medieval Jewish Apostate: Peter Alfonsi, Hermann of Cologne, and Pablo Christiani." In *Jewish Apostasy in the Modern World*, edited by Todd M. Endelman, 20–47. New York/London: Holmes and Meier.

Daneel, Inus. 1984. "Life around the Pool in African Independent Churches." In *New Faces of Africa: Essays in Honour of Ben Marais*, edited by W. Hofmeyr and W. S. Vorster, 36–79. Pretoria: University of South Africa.

Kleinberg, Aviad M. 1992. "Hermannus Judaeus's Opusculum: In Defence of its Authenticity." *Revue des Etudes Juives* 151: 337–53.

Martin, Luther H. 2004. "Performativity, Narrativity, and Cognition: Demythologizing the Roman Cult of Mithras." In *Rhetoric and Reality in Early Christianity*, edited by W. Braun, ch. 8. Waterloo: Wilfrid Laurier University Press.

Migne, J.-P. 1996. *Patrologia Latina, the Full Database*. Alexandria, Va.: Chadwyck-Healey.

Morrison, Karl F. 1992. *Conversion and Text: The Cases of Augustine of Hippo, Hermann-Judah, and Constantine Tsatsos*. Charlottesville: University Press of Virginia.

Olayiwola, David O. 1995. "Joseph Ayo Balalola (1904–1959)." In *Makers of the Church in Nigeria*, edited by Joseph Akinyele Omoyajowo, 138–49. Lagos: CSS Bookshops Limited.

Omoyajowo, Justus Akinwale. 1998. "The Emergence and Shaping of an African Independent Church: Christ Apostolic Church, Nigeria." Diss.Phil. Bayreuth.

Papini, Robert. 1999. "Carl Faye's Transcript of Isaiah Shembe's Testimony of his Early Life and Calling." *Journal of Religion in Africa* 29: 243–84.

Peel, J. D. Y. 2004. "Divergent Modes of Religiosity in West Africa." In *Ritual and Memory: Toward a Comparative Anthropology of Religion*, edited by Harvey Whitehouse and James Laidlaw. Walnut Creek, Calif.: AltaMira Press.

Probst, Peter. 1989. "The Letter and the Spirit: Literacy and Religious Authority in the History of the Aladura Movement in Western Nigeria." *Africa* 59: 478–95.

Ricklin, Thomas. 1999. "Der 'Dialogus' des Petrus Alfonsi. Eine Annäherung." In *Gespräche Lesen: Philosophische Dialoge im Mittelalter*, edited by Klaus Jacobi. Tübingen: Gunter Narr Verlag, 39–155.

Roos, Lena. 2002. *The Stranger Who Lives Next Door: Jewish-Christian Relations in Germany during the High Middle Ages*. Uppsala: Swedish Science Press.

Saltman, Avrom. 1988. "Hermann's Opusculum de Conversione Sua: Truth or Fiction?" *Revue des Etudes Juives* 147: 31–56.

Seeberg, Reinhold D. 1891. *Hermann von Scheda. Ein jüdischer Proselyt des zwölften Jahrhunderts*. Leipzig: Akademische Buchhandlung.

Sjöblom, Tom. Forthcoming. "Storytelling—Narratives of the mind and Modes of Religiosity." In *History, Memory, and Cognition*. Special issue of *Historical Reflections/Réflexions Historiques*.

Tolan, John. 1993. *Petrus Alfonsi and His Medieval Readers.* Gainesville: University Press of Florida.

Whitehouse, Harvey. 1995. *Inside the Cult: Religious Innovation and Transmission in Papua New Guinea.* Oxford: Oxford University Press.

———. 2000. *Arguments and Icons: Divergent Modes of Religiosity.* Oxford: Oxford University Press.

Medieval Sources

Hermannus quondam Judaeus opusculum de conversione sua, herausgegeben von Gerlinde Niemeyer. 1963. Monumenta Germaniae Historica. Die Deutschen Geschichtsquellen des Mittelalters 500–1500. Quellen zur Geistesgeschichte des Mittelalters. IV.Band. Weimar: Hermann Böhlaus Nachfolger.

"Der Dialog des Petrus Alfonsi. Seine Überlieferung im Druck und in den Handschriften." 1982. Text edition, Diss.Phil. Berlin, vorgelegt von Klaus-Peter Mieth.

Die Disciplina Clericalis des Petrus Alfonsi (das älteste Novellenbuch des Mittelalters), nach allen bekannten Handschriften, herausgegeben von Alfons Hilka und Werner Söderhjelm (Kleine Ausgabe). 1911. Sammlung mittellateinischer Texte, herausgegeben von Alfons Hilka I. Heidelberg: Carl Winter's Universitätsbuchhandlung.

Lullus, Raimundus. 1971–1973. *Opuscula,* edited by E.-W. Platzech. 3 vols. Hildesheim: Dr. Gerstenberg.

———. 1980. *Vita Coaetanea.* In *Opera Latina.* Vol. VIII, CCCM, 34: 259–309, edited by F. Stegmüller. Turnhout, Belgium: Brepols.

Corrupt Doctrine and Doctrinal Revival: On the Nature and Limits of the Modes Theory   11

ILKKA PYYSIÄINEN

THIS CHAPTER EXPLORES THE DYNAMICS of doctrinal revival, using as a case example the emergence of the Laestadian revivalist movement within the Lutheran churches in Finland, Norway, and Sweden. I try to show to what extent the modes theory helps explain this phenomenon and also how the case of Laestadianism helps modify some elements of the modes theory. A central theoretical issue is the relationship of the modes theory with the theory of the cognitive optimum as put forward by Pascal Boyer. I start, therefore, by presenting the two theories; then follows an analysis of the nature of the Laestadian revival. I conclude with a few remarks about the modes theory, based on the case of Laestadianism.

Natural Domains, Nonnatural Constructs, and Religion

People have many kinds of ideas and beliefs that influence their behavior. There are various ways of grouping them into both overlapping and nonoverlapping categories. Some such categories result from the fact that cognition is domain-specific in the sense that any given constraint applies to some, but not all, actions and properties of the mind. By constraint I mean any theoretical statement tied to an empirical phenomenon and narrowing the number of possibilities for how the mind may function. Constraints may relate to cognitive processing, its neuronal implementation, or to the general learning conditions underlying different learning objectives. Domain specificity and domain generality are thus the endpoints on the applicability continuum. Domains are always relative to constraints; it is the range of applicability of a constraint that defines a domain (Frensch and Buchner 1999).

One instance of domain specificity is the intuitive ontological division of objects of cognition into the categories of solid objects, nonliving natural things, living kinds, and personal agents (Boyer 1994b, 2001; Barrett 2000). Knowing, for example, that something has the attribute of "being hungry" enables us to know that this something may also have the attribute of "being sad," but not that of "needing some hammering." As it has been shown that even very small children can correctly make such inferences and that they thus implicitly understand the domain-specific nature of ontological knowledge (Keil 1996), there is speculation that at least some of these domains of knowledge are genetically encoded in our brains: we are born with, for example, a readiness to reason about living kinds in a certain prespecified manner (Atran 1990, 1998, 2002; Cosmides and Tooby 1994; Sperber 1994; see Hirschfeld and Gelman 1994).

This knowledge is implicit in two senses: (1) it is not necessary that we be consciously aware of the domain-specific nature of our cognition, and (2) implicit knowledge of the domain-specific nature of cognition comes naturally, as a by-product of learning and maturation, requiring no deliberate teaching and education in this respect. From this it follows that we need to make a distinction between natural and nonnatural cognition: while natural cognition is spontaneous, implicit, and culture independent, nonnatural cognition is something that must be learned through an arduous process of education. It is therefore explicit and depends on cultural institutions (Boyer 1994b; McCauley 2000). The prime example of nonnatural cognition is science (see Wolpert 1994), but there are other such domains as well. Donald Wiebe (1991), for example, has argued persuasively that theology is in this sense comparable to science: it consists of theoretical reflection on the natural content of folk religion, requiring complicated processes of learning supported by cultural institutions (See Pyysiäinen 2000a; 2001: 197–236; 2002).

Calling religion (in contrast to theology) natural seems to raise a problem, however. Is religion not something supernatural, after all? It has often been presupposed that supernatural ideas cannot be produced by natural minds; religion is a dramatic alternative for ordinary cognition and, therefore, needs a dramatic explanation. Such an explanation frequently has been sought in some kind of "religious experience" (Boyer 2001: 307–11). The newly emerged discipline of cognitive science of religion proceeds from the contrary assumption that religious thought and action are produced by quite ordinary cognitive mechanisms; it is only certain outcomes of this processing that seem to contradict our natural intuitions. They are exemplified by such ideas as, for example, ghosts, ancestors, gods, mana, karma, kami, and so forth. They all involve some such element that makes it impossible to place them in any natural ontological domain. Boyer (1994b: 91–124; 2001: 51–91) therefore calls them counterintuitive or counterontological.

A counterintuitive mental representation has the default properties of the intuitive domain, plus one violation of intuition. *Violation* means that a representation either lacks a feature that we intuitively expect it to have or it has an additional feature we intuit that it should not have. In this sense, religious representations are constructed by violating the boundaries between ontological categories; they are nonnatural combinations of natural building blocks. Although the conceptual outcomes of transferring and deleting attributes across ontological boundaries are counterintuitive, they are natural in the sense that they are the products of natural cognitive processes. The human mind is, by its very nature, not only capable of dividing up the world into separate domains, but also of reshuffling knowledge derived from these domains. Religion thus comes about naturally, while both science and theology require specific education (Boyer 1994b: 91–124; 2001: 51–167; Mithen 1996; Barrett 2000; McCauley 2000; Pyysiäinen 2001: 9–23; 2003).

Boyer predicts that, at least in oral cultures, optimally counterintuitive representations become selected for cultural transmission. They have staying power because of their cognitive form. But in actual practice, we do not adopt, represent, and transmit isolated individual ideas. Ideas tend to form clusters in which certain ideas are linked together, thus excluding certain other ideas (see Barabási 2002). A Christian, for example, is more likely to have Christian ideas than Buddhist ones. Although both traditions contain optimally counterintuitive ideas, these ideas are not equally likely to appeal to a Christian and a Buddhist, respectively. The cognitive optimum only works ceteris paribus; in real life, it is not the only thing contributing to the staying power of beliefs (as also noted by Nuckolls 2001). This seems to follow from the fact that the concepts we have in mind are not isolated from each other, but rather form networks in which concepts are nodes linked by associations; mental contents thus are always more or less organized (although concepts are rather constructs than unitary entities). We therefore can infer attributes of concepts from other attributes (Saariluoma 1997: 62–70; 2002; Lindeman, Pyysiäinen, and Saariluoma 2002; Goldblum 2001: 35–53).

Another important thing is that we are not only dealing with separate individuals and free-floating ideas invading their minds one by one. Individuals can join together to pursue common interests. In an "I mode" an actor acts qua a private person, whereas in a "we mode" he or she acts qua a group member, to use the expressions coined by Raimo Tuomela. We do not have to trade cognitive processes for the metaphysical hypostatization called "culture" in order to appreciate the irreducible difference between these two modes. Quite briefly, acting in the we mode in a structured group means acting or attempting to act intentionally with the purpose of following and advancing (or, at least, of not contradicting) the norms, values, goals, and so forth, of the group. Although these are represented in individual minds only, they nevertheless are different representations than representations of individual goals and the like. A we mode necessitates that members of the group represent something about the group in their minds, believe that others also represent the same thing, and believe that others believe them to be representing the same thing (Tuomela 1995, 2003). Michael Suk-Young Chwe (2001) has recently suggested that such mutual knowledge is established in social rituals. This entails that people construct organizations and institutions to advance the beliefs and practices they as a group find worth advancing.

Boyer, however, suggests that counterintuitive representations constitute the category of "religious ideas" and that concepts merely confirming intuitive ontologies are ipso facto nonreligious, although counterintuitiveness as such is not a sufficient criterion for religion (Boyer 1994a: 408; 1994b: 122, 124). It is difficult to differentiate between religious and other kinds of counterintuitiveness, though. Counterintuitive representations are also found in fiction and mental disturbance, for example. Even scientific concepts and theories are in some sense counterintuitive. Some might also want to differentiate between magic, folklore, and religion, all of which involve counterintuitive representations (see Pyysiäinen 2000a; 2001: 9–22; 2002). Distinguishing between religion and folklore has also been an important element in the modes theory: the modes canalize "natural" religiosity into something more difficult to represent (see chapter 13).

Whitehouse's (1995, 2000, 2001a, 2001b, 2002a, 2002b) theory of the two modes thus could be understood as an attempt to identify and explain some stable and recurrent patterns in the multiplex world of the counterintuitive. However, for Whitehouse counterintuitiveness is neither a sufficient nor a necessary feature of religion. Religion does not come naturally to humans because, as a concept, it is defined by modal transmission of ideas; religious ideas are ideas that can only be transmitted "modally" (see Whitehouse 2001a: 208 and chapter 13). Thus, the modes theory is essentially a theory of religion, not of cultural transmission of ideas in general. The modes define religion, and religion defines the modes. Yet, defining religion and explaining durability in cultural transmission can also be treated as separate issues. As I see it, confounding them only creates unnecessary problems for the modes theory.

I would like to disentangle the problems of defining religion from Whitehouse's theory and to view it as a theory that explains why particular ideas (whether counterintuitive or not) and particular practices in particular contexts are selected for transmission. Boyer's theory explains the role of optimal counterintuitiveness in cultural transmission; it cannot help us explain why people have some particular religious ideas and not others. Here the modes theory can complement it in suggesting that there are two differing ways of ensuring a more or less faithful transmission of ideas and practices. One is based on the supposition that emotional coloring enhances recall, the other on the fact that repetition can serve the same function. If you want people to remember what you are saying, either stir their emotions or repeat your message at proper intervals. Making a choice between these alternatives then also has predictable social consequences. There is no need to argue that this only happens in religion.

Whitehouse might object to this by saying that in actual fact imagistic and doctrinal effects are only found in what is commonly regarded as religion. But, if this is presented as an empirical observation, then religion must be defined in some other way than with reference to modal effects as a defining characteristic. If the modes are defined as modes of religiosity, religion cannot be defined with reference to the two modes, because this leads to a tautological argument and makes the theory immune to criticism. If, on the other hand, the objection is not meant as an empirical observation but as a conceptual, analytical statement, then it cannot be a counterargument for the empirical observation that there is religiosity outside the scope of the two modes.

There also seems to be no need to postulate that the modes theory only concerns ideas and beliefs that are more difficult to acquire, represent, and transmit than cognitively optimal ideas. I think this claim soon leads to trouble because there is empirical evidence to support the claim that in doctrinal contexts theological ideas always get simplified when transmitted orally in everyday contexts (Barrett and Keil 1996; Barrett 1998, 1999, 2002). Scott Atran (2002: 155–59) even argues that there is no evidence that doctrinal mode religion tends toward some logically integrated and coherent ideology employing implicational logic; if the doctrines really were logically integrated, then repetition would be unnecessary to ensure coherence. In imagistic contexts, ideas and beliefs are simple for very much the same reason; they just are not distortions of a theology (see Rubin 1997; Pyysiäinen 2000b).

In what follows, I wish to provide one example of the inner dynamics of the doctrinal mode and to discuss the limits of the modes theory. I use the so-called Laestadian revivalist movement within the Lutheran churches of Sweden, Finland, and Norway as a case study, trying to show how a weakened doctrinal mode produces a doctrinal revival.

Laestadius and Laestadianism

The Laestadian movement received its name from its founder, Lars Levi Laestadius (1800–1861), who was a minister of the Swedish Lutheran Church. Laestadius was born in Jäckvik, in South Swedish Lappmark (Piteå Lappland) in January 1800. His father was a Swedish settler, and his mother belonged to the Southern Sami (Lapp) people who were converted to Christianity as late as the beginning of the nineteenth century (Miettinen 1943: 101–13, 166; Rydving 1993). His home language was Swedish, but he also spoke Southern Sami. Later, as he moved to Pajala in 1849, he also learned Finnish. Finnish subsequently became the *lingua sacra* of Laestadianism, as Laestadius's sermons, published in four postillas (1876, 1894, 1897, 1924), were in Finnish (*Hernösands Stifts Historia och Herdaminne* III 1879: 155–56; *Kansallinen elämäkerrasto* III 1930: 328–30; Pentikäinen 1998: 110, 113).

In 1825 Laestadius was ordained as a minister in the Lutheran Church in Härnösand. At first he was appointed as the minister of the nomadic Sami in Piteå Lappland. For about a year he traveled around with them, until in 1826 he was appointed as the vicar of Karesuando, the northernmost parish in Sweden, where three-fourths of the population was Sami. In 1827 Laestadius married Brita Kajsa Alstadius, who had Sami ancestors in several generations (*Hernösands Stifts Historia och Herdaminne* III 1879: 155; *Kansallinen elämäkerrasto* III 1930: 328–29; Pentikäinen 1998: 108–11).

At first Lestadius did not take his ministry with the same seriousness as he did later on. Then, in 1832, he fell severely ill; after a year he also lost his three-year-old son who had been very dear to him. In 1842 he again fell ill and was afraid of dying. Fear of death made him think about the sins of his youth; he now thought that he had lead a godless life, although he had been admired by many as a truly religious man. This mental turmoil is reflected in Laestadius's nineteen-page pastoral thesis *Crapula mundi*, which he defended in 1843. A year later, he met a young Sami woman, Milla Clements' daughter, who has come to be known as Mary (Maria) of Lappland and who "opened her whole heart" to Laestadius in a conversation and thus brought him to a "conversion" (Laestadius 1909: 23; *Kansallinen elämäkerrasto* III 1930: 329; Pentikäinen 1998: 108–11, 117; Larsson 1999: 10–25, 47–61).

Laestadius started to preach with new vigor against sinful life, drinking, and worldliness, calling things by what he took to be their right names. His style was folksy and he certainly knew how to use irony. In 1845 the first so-called signs of grace appeared. Laestadius describes how he, in the early spring, saw that some of his Sami listeners were touched by his sermons and showed signs of "waking up" (*heräys*). They lamented that their hearts had been cold and that their minds now were restless. On December 5, a certain Sami woman suddenly felt the amazing grace so vividly that she started to jump high up in the air. According to Laestadius, this was accompanied by nothing more or less than an earthquake that lasted for a few seconds. In due course many others obtained similar experiences, which were subsequently referred to as "being moved" (Finnish *liikutukset*, Swedish *rörelser*, Sami *libkahusat*) (Laestadius 1909: 40–42; *Kansallinen elämäkerrasto* III 1930: 329–30; Miettinen 1942: 47–53; Pentikäinen 1998: 109). A few descriptions of the revelations seen by his parishioners in a *liikutus* have been published in Finnish by Laestadius (1850–1851; 1909: 56–62).

In 1849 Laestadius was appointed the vicar of Pajala, a Finnish-speaking parish south of Karesuando. There he met criticism because of the radical nature of the religiosity of his followers; especially the *liikutukset* were something outsiders could not accept as becoming behavior. Then, on November 8, 1852, after the Norwegian border had been closed from the traveling reindeer herders, an uprising took place in Koutokeino (Guovdageaidnu, Norway). A frenzied mob of about thirty-five to forty "enthusiasts" (*hurmahenget*) attacked the settlers in the village, stabbed a Norwegian merchant and also the sheriff, and burned the local store to the ground. They also gathered many of the villagers into a house that they intended to set on fire, but other people came to help in the last minute, and those in the house were saved. A small baby, however, was killed in the fight between the two groups. Forty-six people were sued; five of them were sentenced to death, but only two were finally executed. Lars Hætta and Anders Bær, who were sentenced for life, wrote their memoirs in prison. Also some eyewitnesses were interviewed at the end of the nineteenth century (Hætta and Bær 1993; Bjørklund 1992: 37; Pentikäinen 1995: 296–99).

Laestadius was accused of having caused the revolt by his preaching, but he most probably had never even been to Koutokeino (Pentikäinen 1995: 296). After this incident, the spread of Laestadianism among the Sami was somewhat blocked; instead, it started to attract Finnish peasants (*Hernösands Stifts Historia och Herdaminne* III 1879: 156; *Kansallinen elämäkerrasto* III 1930: 330–31; Miettinen 1942: 24–152; Raittila 1976: 15–160; Suolinna and Sinikara 1986: 15–19; Larsson 1999: 51–54, 106–8).

Laestadius died in 1861. After his death the movement quickly spread both to the north and to the south (and also overseas); at the turn of the century it was the dominant religious movement in the whole northernmost Fenno-Scandinavia (the so-called Nordkalotten). The quick and effective spread of the movement soon led to it being split into several branches (Raittila 1976: 31–160; Suolinna and Sinikara 1986: 19–24; Pentikäinen 1998: 103–8). The largest branch, The Conservative Laestadians, is still the largest religious revivalist movement in Finland (*Kansallinen elämäkerrasto* III 1930: 331; Miettinen 1942: 24–152; Raittila 1976: 15–160; Suolinna and Sinikara 1986: 15–24; Laestadius 1843; Bjørklund 1992: 37; Larsson 1999: 51–54, 106–8. See the websites of the Conservatives and the Neoawakenists, and also a general introduction to Laestadianism at www.srk-oulu.net; www.uusherays.fi/heinis/index.html; members.tripod.com/ makkeri, last accessed August 2002).

Scandinavian church historians have often described Laestadius as only a Lutheran minister and the founder of a Lutheran revivalist movement. Yet, I think that Juha Pentikäinen (2000: 44) cannot be totally wrong when he emphasizes that the Sami pre-Christian traditions had had a very deep impact on Laestadius (see also Gjessing 1953: 97). Laestadius knew well the folk customs and daily life of the Sami. He was also interested in the Sami religion, the beliefs of which he frequently employed in his sermons (Laestadius 1997; 2002; Gjessing 1953: 97; Outakoski 1991; Pentikäinen 2000: 44; see Marmier 1842–1845). Christian Mériot (1975) emphasizes most strongly the fact that the Christianization of the Sami had destroyed their traditional culture with nothing to offer in its stead and that Laestadianism thus was an attempt to construct a version of Christianity that would be compatible with the Sami traditions and way of life. It was essentially a movement of national liberation. Here Mériot may, however, underestimate the role of similar Protestant revivals in other parts of Scandinavia and the whole of Western Europe.

Henry Minde (1998: 16–17, 21), for example, is clear that Laestadianism was but one example of the revivals that took place from the Urals in the east to the American frontier in the west and that it must be seen against the backcloth created by the French Revolution. Laestadianism was not primarily a reflection of Sami religion and temperament but a manifestation of the northern European pietistic spiritual tradition and a reaction to the Enlightenment. The various ethnic and local characteristics of the revival were very soon suppressed as something non-Christian.

Laestadianism can indeed be seen on a continuum with the large-scale folk revivals that reached western Finland in the latter part of eighteenth century, when some of the clergy also became receptive to pietistic ideas. The beginnings of this awakening have been traced to the vision seen by a certain young maid, Lisa Eerontytär (or Eerikintytär), in 1756. In a couple of years the new revival was widespread throughout the whole province (Sulkunen 1999: 13–45; Heino 1976: 31–33). Spontaneous preparedness for trances, speaking in tongues, intimate experiences of God's presence, and the like spread from the west through all parts of Finland in the 1770s and subsequent decades (Siltala 1992: 27–28; see Siltala 1990). The spontaneous awakenings in due course lead to the emergence of revivalist movements organized around lay preachers and clergymen alike (see Pentikäinen 1975). Heikki Ylikangas (1979: 24) notes that it was the lay leaders who needed the authority of ecstatic experiences; ministers had the authority of their established socioreligious position. However, ecstatic experiences were rejected also by the lay leaders as soon as they had established their reputation and status.

Kirsti Suolinna (1969: 61–64, 71–73) takes the revivals to be a protest against the ideals of the Enlightenment. She observes that the revivals relate to the rapid growth of the population that preceded industrialization in Finland. Nineteenth-century Finland also was strongly touched by the national-romantic ideas that were popular throughout Europe (see Jutikkala and Pirinen 1984: 179–84). National romanticism was the ideology of urban elites; it led to a schism between center and periphery, the periphery protesting against modernization and its alien values. The Industrial Revolution led to a conflict of interests between landowners and industrial entrepreneurs, on the one hand, and between tenant farmers and workers, on the other hand. The protests of the revivalist movements were thus aimed at the urban nobility. In the mid-nineteenth century, only 1.4 percent of the population belonged to the estates; the gap between them and common people was deep. One manifestation of this divide was language: Swedish was the language of the elite, while common people spoke Finnish. Literacy, however, was widespread also among common people, unlike in many other feudal societies. This was due to the Lutheran ideal that everybody should be able to read the Bible; the church thus had organized a large-scale teaching of literacy skills. In Sweden, the revival lead by Erik Ståhlberg and Anders Larsson, in the beginning of the nineteenth century, was even called *Läseriet* ("Readerism"). In both countries the movements were swiftly organized, partly because of a need to spread religious literature effectively throughout the country. Also, lower clergy, who had difficulties in earning their living, played an active role in the revivals (see Siltala 1992: 27; Ylikangas 1979: 34, 40, 47, 53, 104, 199–209, 271–72). This probably contributed to revivals soon developing in a doctrinal direction.

In 1726 the *konventikkeliplakaati*, a statute that prohibited private devotions, had become effective, only to be repealed in 1869 when a new ecclesiastical law was enacted. The statute could not prevent the revivals; however, the *konventikkeliplakaati* well expressed the attitude of the church and the state of Sweden-Finland toward Pietism: it was not the ecstatic behavior as such that was under suspicion, but the possibility that it might lead to "separatism" (i.e., doctrinal innovation threatening the authority of the Lutheran Church and, thus, also the state) (Sulkunen 1999: 22–26). As Boyer (2001: 292–96) suggests, modernization is generally felt as a threat in religious coalitions because it brings along the possibility of other, competing commitments; thus modernization is condemned in order to raise the costs of defection. (According to Laestadius [1843: 9], "The greatest of vices lurk in the protection of urban civilization.")

Pietistic awakenings seem to have reached the Sami even before Laestadianism in the form of the *Čuorvut* movement ("Shouters/Callers"). It may have been a Sami offshoot of the earlier Wiklundian movement (as Miettinen opines). The heyday of the *Čuorvut* movement was experienced in 1760 to 1770. Its name derives from the practice of its nomadic preachers to urge people to repent by preaching in a shouting voice. Ecstatic preaching was also practiced. The shouters managed to bring about a change in the moral life in Koutokeino, but the influence was not long lasting. Not much is known about this movement, however; the only source seems to be the memoirs of Lars Hætta and Anders Bær (1993: 9–14; cf. Miettinen 1943: 308–11; Outakoski 1987; 1991: 16–18).

The Sami had been trading fish, fur, and game for alcohol and thus had incurred considerable debts. Many lost their whole property in drinking. Historians and chroniclers have provided vivid descriptions of the collective depravity of the Sami: fathers were drinking and gambling, starving infants were crying beside their passed out mothers, and so on (see, e.g., Laestadius 1909: 65–69; Hætta and Bær 1993: 15–18; Havas 1927: 3–5; Miettinen 1943: 114–58). Although these descriptions may exaggerate the depravity of the Sami in order to emphasize Laestadius's achievements, there is no doubt that alcohol was causing very real social problems. Importing alcoholic beverages to Lappland had been prohibited by law at the beginning of the nineteenth century, but the prohibition remained a dead letter. When Laestadius spoke about the evils of drinking, he not only accused the Sami for their bad habit, but especially the settlers who sold liquor to the Sami. He even claimed that his preaching activity was so strongly opposed because his demand on temperance ruined the liquor business of many traders in spirits (Laestadius 1909: 90–94, 328–61).

It thus seems that both Minde's and Mériot's claims merit serious consideration. Laestadianism is one example of the pietistic revivals of western Europe and a reaction to modernization. But, at the same time, it is also an expression of the peculiar sociocultural situation of the Sami. Laestadius's interest in the Sami religion itself may partly explain his views on some theological questions (see Laestadius 1909: 45–56, 62–63). For him, the Christian visions and revelations were real because they derived from the spiritual world that was within every human being. This might somehow reflect the Sami religion and its shamanistic elements with the spirit travels in other worlds, although this is somewhat speculative (see Gjessing 1953). It is clear, however, that Laestadius strongly opposed the philosophy of the Enlightenment and what he called "rationalist theology." I cannot help seeing in his arguments some parallelism with Stephen Toulmin's (1992) famous thesis that Enlightenment philosophy, especially Cartesianism, destroyed what Toulmin takes to be the Renaissance holistic view of humanity: humans were at once spiritual/rational and bodily beings, and the rational had no priority over the bodily.

In his huge posthumously published formal treatise Dårhushjonet ("The Madhouse Man"), which he wrote over a twelve-year period, Laestadius (1949–1964: #140–46, #185, #192) argued against the rationalist philosophers of the Enlightenment that the self that thinks is the same self that has sense experience; this is proved by our immediate feeling. There is no rational soul, apart from sense organs, nerves, and the brain; all thinking presupposed movement in the material brain. That thinking was carried out through the "organs of the soul" was proved by brain injuries that caused impairments in mental functions, as well as by intoxication; one only had to get drunk to realize that the blood could indeed affect thinking.

This was something "rationalist theologians" could not understand. They had adopted the rationalist philosophical doctrine of the soul as though it was based on the Word of God; they did not want to listen to what medical doctors had to say about the soul. Therefore, the secret forces of the heart, as they every now and then were evoked to work, were regarded as madness. For the rationalist theologians, God did not have a heart or a conscience, only will and reason; the Devil did not exist for them at all. They wanted to deny the existence of *sensationes internae* and had obscured the order of grace so that it was impossible for anyone to gain any understanding about the things that belong to true conversion and being born again. Gone was the idea of reward and punishment in another world; it was enough merely to show the outward signs of a decent life. Therefore, the rationalist theologians could not recognize justification as an actually felt effect of grace. For them, all living religion was "enthusiasm" (*svärmeri*, < German *Schwärmerei*) and an offence against the church (Laestadius 1909: 43–45, 50–52).

Laestadius felt deeply that the church and the political elite, infatuated with the ideals of modernization, were morally bankrupt and had nothing to offer to suffering people, let alone to the miserable, impoverished, and corrupt Lappland (e.g., Laestadius 1843: 1). He thought that people were living the end of times; manners had changed, and all of humankind had been corrupted in only two generations. People sought the highest happiness not in religion and faith but in gluttony, drinking, and gambling. They fought against each other in the streets, scolded and cursed each other, and "an immoderate craving for novel things" had replaced former moderation. The Sami and the Finns, like all other nations, were demoralized; they had forsaken true religion so that they only had the outward form of religion, with all content gone, while the heart was empty (Laestadius 1843: 1–4, 11–12; 1909: 143–45). Much in accordance with Minde's interpretation, Laestadius (1843: 12–13, 19) was quite explicit in writing that the French Revolution was characterized by "barbarism."

Emotional Experience and Doctrine

The Laestadian emphasis on "religion of the heart" can be understood as an alternative for the rationalist theology that no longer seemed to have the inferential potential that is required from beliefs that are to become widespread in a population of nonspecialists. Laestadius brought the Lutheran message back to people's everyday lives by putting emphasis on personal experience.

An especially salient feature of Laestadianism came to be the experience of "being moved" (*liikutus*). It was these spontaneous and uncontrolled expressions of emotion that non-Laestadians most opposed in this movement. The *liikutukset* could take place during the sermon, the singing of hymns, or, especially, the Eucharist.

Some Laestadians even went into a *liikutus* when they were prosecuted in the court for their unbecoming behavior. Yet, some also experienced a *liikutus* alone while reading the Bible. The *liikutukset* can be divided into those caused by the emotions of sorrow and of joy. Sorrow and grief were due to feelings of sinfulness that were so overwhelming that people were unable to talk, pray, cry, or even sigh; they felt as though they were suffocating and could only let out some unarticulated sounds of despair, feeling that they were going to die. As the preachers then powerfully proclaimed that all sins were forgiven in the name and blood of Jesus Christ, this resulted in such relief that it made people hop and jump and cry out loud (Miettinen 1943: 162–66).

The *liikutukset* were manifested most importantly in the form of sounds. They were preceded by heavy breathing and sighing, as in the case of Erkki Barsk who experienced a *liikutus* in court. As his emotions became stirred, his body is reported to have somehow shrunk. His pupils were dilated, "blood arouse in the head," and breath was taken away as he pressed his hands against his breast, waving his torso back and forth and uttering both low- and high-pitched sounds. In a *liikutus* people sobbed, moaned, wailed, wept, howled, or sighed, hollered, bellowed, and cried out of pain or joy. Also, laughing, hiccupping, and imitations of animal voices were known signs of *liikutus*, as were various bodily motions, such as clapping of hands, stomping of feet, and jumping and swinging around. Some even jumped on the table or bench, starting to dance or leap. Some shook, convulsed, and waved their hands; especially in the *liikutukset* of sorrow, people could even fall to the ground. *Liikutukset* could set on all of a sudden, without any preceding signs, and people's ability to control them varied both individually and according to the situation (Miettinen 1942: 166–70).

The *liikutukset* are the result of individual people personally realizing the relevance of the collective tradition. It is especially through rituals that tradition appeals to individuals. It is doubtful, however, that the spread of the Laestadian movement could, in the long run, have been built only on subjective experiences. It may be that the idea of *liikutukset* was more important for the movement than the actual experiences. The first stories of *liikutukset* created episodic memories that had attention-grabbing potential; these memories then became attractors around which a precipitate of religious ideas was centered.

For Laestadius himself, visions and revelations were not mere belief in ghosts or empty imagination. They were real because they derived from the spiritual world that was within every human being. Laestadius deliberately wanted to "sharpen the intellect and revive religious feeling" by his sermons. As the parishioners of Pajala put it, the purpose was to "move hearts" but not to "create liikutuksia" (Miettinen 1942: 161). This contradiction may be explained by two facts: first, it is important for the believers to make a distinction between divinely caused emotional effects and mere natural feelings, as Ann Taves (1999) has shown with regard to Methodism; second, the Laestadians had to defend themselves against the allegations that their religious life deviated from what was commonly accepted within the Lutheran Church. In other words, they have had to find the conceptual means to reconcile their imagistic-like practices with the doctrinal context from which they emerged. Even today, the attitude toward the Lutheran Church among the Laestadians is at once critical and respectful. The church is respected as a social institution, although in religious matters it is not considered a binding authority (see Suolinna 1969: 66; Kurvinen 1980; Talonen 1988: 48–51, 91–94). It is only the Laestadian movement (or a given branch of it) that is regarded as the true church of God.

Laestadius emphasized that one had to have clear insight into both the order of grace and the high emotions, although these two were actually rarely found together. This was why there was often tension between reason and revelation in religion. Yet, reason without revelation was blind, and strong faith with little knowledge could lead to enthusiasm (svärmeri). In the last analysis, it was the one who had clear insight who had to lead those with only high emotions and little reason. Although high and living emotions were an absolutely necessary part of a living faith, they did not have to be expressed as noisy liikutukset, which were not a necessary concomitant of grace. They were good and useful but did not form the necessary condition for salvation. Liikutukset alone were no good; one also had to read the Bible and understand the difference between the "old" and the "new" human being (i.e., the sinful and the saved) (Laestadius 1909: 45, 89, 90, 291–93; see Miettinen 1942: 190–96).

For the ordinary followers, the distinction between emotions caused by the Holy Spirit and the humanly caused outward manifestations of these emotions seems to have been too difficult to grasp. What was theologically correct was inapplicable in practical reasoning. Also, the outward expressions of divine emotions were regarded as unmediated manifestations of the Holy Spirit. They were even considered to prove that one was advanced in the holy life (Miettinen 1942: 200–5).

Many non-Laestadian vicars, ministers, and government officials, however, criticized the liikutukset as dangerous enthusiasm. Laestadius thought that this hostility was due to the rationalist reluctance to accept religious truth or to the fact that his demand on temperance had ruined the liquor business in Lappland. He tried to convince the church authorities that the movement initiated by his sermons was not a threat to the church. Yet, the liikutukset were believed to be an acute problem in many parishes, and various precautions had to be taken to prevent them. In Pajala, the bishop then gave the orders that, in an ordinary Sunday service, no one was allowed to express a liikutus; Laestadius was willing to arrange a separate vesper for the "awakened," where they were allowed to express their emotions freely, while others were not allowed to complain about that (Laestadius 1909: 90–94, 328–61; Miettinen 1942: 178–90). In Norway, at Ankenes Church in 1887, the Laestadians were even excluded from communion, and the services had to be conducted under police protection (Minde 1998: 18).

During the last years of Laestadius's activity, the practice of *liikutukset* waned at least in some parishes. In the Swedish parishes of Ylitornio and Karunki, the *liikutukset* seemed still to be a problem in 1858 and 1859, however; the misbehaving parishioners had to be dragged out of the church to cool down. As this increasingly caused trouble, the vicar of Karunki demanded that the troublemakers be drawn to court and fined. These attempts at control seem to have been successful, although the *liikutukset* soon waned also in such parishes where no actions against the awakened ones were taken (Miettinen 1942: 184–90).

Conclusion

The Laestadian protest was aimed at a form of religion that apparently belongs to the category of doctrinal religion but shows signs of degeneration. However, neither the nature of this degenerated religion nor the Laestadian protest against it can be properly understood without making the distinction between people's actual religiosity and theological doctrine. The theological elite had introduced doctrinal novelties in the spirit of rationalistic philosophy, or what is sometimes called "neology"; this, then, deepened the gap between theology and people's everyday religion.

Here Whitehouse's (e.g., 2002a, 2002b) notions of "spontaneous exegetical reflection" (SER) and the "principle of agreement" are a bit problematic in the sense that it is not clear which doctrinal innovations are to be considered unauthorized. I agree with Whitehouse that unauthorized doctrinal innovations are banned in doctrinal religions, but merely stating this overlooks the fact that there often are debates about innovations that yet are authorized in some sense (e.g., the debates on women's ministry in the Protestant churches). Folk religiosity cannot be changed by new official declarations; nor are the authorities themselves always in agreement about the innovations. Laestadius, for instance, was a minister of the Lutheran Church who did not accept the doctrinal novelties infiltrating the church via university theology. How do we explain such inner dynamics in the doctrinal mode?

The Laestadian protest was directed against a supposedly wrong kind of theology, on the one hand, and against the new ways of life of common folk, on the other hand. It might even be said that Laestadius thought that it was the doctrinal lapses that, at least in part, had caused serious problems in everyday life. But he also seems to have thought that the Sami way of life was good and right in itself, and that it was the settlers who had caused all the trouble (Minde 1998: 16). From the Laestadian point of view, the church had both introduced theological novelties and fostered wrong kinds of cultural innovations; from the point of view of the church, it was the Laestadians who had introduced unauthorized doctrinal and ritual innovations. As Whitehouse's theory is constructed to explain regularities in traditions, it is not particularly helpful in explaining these kinds of dynamics in religious life.

My own first hunch that Laestadianism might be understood as an imagistic religion did not work. Laestadianism is very clearly a doctrinal religion. The only imagistic-like feature in it is the presence of strongly emotional experiences. But, on this basis alone, it cannot be classified as imagistic, especially as emotions have so clearly been subsumed under doctrinal control. Therefore, if we want to use Whitehouse's theory, Laestadianism must be interpreted and explained within the inner dynamics of the doctrinal mode.

It seems that loosening of the principle of agreement ("liberal theology") generally tends to have the effect of bringing about revivalist movements that emphasize a more rigorous reading of the doctrine, as well as the necessity for a personally felt relationship with the doctrine. Laestadianism seems to be a good case along these lines. By inversion of the argument, it could also be predicted that a too-strict principle of agreement will tend to produce revivalist movements whose primary aim is to evoke personal, ecstatic experiences to ensure that the individual relevance of religion is not lost. We might analytically distinguish between two kinds of revivalist movements: those that direct their protest against the dry routine of theological traditions, and those that direct their protest primarily against a too-loose interpretation of doctrine within the theological tradition. To the former category belong elements of religious revivals aspiring toward heightened personal experience (i.e., various kinds of ecstatic phenomena). They are more imagistic in their orientation. To the latter category belong elements that primarily aim at restoring "the original doctrine." They are clearly doctrinal in their orientation. In practice, however, these features may combine in one and the same movement. It is also very difficult to measure the looseness or strictness of the principle of agreement or the intensity of personal commitment. Especially if we want to make predictions, there is the danger of slipping into mere "just-so" stories. But analytically, this distinction seems to capture an important difference, and, thus, the modes theory can be used as an analytical tool in explaining the nature of various kinds of revivalist movements. It is neither a typology of religion nor a realistic classificatory scheme.

One problem, however, is explaining how phenomena in one mode can emerge from the other mode if the modes are mutually exclusive (see chapter 12). Much of that discussion revolves around the concept of a "tedium effect" (i.e., people getting bored with their dry and routinized rituals). This expression was originally employed to describe the reactions of the aboriginals of the Pacific Islands after they were converted to Christianity. According to Aarne Koskinen (1953: 91–94), it was generally admitted that the influence of Christianity on them remained superficial; the natives "had none of the ambition of real Christians." They did not discard their old beliefs and practices, and the conversions often were "immense mass phenomena." Although Christianity at first was popular, "disappointment and tedium soon made their appearance." The natives felt that Christianity had promised more than it had been able to give; they did not gain the expected worldly advantages from "white man's magic" (see Whitehouse 2000: 44–45, 142–43). It surely is a long leap from this observation to the assumption that the tedium effect is a necessary and intrinsic element of doctrinal religion as such. Frequent repetition of an unemotional ritual may, for example, be boring but still considered relevant precisely because of the repetition (see Malley 2002; Pyysiäinen 2001: 229). There is, for example, empirical evidence for the so-called illusory truth effect: a mere repetition of a statement can lead to increases in the strength of one's belief that the statement is true (Begg, Anas, and Farinacci 1992; Schacter and Scarry 2000). Thus, tedium need not be a necessary consequence of all repeated rituals; there are actually many counterexamples to the claim that there is an inverse relation between emotional arousal and frequency of performance (see Atran 2002: 155–59, 290–92; McCauley and Lawson 2002: 179–212; Pyysiäinen 2001: 78–97; Boyer 2001: 260–62).

It can be argued that features that deviate from a ritual script formed by repetition are attention grabbing and, thus, a potential source of arousal. Repetition habituates us to take the repeated representations and behaviors as natural and self-evident. Possible episodic memories of instances that deviate from the script are then stored in memory along with the script (see Klein et al. 2002 for experimental evidence). Normally, this storing happens because episodic memories of specific instances enable us to reevaluate our conclusions, to evaluate the credal value of people's statements, and to specify the scope of summary judgments. Semantic and episodic memory need to cooperate to be able to recognize surprising and exceptional events and phenomena: semantic memory represents what is common across situations, while episodic memory represents the exceptions. Enduring episodic memories are formed when problems arise in the functioning of an intuitive and spontaneous inference system, and a systematic and reflective system thus gets activated (see Pyysiäinen 2004). This means that situations requiring more conscious control tend to give rise to stronger episodic memories (Lieberman et al. 2002: 228, 233–34; see Tulving 1995; Frith and Dolan 2000; Brown and Craik 2000; Zola and Squire 2000; Schacter et al. 2000).

In the case of religious doctrines, this is more complicated than in Stanley Klein et al.'s material concerning judgments about the self and others. People do not necessarily evaluate the credal value of religious claims in the same fashion. Yet, it is at least a good hypothesis that in religious judgments people draw information from both doctrinal summaries and from their episodic memories of specific events. Episodic instances help us to reevaluate our own religious conclusions, to evaluate the credal value of others' statements, and to specify the scope of doctrinal summaries. Ritual repetition creates scripts and routines; people carry on with the rituals even if they are boring if the cost of neglecting them is believed to be high enough (see Pyysiäinen 2001: 130–39; Boyer 2001: 229–63). Various episodic memories then help people to evaluate this question. The interplay of personal judgment and the collective tradition is expressed in the continuum of "theological correctness," on which natural intuitions occupy one end and "off-line" theological doctrines the other (Barrett and Keil 1996; Barrett 1998, 1999). No doctrinal mode can exist without such a continuum.

This seems to go well with the case of Laestadianism. Laestadius accused the theological elite of having obscured the order of grace and of neglecting important aspects of natural life. The theologized religion was not only considered wrong but also useless. Only by reviving the personal dimension could Laestadius bring individual people into awakening (*heräys*) (i.e., to a personal realization of the relevance of religion). Yet, people do not adhere to the doctrine as a coherent whole, but rather pick and choose what is relevant for them in their daily lives. Only a precious few even know the doctrine in all its detail. All attempts at educating people to believe in sophisticated theology, without the personal dimension of episodic memories, are doomed in the long run; they inevitably lead to various kinds of pragmatic reactions, such as the Laestadian revival.

Note

I want to thank Veikko Anttonen, Kimmo Ketola, Juha Pentikäinen, Juha Siltala, Tom Sjöblom, Don Wiebe, and, of course, Harvey Whitehouse for comments on earlier drafts of this chapter. The writing of this paper was supported by the Academy of Finland (project 200827 and Academy Research Fellow's post 00920).

References

Atran, Scott. 1990. *Cognitive Foundations of Natural History*. Cambridge: Cambridge University Press and Editions de la Maison des Sciences de l'Homme.

———. 1998. "Folk Biology and the Anthropology of Science: Cognitive Universals and Cultural Particulars." *Behavioral and Brain Sciences* 21: 547–609.

———. 2002. *In Gods We Trust: The Evolutionary Landscape of Religion*. New York: Oxford University Press.

Barabási, Albert-László. 2002. *Linked: The New Science of Networks*. Cambridge, Mass.: Perseus Publishing.

Barrett, Justin L. 1998. "Cognitive Constraints on Hindu Concepts of the Divine." *Journal for the Scientific Study of Religion* 37: 608–19.

————. 1999. "Theological Correctness: Cognitive Constraint and the Study of Religion." *Method and Theory in the Study of Religion* 11: 325–39.

————. 2000. "Exploring the Natural Foundations of Religion." *Trends in Cognitive Sciences* 4: 29–34.

————. 2002. "Dumb Gods, Petitionary Prayer and the Cognitive Science of Religion." In *Current Approaches in the Cognitive Science of Religion*, edited by Ilkka Pyysiäinen and Veikko Anttonen, 93–109. London: Continuum.

Barrett, Justin L., and Frank Keil. 1996. "Conceptualizing a Nonnatural Entity: Anthropomorphism in God Concepts." *Cognitive Psychology* 31: 219–47.

Barrett, Justin L., Rebekah A. Richert, and Amanda Driesenga. 2001. "God's Beliefs Versus Mother's: The Development of Nonhuman Agent Concepts." *Child Development* 72(1): 50–65.

Begg, Ian Maynard, Ann Anas, and Suzanne Farinacci. 1992. "Dissociation of Processes in Belief: Source Recollection, Statement Familiarity, and the Illusion of Truth." *Journal of Experimental Psychology: General* 121(4): 446–58.

Bjørklund, Ivar. 1992. "The Anatomy of a Millenarian Movement: Some Organizational Conditions for the Sami Revolt in Guovdageaidnu in 1852." *Acta Borealia* 2: 37–46.

Boyer, Pascal. 1994a. "Cognitive Constraints on Cultural Representations: Natural Ontologies and Religious Ideas." In *Mapping the Mind: Domain Specificity in Cognition and Culture*, edited by Lawrence A. Hirschfeld and Susan A. Gelman, 39–67. Cambridge: Cambridge University Press.

————. 1994b. *The Naturalness of Religious Ideas: A Cognitive Theory of Religion*. Berkeley: University of California Press.

————. 2001. *Religion Explained: The Evolutionary Origins of Religious Thought*. New York: Basic Books.

Brown, Scott C., and Fergus I. M. Craik. 2000. "Encoding and Retrieval of Information." In *The Oxford Handbook of Memory*, edited by Endel Tulving and Fergus I. M. Craik, 93–107. Oxford: Oxford University Press.

Chwe, Michael Suk-Young. 2001. *Rational Ritual: Culture, Coordination, and Common Knowledge*. Princeton, N.J.: Princeton University Press.

Cosmides, Leda, and John Tooby. 1994. "Origins of Domain Specificity: The Evolution of Functional Organization." In *Mapping the Mind: Domain Specificity in Cognition and Culture*, edited by Lawrence A. Hirschfeld and Susan A. Gelman, 85–116. Cambridge: Cambridge University Press.

Frensch, Peter A., and Axel Buchner. 1999. "Domain-Generality Versus Domain-Specificity in Cognition." In *The Nature of Cognition*, edited by Robert J. Sternberg, 137–72. Cambridge, Mass.: MIT Press.

Frith, Chris, and Raymond J. Dolan. 2000. "The Role of Memory in the Delusions Associated with Schizophrenia." In *Memory, Brain, and Belief*, edited by Daniel L. Schacter and Elaine Scarry, 115–35. Cambridge, Mass.: Harvard University Press.

Gjessing, Guttorm. 1953. "Sjamanistisk og laestadiansk ekstase." In *Liber saecularis in honorem J. Qvigstadii*, pars II, *Studia Septentrionalia* 5(II): 91–102. Oslo: H. Aschehoug and Co. (W. Nygaard).

Goldblum, Naomi. 2001. *The Brain-Shaped Mind: What the Brain Can Tell Us about the Mind.* Cambridge: Cambridge University Press.

Hætta, Lars, and Anders Bær. 1993 (1958). *Usko ja elämä,* translated by Pekka Sammallahti. Utsjoki: Girjegiisá.

Havas, Wäinö. 1927. *Laestadiolaisuuden historia pääpiirteissään.* Oulu: Suomen lähetysseuran laestadiolainen haaraosasto.

Heino, Harri. 1976. *Hyppyherätys—Länsi-Suomen rukoilevaisuuden synnyttäjä* (The Jumping Revival as the Origin of the Supplicationism of West-Finland). Helsinki: Suomen Kirkkohistoriallinen Seura.

Hernösands Stifts Historia och Herdaminne III. 1879. Hernösand: Hernösands-postens tryckeri-aktiebolag.

Hirschfeld, Lawrence A., and Susan A. Gelman. 1994. "Toward a Topography of Mind: An Introduction to Domain Specificity." In *Mapping the Mind: Domain Specificity in Cognition and Culture,* edited by Lawrence A. Hirschfeld and Susan A. Gelman, 3–35. Cambridge: Cambridge University Press.

Jutikkala, Eino, and Kauko Pirinen. 1984 (1962) *A History of Finland,* translated by Paul Sjöblom. 4th rev. ed. Helsinki: Weilin+Göös.

Kansallinen elämäkerrasto III. 1930. Porvoo: WSOY.

Keil, Frank C. 1989. *Concepts, Kinds, and Cognitive Development.* Cambridge, Mass.: MIT Press.

Klein, Stanley B., Leda Cosmides, John Tooby, and Sarah Chance. 2002. "Decisions and the Evolution of Memory: Multiple Systems, Multiple Functions." *Psychological Review* 109: 306–29.

Koskinen, Aarne A. 1953. *Missionary Influence as a Political Factor in the Pacific Islands* (*Suomalaisen tiedeakatemian toimituksia* B; 78, 1). Helsinki: Suomalainen tiedeakatemia.

Kurvinen, Jorma. 1980. *Raportti lestadiolaisuudesta.* Helsinki: Kirjapaja.

Laestadius, Lars Levi. 1843. *Crapula mundi seu morbus animi contagiosus, cujus causam sub libertatis specie occultam, in servitute morali, symptomata visibilia in turbulentis gentium motibus, nec non exitums tristem in morte spirituali, indagavit, omniumque ordinum vitae genus percurrendo adumbravit L. L. Laestadius.* Hernoesandiae.

———. 1850–1851. *Suomenkielisiä kirjoituksia* 1–6. A microfilm copy of the original (HYK microfilm B 4139), housed at the Helsinki University Library.

———. 1909 (1852–1854). *Tidskriften Ens ropandes röst i öknen, åren 1952–1954,* edited by J. F. Hellman. Uleåborg: Aktiebolaget "Oma kanta's" tryckeri.

———. 1949–1964. *Dårhushjonet. En blick i nådens ordning,* edited by Erik Bäcksbacka. (*Suomen Kirkkohistoriallisen Seuran Toimituksia;* L:1, 2, 3.) Helsinki: Suomen Kirkkohistoriallinen Seura.

———. 1925. *The New Postilla of Lars Laestadius,* translated by Arthur Niska et al. Hancock, Mich: Finnish Lutheran Book Concern.

———. 1964 (1876). *Postilla I–II.* Helsinki: Akateeminen kustannusliike. (Contains all previously published Finnish sermons from 1876.)

———. 1997. *Fragmenter i lappska mythologien,* edited by Reimund Kvideland. *NIF Publications* 37. Åbo: Nordic Institute of Folklore.

———. 2002. *Fragments of Lappish Mythology,* edited by Juha Pentikäinen, translated by Börje Vähämäki. Beaverton, Ontario: Aspasia Books.

Larsson, Bengt. 1999. *Lars Levi Laestadius—hans liv ock verk* and *den laestadianska väckelsen.*

Skellefteå: Artos.

Lieberman, Matthew D., Ruth Gaunt, Daniel T. Gilbert, and Yacoov Trope. 2002. "Reflexion and Reflection: A Social Cognitive Neuroscience Approach to Attributional Inference." *Advances in Experimental Social Psychology* 34: 199–249.

Lindeman, Marjaana, Ilkka Pyysiäinen, and Pertti Saariluoma. 2002. "Representing God." *Papers on Social Representations* 11: 1.1–13.

Malley, Brian. 2002. "*Arguments and Icons*: A Review." *Journal of Ritual Studies* 16(2): 5–7.

Marmier, Xavier. 1842–1845. *Relation du voyage*. Voyages de la commission scientifique du Nord, publiés sous la direction de M. Paul Gaimard, I–II. Paris: Arthus Bertrand.

McCauley, Robert N. 2000. "The Naturalness of Religion and the Unnaturalness of Science." In *Explanation and Cognition*, edited by Frank Keil and Robert Wilson, 61–85. Cambridge, Mass.: MIT Press.

McCauley, Robert N., and E. Thomas Lawson. 2002. *Bringing Ritual to Mind: Psychological Foundations of Cultural Forms*. Cambridge: Cambridge University Press.

Mériot, Christian. 1975. "Une reponse religieuse a une situation de depersonnalisation ethnique." *Cahiers de Centre d'Études et de Recherches Ethnologiques* 3: 31–73.

Miettinen, Martti E. 1942. *Lestadiolainen herätysliike* I. Mikkeli (privately printed).

———. 1943. *Pohjoisen Tornionlaakson Oloista Lestadiolaisen Herätysliikkeen Syntyaikoina*. Pohjois-Pohjanmaan Maakuntaliiton Julkaisuja I. Oulu (privately printed).

Minde, Henry. 1998. "Constructing Laestadianism: A Case for Sami Survival?" *Acta Borealia* 15(1): 5–25.

Mithen, Steven. 1996. *The Prehistory of the Mind: The Origins of Art, Religion, and Science*. London: Thames and Hudson.

Nuckolls, Charles W. 2001. "Steps to an Integration of Developmental Cognitivism and Depth Psychology." In *The Debated Mind: Evolutionary Psychology Versus Ethnography*, edited by Harvey Whitehouse, 181–201. Oxford: Berg.

Outakoski, Nilla. 1987. "Čuorvvot." In *Sami Religion*, edited by Tore Ahlbäck, 208–10. Sripta Instituti Donneriani 12. Åbo: The Donner Institute for Research in Religious and Cultural History.

———. 1991. *Lars Levi Laestadiuksen saarnojen maahiskuva verrattuna Kaaresuvannon nomadien maahiskäsityksiin* (Underground Spirits in the Sermons of Lars Levi Laestadius and Lappish Folklore). Acta Societatis Historicae Ouluensis. Scripta Historica 17. Oulu: Oulun Historiaseura.

Pentikäinen, Juha. 1975. "Revivalist Movements and Religious Contracultures in Finland." In *New Religions*, edited by Haralds Biezais, 92–122. Scripta Instituti Donneriani Aboensis 7. Åbo: The Donner Institute for Research in Religious and Cultural History.

———. 1995. *Saamelaiset—pohjoisen kansan mytologia*. Helsinki: Suomalaisen kirjallisuuden seura.

———. 1998. "Lars Levi Laestadius Revisited: A Lesser Known Side of the Story." In *Exploring Ostrobothnia*, edited by Börje Vähämäki, special issue of *Journal of Finnish Studies* 2(2): 103–35.

———. 2000. "Esipuhe" (preface). In *Lappalaisten mytologian katkelmia*, by Lars Levi Lestadius and Juha Pentikäinen, translated by Risto Pulkkinen, 1–16. Helsinki: Suomalaisen kirjallisuuden seura.

Pyysiäinen, Ilkka. 2000a. "No Limits? Defining the Field of Comparative Religion." In *Ethnography Is a Heavy Rite: Studies of Comparative Religion in Honor of Juha Pentikäinen*, edited by N. G. Holm et al., 31–40. Religionsvetenskapliga Skrifter 47. Åbo: Åbo Akademi.

———. 2000b. "Variation from a Cognitive Perspective." In *Thick Corpus, Organic Variation and Textuality in Oral Tradition*, edited by Lauri Honko, 181–95. Studia Fennica Folkloristica 7. Helsinki: Finnish Literature Society.

———. 2001. *How Religion Works: Towards a New Cognitive Science of Religion*. Cognition and Culture Book Series 1. Leiden: Brill.

———. 2002. "Religion and the Counter-Intuitive." In *Current Approaches in the Cognitive Science of Religion*, edited by Ilkka Pyysiäinen and Veikko Anttonen, 110–32. London: Continuum.

———. 2003. "True Fiction: Philosophy and Psychology of Religious Belief." *Philosophical Psychology* 16(1): 109–25.

———. 2004. "Intuitive and Explicit in Religious Thought." *Journal of Cognition and Culture* 4.

Raittila, Pekka. 1976. *Lestadiolaisuus 1860–luvulla*. Helsinki: Akateeminen kustannusliike.

Rubin, David C. 1997 (1995). *Memory in Oral Traditions*. New York: Oxford University Press.

Rydving, Håkan. 1993. *The End of Drum-Time: Religious Change among the Lule Sami, 1670s–1740s*. Acta Universitatis Upsaliensis, Historia Religionum 12. Uppsala.

Saariluoma, Pertti. 1997. *Foundational Analysis: Presuppositions in Experimental Psychology*. London: Routledge.

———. 2002. "Does Classification Explicate the Contents of Concepts?" In *Current Approaches in the Cognitive Science of Religion*, edited by Ilkka Pyysiäinen and Veikko Anttonen, 230–60. London: Continuum.

Samuels, Richard. 2000. "Massively Modular Minds: Evolutionary Psychology and Cognitive Architecture." In *Evolution and the Human Mind: Modularity, Language and Meta-Cognition*, edited by Peter Carruthers and Andrew Chamberlain, 13–46. Cambridge: Cambridge University Press.

Schacter, Daniel L., and Elaine Scarry. 2000. *Memory, Brain, and Belief*. Cambridge, Mass.: Harvard University Press.

Schacter, Daniel L., Anthony D. Wagner, and Randy L. Buckner. 2000. "Memory Systems." In *The Oxford Handbook of Memory*, edited by Endel Tulving and Fergus I. M. Craik, 627–43. Oxford: Oxford University Press.

Siltala, Juha. 1990. "On the Application of Fantasy Analysis in the Study of the Pietist Awakening Movement in Finland during the Early 19th Century." *Mentalities/Mentalités* 7(1): 9–14.

———. 1992. *Suomalainen ahdistus. Huoli sielun pelastuksesta*. Helsinki: Otava.

Sperber, Dan. 1994. "The Modularity of Thought and the Epidemiology of Representations." In *Mapping the Mind: Domain Specificity in Cognition and Culture*, edited by Lawrence A. Hirschfeld and Susan A. Gelman, 39–67. Cambridge: Cambridge University Press.

———. 1996. *Explaining Culture: A Naturalistic Approach*. Cambridge, Mass.: Blackwell.

Sulkunen, Irma. 1999. *Liisa Eerikintytär ja hurmosliikkeet 1700–1800–luvuilla*. Helsinki: Gaudeamus.

Suolinna, Kirsti. 1969. "Herätysliikkeet sosiaalisina liikkeinä." *Sosiologia* 6: 61–77.

Suolinna, Kirsti, and Kaisa Sinikara. 1986. *Juhonkylä. Tutkimus pohjoissuomalaisesta lestadio-laiskylästä.* Helsinki: Suomalaisen kirjallisuuden seura.

Talonen, Jouko. 1988. *Pohjois-Suomen lestadiolaisuuden poliittis-yhteiskunnallinen profiili 1905–1929* (The Sociopolitical Profile of the Laestadian Movement in Northern Finland between 1905–1929). *Suomen kirkkohistoriallisen seuran toimituksia* 144. Helsinki: Suomen Kirkkohistoriallinen Seura.

Taves, Ann. 1999. *Fits, Trances, and Visions: Experiencing Religion and Explaining Experience from Wesley to James.* Princeton, N.J.: Princeton University Press.

Toulmin, Stephen E. 1992 (1990). *Cosmopolis: The Hidden Agenda of Modernity.* Chicago: University of Chicago Press.

Tulving, Endel. 1995. "Organization of Memory: Quo Cadis?" In *The Cognitive Neurosciences,* edited by Michael S. Gazzaniga et al., 839–47. Cambridge, Mass.: MIT Press.

Tuomela, Raimo. 1995. *The Importance of Us: A Philosophical Study of Basic Social Notions.* Palo Alto, Calif.: Stanford University Press.

———. 2003. "The We-Mode and the I-Mode." In *Socializing Metaphysics: The Nature of Social Reality,* edited by F. Schmitt, 93–127. Lanham, Md.: Rowman & Littlefield.

Wiebe, Donald. 1991. *The Irony of Theology and the Nature of Religious Thought.* McGill-Queen's Studies in the History of Ideas 15. Montreal: McGill-Queen's University Press.

Whitehouse, Harvey. 1995. *Inside the Cult: Religious Innovation and Transmission in Papua New Guinea.* Oxford: Oxford University Press.

———. 2000. *Arguments and Icons: Divergent Modes of Religiosity.* Oxford: Oxford University Press.

———. 2001a. "Conclusion: Towards a Reconciliation." In *The Debated Mind: Evolutionary Psychology Versus Ethnography,* edited by Harvey Whitehouse, 203–23. Oxford: Berg.

———. 2001b. "Transmissive Frequency, Ritual, and Exegesis." *Journal of Cognition and Culture* 1(2): 167–81.

———. 2002a. "Conjectures, Refutations, and Verification: Towards a Testable Theory of 'Modes of Religiosity.'" *Journal of Ritual Studies* 16(2): 44–59.

———. 2002b. "Modes of Religiosity: Towards a Cognitive Explanation of the Sociopolitical Dynamics of Religion." *Method and Theory in the Study of Religion* 14(3–4): 293–315.

Wolpert, Lewis. 1994 (1992). *The Unnatural Nature of Science.* Cambridge, Mass.: Harvard University Press.

Ylikangas, Heikki. 1979. *Körttiläiset tuomiolla. Massaoikeudenkäynnit heränneitä vastaan.* Helsinki: Otava.

Zola, Stuart, and Larry R. Squire. 2000. "The Medial Temporal Lobe and the Hippocampus." In *The Oxford Handbook of Memory,* edited by Endel Tulving and Fergus I. M. Craik, 485–500. Oxford: Oxford University Press.

Websites

www.srk-oulu.net (website of the Conservative Laestadians)

www.uusherays.fi/heinis/index.html (website of the Neo-Awakenism)

members.tripod.com/makkeri (website that contains information about Laestadianism in Finnish, partly in English)

CRITICAL DISCUSSION V

Critical Reflections on the Modes of Religiosity Argument[1]

12

DONALD WIEBE

CCORDING TO HARVEY WHITEHOUSE (1995, 2000), ethnographic research
—his own as well as that of others—reveals the existence of two contrasting modes of religiosity and has given rise to a variety of dichotomous
models and theories of religion. He maintains, however, that none of the theories
proffered has persuasively accounted for the divergent ways of being
religious—which he labels "doctrinal" and "imagistic"—because none provides an
adequate causal explanation of these two modalities (2002: 294). For Whitehouse,
an adequate account of the existing modes of religiosity must explain both why the
diverging modes came about in the first place (2002: 294) and why they have different social consequences (2002: 308). His theory of the modes of religiosity, he
claims, fulfills both tasks: it improves upon its predecessors by disclosing the cognitive mechanisms (differential systems of memory) that underlie, and therefore explain, "the differences in the way religious activities are handled psychologically"
and, in turn, explain the sociopolitical features that relate to the differences of expression of religion "in social organization and politics at the level of groups and
populations" (2002: 308). A central idea of Whitehouse's theory is that substantial variations in the frequency with which religious practices are enacted results in
the activation of distinctive memory systems; these variables in turn have demon-
strable effects on the nature and organization of religious ideas and the scale and
structure of religious organizations. According to Whitehouse, that is, the specific
psychological and social (organizational) features of each mode of religiosity coalesce and mutually reinforce each other, forming what he calls "suite[s] of features
that are causally interconnected" (2002b: 302). Thus, the form of codification of
religious experience, thought, and practice provides a causal explanation for why diverging modes of religiosity arise in the first place and, in producing contrasting
sets of sociopolitical features, why they effect different political consequences.

In his most recent summary statement of the theory, Whitehouse describes the "causal interconnectedness" of doctrinal and imagistic religiosity in the following fashion. On the one hand, frequent repetition of a religious teaching or religious ritual (involving low levels of emotional arousal) activates the semantic memory for those teachings and rituals and produces a doctrinal form of knowledge, which in turn encourages the presence of religious leaders responsible for maintaining doctrinal orthodoxy. This kind of knowledge is not intimately tied to any particular experience of the individual members of the community and, consequently, encourages the growth of anonymous, hierarchically structured communities with centralized authority. Further, the presence of religious leaders is conducive to the rapid and widespread dissemination of religion. Frequent repetition of religious rituals with low levels of emotional arousal, moreover, leads to an implicit knowledge of those rituals and enhances the survival of the authoritative teachings stored in semantic memory. On the other hand, low-frequency transmission of religious knowledge associated with high levels of emotional arousal and frequently enacted rituals lead to the coalescence of a different set of "causally connected or mutually reinforcing" (2002b: 304) features that Whitehouse calls "imagistic" rather than "doctrinal." They do so because they activate episodic rather than semantic memory, which results in "lasting autobiographical memories" that tie belief to specific events and experiences (2002b: 304). This "activation of episodic memory triggers spontaneous exegetical reflection"—revelations—experienced by those undergoing the ritual action, making the beliefs held highly personal and, therefore, unlike the more collective beliefs of the doctrinal mode. Such reflection, moreover, inhibits the growth of leadership and the centralization of authority in the community concerned and restricts the formation of an orthodox body of belief. Rather, the high-arousal experience creates intense cohesion among those undergoing the ritual process and, so, fosters localized, exclusive communities that, lacking centralized authority and leadership, are not likely to spread quickly or widely.

Whitehouse's theory of the modes of religiosity will, with justification, find an appreciative audience among scientifically oriented students of religion. His work suggests how fruitful a theory can be that does not rest on the assumption of the sui generis character of cultural reality—a position held, unfortunately, by the majority of scholars in the religious studies community today (McCutcheon 1997). Whitehouse has also shown how important it is for social scientists to recognize that culture (including religion) is, at least in part, the product of psychological mechanisms that are themselves products of our evolutionary development; that is, his theory is worked out within the broader framework of the evolutionary development of the human mind and, therefore, holds out the possibility of providing a genuinely causal, rather than simply hermeneutical, account of religion. However, the theory of the modes of religiosity, in my judgment, is not wholly perspicuous, and if it is to be of more general use to the student of religion, it will need both clarification of some of its central aspects and further elaboration with respect to its relationship to the social sciences. The critical reflections set out here, it is hoped, will be of some assistance in setting out the ambiguities that need clarification and in delineating the elaborations necessary to make clear the theory's relevance for a general theory of religion.[2]

The Problem of Causality

A significant factor in grasping the import of Whitehouse's theory of the modes of religiosity, in my judgment, is the ambiguity that seems to characterize his notion of causality. Whitehouse claims that the key features of doctrinal and imagistic religiosity "stand in stark contrast with each other" (2002b: 308), and he claims that the clustering of these features is explained in terms of psychological causes. However, given that he uses the notion of "cause" interchangeably with the notion of "cognitive constraint" and the phrase "tendency to coalesce" and that he conflates the notions of structure and cause, it is not altogether clear what the import of his causal argument is.

As I understand it, Whitehouse's account of the modes of religiosity presumes the possibility of an evolutionary explanation for the psychological mechanisms that constitute semantic and episodic memory (which I consider unproblematic). He then proceeds on that basis to account for the divergent social structures among religious traditions (the modes of religiosity) by reference to how belief and ritual practice are mnemonically encoded and transmitted. Once activated, the particular set of cognitive mechanisms associated with each type of memory somehow "causes" or "gives rise to" a particular pattern of social existence. But it is not at all clear what he means by "cause." In *Arguments and Icons: Divergent Modes of Religiosity* (2000), he talks of the modes of religiosity as "general tendencies towards the coalescence of particular transmissive, cognitive, and political features" because each of the sets of features of the two modes is "mutually reinforcing" (2000: 2). And, in a more recent account, he describes semantic and episodic memory as "evolved properties of human mental architecture [that] *constrain and shape* religious representations and the forms of action and social morphology in which these are implicated" (2002: 293, emphasis added). Clearly, then, these mental architectural structures account for the modes of religiosity, but not in the sense of constituting efficient causes of them since, without some activation of the mnemonic mechanisms of semantic and episodic memory, they would produce nothing. Whitehouse's theory, therefore, does not explain why any particular mode of religiosity—doctrinal or imagistic—actually comes into existence, but rather sets out what might be called the conditions of the possibility of the existence of the modes: if the inculcation (transmission) of beliefs and if ritual enactment (with a minimum level of emotional arousal) occur frequently, then a doctrinal mode of religion is likely to emerge, but if there is spontaneous exegetical reflection in association with infrequently enacted rituals (with high levels of emotional arousal), an imagistic mode of religion is likely to arise (because of the difference in type of transmission of religious knowledge involved). Semantic and episodic memory might, therefore, be thought of as a kind of "structural causality" in that, given their activation, they constitute constraints on the type of religion likely to develop (because of a difference in mode of transmission of religious knowledge), but do not themselves directly "cause" or "give rise to," in the sense of "originate," anything. I concur with Whitehouse's implicit claim about the political character of doctrinal and imagistic religion in the formulation of his thesis in *Arguments and Icons*, where he points out that his fundamental concern is "whether universal features of human memory, activated in different ways, might be said to mould political organization and ideology" (2000: 5). Nevertheless, semantic and episodic memory are not efficient causes—that is, "things" that directly produce or give rise to something else—and accounting for the emergence of any particular religious group (whatever the mode of religiosity involved), it appears to me, will also require social-scientific analysis and explanation.

It seems to me that a further, related problem with the modes theory emerges with Whitehouse's admission that the "tendencies to coalescence" do not always result in coalescence of the features of these modes of religiosity. If it is true, that is, that the theory of the modes of religiosity does not really provide a basis for strict deductions about the cognitive and sociopolitical dynamics of religion of which Whitehouse speaks, then it is not immediately clear how they function or why they are necessarily divergent and, therefore, mutually exclusive, as Whitehouse maintains (1995: 193; 2000: 1). Nevertheless, theoretically speaking, it seems to me that in Whitehouse's theory any particular religious tradition ought to be either doctrinal or imagistic. The only possible theoretical alternative would be an "inconsistent" tradition in which the two modes were dialectically related to each other in a kind of "creative tension" that must ultimately, however, resolve itself in favor of a purely doctrinal or imagistic mode (see 2000: 124, 130). Thus, in his latest summary of the theory, for example, Whitehouse writes, "Religious traditions founded upon interacting modes of religiosity encompass large populations but, at the same time, they are composed of many locally distinctive ritual communities" (2002b: 309). Despite these comments, however, it is not self-evident why there cannot exist—given the fact that the theory does not provide a basis for strict deductions about the cognitive and sociopolitical dynamics of religions—social conditions that involve behavior that can activate both semantic and episodic memory and, therefore, produce traditions involving a blend of both types of religiosity—that is, behavior that creates larger doctrinal communities within which there are occasions of imagistic religiosity that involve high arousal without disruption to the structure of the broader doctrinal community (see chapter 11). Indeed, in *Arguments and Icons* Whitehouse seems to support precisely such a conclusion in maintaining that the modes of religiosity operate in a fashion that exhibits a complex interpenetration of their contrastive features (2000: 52).

The reason for my skepticism on this matter becomes even clearer, I think, if we look at one of the two basic scenarios in which Whitehouse claims both modes of religiosity are present in a single religious tradition. In the case where core religious teaching is successfully transmitted to the majority of a tradition's adherents, according to Whitehouse, the possibility exists that the imagistic domain of operation may project cohesion "onto (at least some aspects of) the mainstream doctrinal orthodoxy and the large anonymous populations over which it prevails" (2002b: 311). But this, it seems to me, cannot but involve the fusion of the two modes and, therefore, runs contrary to the theory. On the other hand, Whitehouse also claims that it is possible that the imagistic domain projects cohesion "only on the local communities it encompasses" (2002: 311). In that case, however, we seem to have the oddity of two self-sustaining, divergent, and fundamentally contrasting modes of religiosity that, even though in tension with each other, also happen to be mutually reinforcing, which again seems to conflict with the theory.

Further confusion is created by Whitehouse's claim that modes of religiosity can occur separately in a religious tradition (2002b: 294), for it seems to conflict with an earlier claim to the effect that "there is no such thing as a religious tradition that does not depend for its transmission on both semantic and episodic memory" (2000: 11). In fact, Whitehouse insists that the modes have occurred separately and individually in religious traditions, as in the case of the earliest form of religion among Palaeolithic hunter-gatherers (2000: 3) and that of pre-contact Melanesians (2000: 54, 160–61), which are wholly imagistic. Whitehouse nevertheless claims that when these modes of religiosity "interact with each other," they do so in a fashion that does not result "in a fusion of the two types" (2002b: 309), even though in *Arguments and Icons* he maintains that the two modes seem to become "so enmeshed that the analytical distinction" breaks down (2000: 149).

The Role of the Social Sciences

A second problem in understanding the full import of Whitehouse's theory of the modes of religiosity relates to his application of the theory to Melanesian cargo cults. His theory, if I understand it correctly, suggests that the mode of transmission of religious experience alone can account for the sociopolitical nature of any particular group or movement. On this ground Whitehouse insists that there is no need for social-scientific theorizing and, especially, no need for functionalist accounts of religious developments in Melanesia; that a cognitivist theory alone can account for the emergence of the Dadul-Maranagi splinter group in East New Guinea that Whitehouse describes in his *Inside the Cult: Religious Innovation and Transmission in Papua New Guinea* [1995]). It seems to me, however, that Whitehouse's own account of this development reveals an implicit sociological explanatory account of the group rather than one that is simply cognitivist.

"Splinter-group activities tend to recur every few years," asserts Whitehouse, and he claims to have shown "that this periodicity is associated with distinctive patterns of cultural transmission and codification, and political organization" (1995: 65) (although the nature of "associated" here is left without elaboration). Whitehouse, no doubt, is justified in making that connection, but the mere existence of the possibility of "non-verbal, analogic codification, sensual stimulation, and emotionality" cannot in itself be the cause of the rise of the splinter group. However, Whitehouse does not explicitly attempt to provide an alternative causal account of that event. Whitehouse rather argues that this development is a by-product of the tedium effect born of doctrinal rountinzation. But such reasoning, it seems to me, is essentially speculative. Nevertheless, despite the speculative character of his argument, Whitehouse maintains that this splinter group "was in no sense a functional response either to the demands of the wider movement or to common interests manifested at some other (i.e., non-religious) level of social reality" (1995: 207). However, he also talks of the splinter group as a "reformist" community (1995: 175) in which the "promise of salvation was not merely being asserted but physically experienced, and solidarity was not merely demanded but realized through the act of collective participation" (1995: 150), which, it appears, amounts to a kind of functionalist account of the group's existence. The Dadul-Maranagi splinter group, that is, apparently sought a quicker return on their religious investment than was being offered by the mainstream Pomio-Kivung group, who, although not simply conflating their natural and supernatural goals, did not (to all appearances) place primary emphasis on the "pursuit of the miracle" (1995: 46–47). The Dadul-Maranagi splinter group, therefore—whatever the influence of the tedium effect—appears to have believed that it had something to gain from the ancestors by splitting off from the mainstream group. The real cause of the existence of the splinter group may, however, lie at an even deeper level. It might be the case, that is, that the surface interpretation for the actions of the radicals just provided may well be a cover for other, more mundane motives underlying the radical developments in the splinter group. This certainly appears to be the case for Baninge, Tonotka, Lagewago, and others in the splinter group movement who had much to gain by way of power and prestige in splitting from the mainstream community.

Finally, Whitehouse himself seems explicitly to espouse a sociological explanation of these developments, for in his view of the relationship between mainstream and splinter groups, the mainstream group has something to gain from the reformist aspect of Kivung religion (which is expressed in the Dadul-Maranagi splinter group). He writes, "Although such outbursts in any given community only occasionally and temporarily interrupt the repetitive performance of conventional Kivung rituals, people's memories of climactic periods enrich and deepen their experience of orthodox practices and, in the long run, help to sustain commitment to the mainstream Pomio-Kivung movement" (1995: 175, see also 154, 184). That this is simply an unintended consequence of climactic ritual, as Whitehouse maintains (1995: 4), is not established and, further, conflicts with his recognition of these splinter group movements as reformist in character.

Whitehouse follows the same pattern of thought in his discussion of splinter groups in his later book, *Arguments and Icons*, where he once again appears to invoke sociological explanations to account for why such imagistic modes of religiosity arise in the first place. "[I]t is very probable," he claims, "that mainstream movements could not survive without these sporadic outbursts of splinter-group activity, at different times and places, at a local level" (2000: 128). He continues, "The imagistic practices of the Noise and the Second Cult took from the mainstream movement basic ideas and themes but they gave back a renewed sense of the revelatory power of these ideas and of the solidarity uniting those who upheld and obeyed them" (2000: 143–44). Moreover, he clearly recognizes other, broader, nationalist and secessionist ends sought by the Melanesians and the role their religious activity played in that regard. As he puts it,

> More radical forms of experimentation in Melanesia began largely after the Second World War, with the rise of leaders such as Yali, Paliau, and Koriam. These new leaders and their supporters, drawing on their experience of missionization and other imported colonial forms, developed the first Melanesian religions operating in the doctrinal mode. Such adaptations made possible new kinds of political formation, including micronationalist groupings (2000: 128).

Whitehouse provides no explicit explanation of what inspired the radical forms of religious experimentation, yet he acknowledges that this development was to some extent "facilitated by astute management on the part of the mainstream leaders" (2000: 129). Moreover, in calling them "messianic movements," he implies a teleology that in my judgment requires a psychosociological account of them. And this further implies that the existence of distinctive memory systems and the modes of codification by themselves can only explain how the distinctive modes of religiosity function, but not why they emerged. What is of special interest in this example is that it reveals the peculiar conditions that made possible the transformation of imagistic Melanesian religion into a religion dominated by a doctrinal type of religiosity by providing it a model of religiosity of which it was, until then, according to Whitehouse, wholly ignorant.[3] However, Whitehouse has simply not shown here that either the tedium effect or the mere availability of the new model is—singly or in tandem—the cause of the transformation.

In addition to the examples I have already presented, I note that in a discussion of "Modes of Religiosity and Political Evolution" (2000: 160–88), Whitehouse accounts for the original emergence of imagistic religion as a result of palpable adaptive advantages it conferred upon hunter-gatherer groups in Upper Palaeolithic times (2000: 167), which clearly undermines interpreting "constrain" and "shape" in his account of the role of semantic and episodic memory in the formation of religion as synonyms for "cause."[4] I have more to say about the ambiguity of his account of hunter-gatherer religion below.

On the Theory-Data Fit

Whitehouse's remarks about how the modes of religiosity operate (function) in relation to each other as elements or aspects of religion—already touched on above—in my estimation create further difficulties for understanding the exact import of his theory of the modes of religiosity. This is, in some ways, the most problematic aspect of his theory, for he seems to affirm contradictory accounts of his own ethnographic data. In Whitehouse's theoretical view, religious traditions are either predominantly doctrinal or imagistic, or present a structure that involves both modes in a dialectical kind of relationship but do not blend the two modes; yet, his own data and interpretation of the data suggests to me the contrary. I turn first to the ambiguities in Whitehouse's account of the relationship of the modes to each other.[5]

In *Inside the Cult* Whitehouse denies that "a given religion or ritual is either [simply] imagistic or doctrinal," yet he maintains that a particular religious tradition may "utilize one or other or both modes of religiosity" (1995: 207), suggesting that a religious tradition may actually be either imagistic or doctrinal with one or other mode of religiosity dominating a cult "at the expense of another" (1995: 198). Whitehouse is not, unfortunately, much clearer about these matters in *Arguments and Icons*. Early in the introduction to the book he writes, "These fundamentally contrasting dynamics are often found within a single religious tradition, where they may be associated more or less strongly with different categories or strata of religious adherents" (2000: 1). There is no further elaboration provided here, however, of the nature of the connection between the strata of religious adherents and modes of religiosity. But that matter aside, Whitehouse insists that the clusters of features of the two modes of religiosity combined in any particular religious tradition that "uses" both function "within readily distinguishable domains of operation" (2000: 2). This latter claim makes sense, of course, in light of his theoretical understanding of the clusters of features characteristic of each mode of religiosity (both psychological and sociopolitical) being mutually reinforcing and the modes being divergent; a true blending of these features would hardly be possible. For Whitehouse, then, it appears as if the imagistic and doctrinal modes of religiosity can only operate dialectically—in tension with each other—within any single religious tradition. Historically, however, these matters are considerably messier, as Whitehouse's account indicates:

> The terms "break away" and "splinter group" suggest a radical division between mainstream and local religious ideology, but this is in reality seldom the case. . . . What crucially takes place in these splinter groups is not so much a reformulation of orthodox dogma but a recodification of it. The central principles of mainstream ideology are recast in iconic imagery (2000: 129).

The modes of religiosity for Whitehouse, then, are not mutually exclusive in their operation; even though a religion may incorporate imagistic and doctrinal modes of operation, these modes must be understood to be "aspects of a single, coherent religious tradition" (2000: 130). Whitehouse, however, reads them as still divergent and fundamentally contrastive for, he claims, the Paliau movement must be seen as a "routinized orthodoxy, operating in the doctrinal mode, punctuated by sporadic and temporary outbursts of climactic, imagistic practices" (2000: 130). It is not altogether clear, however, that he would make the same claim about the Dadul-Maranagi splinter group since the earlier pattern of (mainstream Pomio-Kivung) religious existence in this case was eventually restored, as if the disruption had never occurred, except for the personal influence of the ecstatic experiences shared by members of the splinter group. As Whitehouse puts it, those events "enrich[ed] and deepen[ed] their experience of orthodox practices and, in the long-run, help[ed] to sustain commitment to the mainstream Pomio-Kivung movement" (1995: 175).

Despite the tensions in Melanesian religion described by Whitehouse, we see that his so-called modes of religiosity actually work together, as I have just noted, to form, as he puts it, "a single coherent religious tradition" (2000: 129). And despite the tensions in these specific traditions, there does not seem to be any reason in principle why a routinized orthodoxy could not incorporate climactic imagistic practices in a conscious and deliberate fashion and so prevent the tension and conflict that accompanied the developments in the Melanesian traditions described by Whitehouse. In fact, many Protestant Christian traditions seem to do precisely this.[6]

Even given the claims for the possible mutual participation of both modes of religiosity within any particular religious tradition just outlined above, Whitehouse also espouses the claim that a religious tradition may well exhibit only one or other of these modes. This is indisputable, I think, given his account of their origins. In this regard Whitehouse writes,

> On the basis of archaeological evidence, it is tentatively suggested in this volume that the imagistic mode first appeared among Upper Palaeolithic hunter-gatherers through processes of religious experimentation that turned out to be highly adaptive in conditions of intensified competition for resources, not least because they fostered forms of especially intense local cohesion, facilitating more effective forms of group defense. The doctrinal mode appears to have been invented very much later, precipitated by the advent of writing technologies just a few thousand years ago (2000: 3).

With this great disparity in the timing of the appearance of the two modes of religiosity, there can be no doubt that at least the earliest mode of religiosity wholly characterized all religion until the invention of the doctrinal mode thousands of years later. Whitehouse is clearly aware of this implication:

> It would seem that the imagistic mode of religiosity is very ancient, perhaps as old as our species. Among prehistoric hunter-gatherers, we do not encounter the problem that modes of religiosity can be entwined or enmeshed. Such populations, like the peoples of pre-contact Melanesia, *had no experience of doctrinal practices* (2000: 160–61, emphasis added).

However, Whitehouse does not appear to recognize the problem this produces for his theory, which presumes not only that both episodic and semantic modes of memory are involved in the transmission of religion, but also presumes that all religious traditions involve, in various measures, both modes of religiosity. This problem becomes even more obvious with his implicit suggestion that literacy may be "a necessary condition of the *independent* invention of a doctrinal domain of operation" (2000: 161, emphasis added).[7] If each mode of religiosity has emerged wholly independently, the question of the nature of the relationship between them becomes rather mysterious.

I assume (with Whitehouse) that we are justified in talking of religion appearing among Upper Palaeolithic hunter-gatherers (2000: 161). I also accept his claims that "there is no such thing as a religious tradition that does not depend for its transmission on both semantic and episodic memory" (2000: 11) and that, therefore, no religious tradition can be simply imagistic or doctrinal (1995: 207).

In light of these claims, however, one cannot help but conclude that his talk of Upper Palaeolithic religion as a purely "imagistic mode of religiosity" or that we do not encounter among the hunter-gatherers "the problem that modes of religiosity can be intertwined or enmeshed" becomes problematic (2000: 161). This is not to say that I disagree with his claim that the form of Upper Palaeolithic religion exhibits predominantly the aspects he attributes to what he calls the imagistic mode of religiosity; it means only that I find it unlikely, both in light of cognitive theory and the empirical evidence, that those aspects are not intertwined with elements he attributes to doctrinal religiosity, and not simply in the dialectical fashion he suggests. Thus, given his insistence that both episodic and semantic memory must be involved in the invention of religion, I find his claim that not only prehistoric hunter-gatherers, but even precontact Melanesians, "had no experience of doctrinal practices" (2000: 161) unconvincing, for, on the one hand, the theory implies that the transmission of religion necessarily involves a combination of rhetoric, narrative, and logical integration as well as iconicity and spontaneous exegetical reflection, while, on the other hand, these diverging modes of religiosity preclude any such fusion of these psychological and organizational features. Just how divergent these supposed modes of religiosity really are, therefore, is obviously in question.

It seems to me, then, that it would be more consistent with the archaeological evidence to talk simply about the emergence of religion (not modes of religiosity) with our prehistoric hunter-gatherer forebears and to accept as foundational that religion (including prehistoric religion) is never simply imagistic or doctrinal.[8] That Upper Palaeolithic religion involved complex ceremony and rite—including, as Whitehouse maintains, "a sense of secrecy and revelation through visual special effects" that "bombard the senses in all directions" (2000: 164)—does not necessarily preclude its also involving narratively framed beliefs (and being, therefore, at least protodoctrinal in character [see chapter 4]) in addition to iconicity and spontaneous exegetical reflection, for it is widely agreed that newly emerged *Homo sapiens sapiens* were capable not only of ritual and art but also of mythmaking. Indeed, John E. Pfeiffer, upon whom Whitehouse relies in his discussion of the Upper Palaeolithic hunter-gatherer, admits the role of myth in prehistorical religion: "The people of the Upper Palaeolithic lived at the dawn of the oral tradition, and in a sense started what Homer finished" (1982: 189). This is brought out in even greater detail by others. Alexander Marshak, for example, claims that thinking related to the seasons, the motions in the sky, the growth and movement of plants and animals, and so forth among the hunter-gatherers made possible a form of conceptualization that allowed them to make sense of life in terms of story. The hunter obtained the ability to structure and organize what Marshak calls an increasingly complex time-factored life. "The storytelling skill," he writes, helped [the hunter] to see and recognize process and change, to widen his references and comparisons, to "understand" and to participate in them and foretell them. One assumes, then, that the kind of stories a man tells—in this case a hunter's—helps him to unify the extraordinarily diverse phenomena and processes of his life; and since story is an *equation*, a cognitive form of abstractly structuring and dealing with process and relation, the uses and complexities of the story form would change as the culture becomes more complex" (1972: 133, emphasis in the original).

Furthermore, according to Marshak, this ability to conceptualize gave rise to myths that assisted the hunter to handle time and space "in the skills of the search and hunt, and in the skills of protection and shelter" (1972: 134), as well as in dealing with death (1972: 235ff), sex and divinity (1972: 281ff), and other matters.

Steven Mithen, I think, suggests something similar about the Upper Palaeolithic hunter-gatherer in his account of the Middle/Upper Palaeolithic transition—following Paul Mellars's suggestion that the period marks the crossing of a major cognitive threshold—as one of "a dramatic increase in the degree of accessibility between mental modules" (1994: 35). Although Mithen does not reject the notion of a distinct modular architecture of the brain, he maintains that after the transition, one finds a significant change in human cognitive abilities; as he puts it, "the mind appears to possess a higher degree of generalized intelligence" (1994: 35) that can only be explained by an increased accessibility between mental modules. That increased accessibility, he argues, would allow "[c]ognitive processes evolved for a very specific purpose or use in particular domains, such as stone working or social interaction, [to become] available for other domains" (1994: 35). This would explain not only the significant technological developments in the Middle/Upper Palaeolithic transition, but also the emergence of sets of beliefs—such as those that derive from anthropomorphic thinking—that we now categorize as religious. Mithen suggests, for example, that the activities of prayer, sacrifice, and ritual, and their attendant beliefs, are all likely developments of the supplementation of "[t]he cognitive abilities present in the specialized domain of natural history intelligence . . . with those from other domains" (1994: 35). He continues,

> The most significant source of these is likely to have been the social sphere and the most important cognitive ability the attribution of mental states—now applied to members of other animal species rather than conspecifics. From the Upper Palaeolithic onwards, the non-social world is explored and exploited partly using thought processes which evolved for social interaction (1994: 35).

As Mithen puts it in *The Prehistory of the Mind* (1996), the new behavior that emerged with our Upper Palaeolithic hunter-gatherer forebears after 60,000 BCE suggests that they "were the first to have beliefs in supernatural beings and possibly an afterlife. We are indeed seeing here the first appearance of religious ideologies. This can be explained by the collapse of the barriers that had existed between the multiple intelligences of the Early Human mind" (1996: 174).

Further support for such an interpretation can be found in the work of Esther Goody and her colleagues on the social bias in human intelligence that living in groups requires. "In short," she writes, "effective social living requires anticipation of the actions of others, calculation of short- and long-term costs and gains, and close attention to signals about the consequences of one's own behaviour" (1995: 2). Naming the ability to model this interdependence anticipatory interactive planning (AIP), she notes that language clearly facilitates such planning and suggests that, in light of this, an adaptationist argument can be made for the initial emergence of spoken language.

> With language we construct social worlds that have ultimate reality. . . . It is the sharing of . . . beliefs, impossible without language, which makes them real. And it is this reality which in turn sets premises for shared goals which make possible social action at least part of the time (1995: 8).

Not only are the created worlds "social worlds," they are also "religious worlds," for, as Goody points out, along with the emergence of spoken language, the representation of AIP comes to be expressed dialogically. As she puts it, "[i]n inner speech and in conversation, dialogue and the dyad are built into human cognition" (1995: 12). Thus, spoken language seems to have constructed a dialogue template for social cognition, and that template, along with the dyadic premise, provides a foundation for the social construction of unseen mystical powers and underlies "the human reliance on prayer as 'supplicatory speech addressed to some external force or being'" (Goody 1995: 12). In other words, we have every indication that the cognitive structures of *Homo sapiens sapiens* made possible the construction of religion that involves not only imagistic components and iconic/analogic codification but also beliefs and what Whitehouse calls doctrinal/digital codification.

In my judgment, these contributions by Marshak and Mithen to our understanding of Upper Palaeolithic religion and Goody's account of the likely nature of religion in prehistoric human communities suggest the need for a more holistic view of religion than that provided by Whitehouse to account for the archaeological, anthropological, and historical data we possess on religion.

Culture, Religion, and Religiosity

I have a great deal of sympathy for the type of theorizing represented by Whitehouse's project on the modes of religiosity. I believe it is essential for social scientists to recognize that culture (including religion) is, at least in part, the product of psychological mechanisms that are themselves products of our evolutionary development. Whitehouse's theory clearly, and rightly so, involves a rejection of the assumption of the sui generis character of cultural reality. However, as I have pointed out, his theory of the modes of religiosity is not without its difficulties; nor does it seem to offer an unambiguous account for the ethnographic and historical religious data to which he applies it. Furthermore, Whitehouse seems to be asking more of the cognitive explanation he invokes than it can actually deliver, and this casts some doubt on his claim that it has "profound implications . . . for the comparative study of religion" (2000: 4). The relevant cognitive mechanisms involved in the transmission of religious belief and ritual practice, that is, do not of themselves, for example, account for the emergence of religion on the human scene; nor do they become operative without being externally activated. And it is precisely an account of the activation of these cognitive mechanisms that is missing from his theory. For Whitehouse, it appears, this is not a deficit; for him, alternative social-scientific explanations are not necessary to account for the modes of religiosity that appear in any particular religious tradition. As he puts it, "it is not the vision of a better way of life that determines the political nature of Melanesian movements, it is the way this vision is codified and transmitted" (1995: 203). On the other hand, Whitehouse implicitly relies on precisely such alternative arguments to get him to where he wishes to arrive. This is especially clear in his attempts to illustrate the gist of his theory not only by reference to Melanesian religion(s) but also with respect to other data, including the emergence of the earliest form of religion with the Upper Palaeolithic hunter-gatherer and the first emergence of doctrinal religion considerably later. Furthermore, his theory tells us nothing about religion per se, and he provides no account of how religious phenomena are to be differentiated from nonreligious cultural phenomena or whether the transmission of religious (cultural) information differs from the transmission of nonreligious cultural information.

I do not suggest here that the difficulties which characterize Whitehouse's theory of the modes of religiosity in any way constitute a falsification of the theory. The problems I raise may be more matters of interpretation than of substance and may well find resolution in further clarification of the theory and its application to the psychological, ethnographic, and historical data. The theory, clearly, is in the early stages of development. Whitehouse and his colleagues continue to rework and refine the theory and to evaluate how well it accounts for the empirical data, and only time will reveal whether the theory will present scholars of religion with a broad and cogent research framework for understanding and explaining religion.

Notes

1. I am grateful to Luther H. Martin, Ilkka Pyysiäinen, Tom Sjöblom, Veikko Antonen, and Harvey Whitehouse for critical comments on earlier drafts of this chapter.

2. I have found it difficult not to speak of religion, religious traditions, and theories of religion in discussing Whitehouse's work. I am aware that his theory of the modes of religiosity is concerned exclusively with the transmission of religious knowledge and the effect that the modes of transmission have on the sociopolitical structure of the communities involved; however, it seems to me reasonable to assume that the "end product" of the modes of religiosity is—eventually—particular religions that express different forms, kinds, styles, or types of religiousness. Consequently, I find it reasonable to talk about religious traditions or to raise question about how the modes of religiosity are related to religions and religion without in any way ignoring or undermining the essential point of Whitehouse's work.

3. If I understand Whitehouse here, original Melanesian religion, before the onset of Christian missionization, was imagistic in form. After missionization—which presents a doctrinal mode of religion—Melanesian religion becomes, by imitation, doctrinal in form, only to be transformed again into an imagistic mode by messianic and reform interests produced by splinter groups within the new doctrinal form of Melanesian religion.

4. Given Whitehouse's awareness of selective pressures in the environment that can account for the emergence of religion among our hunter-gatherer forebears, I find it strange that he does not look for the selective pressures that might account for the changes of religion in the Melanesian situation.

5. Others have picked up on the same problem in Whitehouse's formulation of the theory of the modes of religiosity in *Arguments and Icons*. Pascal Boyer, for example, considers Whitehouse's account of the modes as divergent, even though each "can often incorporate elements of the other" as something of a "mystery" (2002: 8, 11). Robert N. McCauley, after noting Whitehouse's cautionary comments about his theory, suggests that "his theory may disallow a good deal less than it seems" and writes, "In the light of such concessions, another way to put the current question is just how divergent are these two modes of religiosity?" (2002: 27). McCauley then suggests that Whitehouse may actually "be conceding that what . . . [he calls] 'mixed mode' phenomena seem a good deal more prevalent than his Melanesian case studies might suggest" (2002: 27). In response to these critiques, Whitehouse seems to admit, "'Pure' examples of modes of religiosity will be hard to find" (2002: 57), thus, in some sense, capitulating to McCauley's criticism, although Whitehouse still maintains that the theory of the modes is the best avenue to account for religious transmission (2002: 57).

6. On this matter, see Ilkka Pyysiäinen's discussion of Laestadianism in chapter 11 of this volume; also see Brian Malley (2002) and Garry Trompf (2002).

7. I find unpersuasive Whitehouse's suggestion of the independent creation of a doctrinal mode of religiosity, which he attributes to the rise of literacy in the period of the temple complexes in ancient Mesopotamia, because it can be shown that it was not until much later, in the period of alphabetic literacy in ancient Greece, that a genuinely new form of thought, radically different from that of all earlier (prehistorical and historical)

human communities, emerged. Prior to the period of missionization, Melanesian religion, I presume, would have been as much entwined with myth as the Upper Palaeolithic hunter-gatherer, but not doctrinal in any systematic sense. I think that the development of alphabetic literacy in ancient Greece gave rise to a radically different mode of thought, but not in the sense of a different mode of religiosity—except, perhaps, indirectly. The emergence of alphabetic literacy, along with other concurrent developments in Greek society, made possible the emergence of a scientific mode of thought that is not only nonreligious but works in quite a contrary fashion to religious thought. (Although this is not to suggest that they cannot become "entwined and enmeshed." In so far as religious thought attempted to accommodate itself to these developments, that is, religion would have been transformed, although the transformation might better be described as a distortion of religion. I shall not, however, pursue this line of thought further here.)

8.   There may be some interesting parallels here between Whitehouse's notions of imagistic and doctrinal religiosity and William Robertson Smith's distinction between ritual and myth in his sociological account of religion. Like Whitehouse, Smith clearly distinguishes ritual from mythic religion and suggests that archaic religions are essentially a matter of institutions and practices and not creeds (creedal belief), yet does not object to the emphasis on creedal belief in the study of modern religion. Nevertheless, unlike Whitehouse, Smith recognized that rituals are not really celebrated without reason, yet he claimed that the "reasons" were not formal declarations of belief but rather stories or myths. Careful analysis of his distinction between dogma, doctrine, and creed on the one hand and myth on the other might be of some help in avoiding the ambiguities and inconsistencies in Whitehouse's theory, but this is not a matter I can follow up here.

References

Barkow, Jerome K., Leda Cosmides, and John Tooby, eds. 1992. "Introduction: Evolutionary Psychology and Conceptual Integration." In *The Adapted Mind: Evolutionary Psychology and the Generation of Culture*. Oxford: Oxford University Press.

Boyer, Pascal. 2002. "*Arguments and Icons*: A Review." *Journal of Ritual Studies* 16(2): 7–12.

Goody, Esther N., ed. 1995. *Social Intelligence and Interaction: Expressions and Implications of the Social Bias in Human Intelligence*. Cambridge: Cambridge University Press.

Johnson, Karen. 2004. "Primary Emergence of the Doctrinal Mode of Religiosity in Prehistoric Southwestern Iran," chapter 4 in this volume.

Malley, Brian. 2002. "*Arguments and Icons*: A Review." *Journal of Ritual Studies* 16(2): 4–7.

Marshak, Alexander. 1972. *The Roots of Civilization: The Cognitive Beginnings of Man's First Art, Symbol and Notation*. London: Weidenfeld and Nicolson.

McCauley, Robert N. 1998. "Comparing the Cognitive Foundations of Science and Religion." Report 37 of the Emory Cognition Project, Department of Psychology, Emory University, Atlanta, Georgia.

———. 2002. "*Arguments and Icons*: A Review." *Journal of Ritual Studies* 16(2): 22–29.

McCutcheon, Russell. 1997. *Manufacturing Religion: The Discourse on Sui Generis Religion and the Politics of Nostalgia*. New York: Oxford University Press.

Mithen, Steven. 1994. "From Domain Specific to Generalized Intelligence: A Cognitive Interpretation of the Middle/Upper Palaeolithic Transition." In *The Ancient Mind: Elements of Cognitive Archaeology*, edited by Colin Renfrew and Ezra B. W. Zubrow. Cambridge: Cambridge University Press.

———. 1996. *The Prehistory of the Mind: The Cognitive Origins of Art, Religion, and Science*. London: Thames and Hudson.

Pfeiffer, John E. 1982. *The Creative Explosion: An Inquiry into the Origins of Art and Religion*. New York: Harper and Row.

Pyysiäinen, Ilkka. 2004. "Corrupt Doctrine and Doctrinal Revival: On the Nature and Limits of the Modes Theory," chapter 11 in this volume.

Smith, William Robertson. 1889. *Lectures on the Religion of the Semites*. First Series. Edinburgh: Adam and Charles Black.

Tooby, John, and Leda Cosmides. 1992. "The Psychological Foundations of Culture." In *The Adapted Mind: Evolutionary Psychology and the Generation of Culture*, edited by Jerome K. Barkow, Leda Cosmides, and John Tooby, 19–136. Oxford: Oxford University Press.

Trompf, Garry W. 2002. "*Arguments and Icons*: A Review." *Journal of Ritual Studies* 16(2): 39–45.

Whitehouse, Harvey. 1995. *Inside the Cult: Religious Innovation and Transmission in Papua New Guinea*. Oxford: Oxford University Press.

———. 2000. *Arguments and Icons: Divergent Modes of Religiosity*. Oxford: Oxford University Press.

———. 2002a. "Conjectures, Refutations, and Verification: Towards a Testable Theory of 'Modes of Religiosity.'" *Journal of Ritual Studies* 16(2): 45–62.

———. 2002b. "Modes of Religiosity: Towards A Cognitive Explanation of the Sociopolitical Dynamics of Religion." *Method and Theory in the Study of Religion* 14(3): 293–315.

Theorizing Religions Past **13**

HARVEY WHITEHOUSE

L IKE ALL DOMAINS OF CULTURE, religious life is extremely complex, multi-
faceted, and riddled with paradox and contradiction. If our aim is to try to
grasp and empathize with religious experience in all its rich subtlety and
variation, the task is an enormous one—even if we restrict ourselves to the study
of a single religious tradition within a tightly circumscribed region and historical
period. As a kind of shorthand, we could call this the challenge of description and
interpretation, though this is not to imply the presence of a single methodology
(indeed, many methodologies, or combinations of them, are possible in this kind
of project).

As noted at the beginning of this book, both by E. Thomas Lawson (chapter
1) and Luther H. Martin (chapter 2), explanatory approaches face a different kind
of challenge. Here, it does not matter if there are features of religious action, feeling, thought, or sensation that fall outside the ambit of a particular theory. What
matters is that the variables with which the theory is concerned conform to patterns of relationships that the theory predicts and that all this is formulated in
such a way that we could agree on what would constitute counterevidence with regard to the theory's predictions. Such an agenda may be alien to many historians,
as it is also to many anthropologists. Where descriptive and explanatory projects
confront one another, there is always a considerable risk of producing intractable
disputes because the terms of the two kinds of projects are simply incommensu-
rable.

The theory of modes of religiosity does not pretend to supply an exhaustive
explanation of all aspects of religious life. Its concern is only to explain certain
aspects of transmission and social organization in religious traditions in terms of
a set of underlying patterns of cognitive processing. It seems to me that the predictions of the modes theory, as originally formulated, have so far withstood the

tests of ethnographers (see Whitehouse and Laidlaw 2004) and of historians and archaeologists (in the present book). The range of ethnographic and historical regions covered in these two books, however, is relatively small. A comprehensive survey would have run into many more volumes and may have thrown up more problematic cases. But the thrust of the evidence we have on the table suggests that the modes dynamics are widespread and robust. Where problems seem to arise most prominently is in relation to the presence of features that were not originally anticipated or that seem to involve the mixing of elements from both the doctrinal and imagistic modes.

Mixed Modes?

According to my original formulation (Whitehouse 1995, 2000), doctrinal and imagistic modes are like oil and water: if they occur together within a single tradition, they remain discernibly separate as domains of operation. One of the most vocal challenges from ethnography, however, has been that religious traditions dominated by the doctrinal mode also may incorporate some elements of the imagistic mode (Whitehouse and Laidlaw 2004). This has been a recurrent theme in the present book as well—figuring prominently, for instance, in the chapters by Anne Clark, Ted Vial, Ulrich Berner, Ilkka Pyysiäinen, and Donald Wiebe.

Consider the case of monastic religious life in the late Middle Ages, discussed with great erudition by Anne Clark (chapter 8). Here, we have evidence for the stable reproduction of a full-blown doctrinal mode of religiosity: routinized transmission and heavy emphasis on verbal and textual codification of a religious orthodoxy, coupled with expansionary, centralizing, and hierarchical dynamics. Although Clark does not explicitly identify all the key variables necessary to confirm the presence of a doctrinal mode of operation, it seems rather likely that the precise concatenation of elements predicted by the modes theory is in fact to be found in medieval monasteries.

Nevertheless, in addition to the predicted variables, Clark identifies the presence of other patterns of religious activity that are not predicted to be essential elements of the doctrinal mode and, yet, would seem to have significant implications for the reproduction of doctrinal-mode elements. The main activities Clark identifies might be characterized as relatively low-frequency epiphanic episodes, usually taking the form of visions or other extraordinary interactions with the divine. Clark stresses that these episodes are quite widely distributed and could therefore have a significant impact on religious meaning and motivation for many (perhaps a majority) of those leading a monastic life in the Middle Ages. The modes theory, of course, does not exclude the possibility of other elements impinging on religious life as well. It only makes the positive prediction that there will be a tendency for certain variables to cluster in a stipulated manner. Clarke's data support that prediction with regard to monastic Christianity, and she offers no alternative explanation for the predicted coalescence of variables. Still, it would be nice to explain the additional features that she identifies.

According to my original formulation, the doctrinal mode is inherently vulnerable to the tedium effect. The cause of this is quite straightforward: arousal broadly correlates inversely with performance frequency, a principle that seems to be well supported in the study of religious rituals cross-culturally. It follows that all traditions in which the doctrinal mode coalesces will harbor selective pressures favoring the establishment of more highly motivating forms of religious experience. One direction in which such forms might develop is through the natural selection of more effective forms of oratory—typically, ones that have increasing levels of relevance to various aspects of daily life. Brian Malley has pioneered some important contributions to our theoretical and empirical knowledge in this area in his ethnographic research on Bible Baptists in Michigan (2004). But, all else being equal, there are also selective pressures in favor of more sensually evocative forms of religious activity, ranging from the banging of tambourines through to the diffusion of very high-arousal, revelatory episodes. On the face of it, this may look like the adoption of elements characteristic of the imagistic mode. And certainly this was a focus of considerable discussion among our colleagues in anthropology (see Whitehouse and Laidlaw 2004). But, in fact, when high-arousal revelations occur as part of a doctrinal mode formation, they often establish effects that contrast very starkly with those found in the imagistic mode of religiosity.

Several issues are significant here, but perhaps the most important is that epiphanic experiences in the doctrinal mode tend to have a dual aspect. On the one hand, they specify information at encoding that may survive in long-term memory as a trigger to processes of spontaneous exegetical reflection (SER). On the other hand, they also tend to be subject to frequent, subsequent rehearsal as more or less formulaic narratives on the theme of conversion, miraculous intervention, visitations and visions, and so on. Clark notes evidence of precisely that pattern in medieval monastic life. It is crucial, however, to note that this latter pattern of cultural transmission is characteristically absent in the imagistic mode. Moreover, these rather special kinds of events that punctuate more routinized religious activity are seldom (if ever) collective experiences. They tend to strike lone individuals rather than groups and, so, are powerless to create the sort of localized group cohesion that typifies the imagistic mode. Thus, what appears to be a fusion or mixing of the two modes is really nothing of the sort. Since the two modes are clustered around fundamentally divergent dynamics, it follows that whenever they draw on a common stock of cognitive mechanisms, they do so in significantly contrasting ways.

Of course, the distinctions I am drawing here are relative rather than absolute. The doctrinal mode privileges verbal transmission of elaborate doctrine and exegesis over private rumination, but we are talking about differences of degree rather than kind. Not only do some imagistic adaptations seem to enhance the survival chances of religious activities based on the doctrinal mode, but as Ulrich Berner (chapter 10) rightly points out, the cognitive mechanisms underpinning doctrinal and imagistic modes are activated in different ways and to different degrees among religious individuals. Within a tradition dominated by the doctrinal mode, for instance, there might be some individuals who attach particular salience to personal revelatory experiences. While reflecting deeply on the significance of those experiences, they might accord rather little importance to authoritative teachings and display a limited grasp of the orthodox canon. Such individuals thus engage in patterns of thinking that are characteristic of the imagistic mode, even though the tradition to which they belong does not exhibit full-blown imagistic features, such as high-arousal, low-frequency collective rituals and concomitant patterns of group cohesion.

Berner and I might differ in our reading of the significance of this sort of individual variation. Berner is wary of generalization beyond the level of individual experience for fear of "reifying abstract concepts—speaking about religions as if they had intentions and acted like human beings" (p. 158). I, too, would be wary of according institutions agentive qualities (see Whitehouse 2003), but that is certainly not what is implied by a notion of modes of religiosity as distributed cognitive patterns that have effects discernible only at a population level. All this approach assumes is that general patterns of mentation and behavior can be analyzed as cumulative properties of the thoughts and actions of individuals. For instance, we can hypothesize that participation in routinized ritual has the effect of suppressing the rate and volume of SER in the minds of a specified number of individuals, whereas participation in very highly arousing and shocking rituals has the effect of increasing the rate and volume of SER in a specified population. Exceptional individual psychology is interesting, but not in any way calamatous, or even mildly problematic, for the modes model. Indeed, it may be very useful, for instance, in explaining how certain forms of inspired or charismatic leadership come into being within routinized religious traditions. And it may even help us to predict variations in the appeal of imagistic-mode activities for different individuals (Berner, pp. 157–58; see also Gragg, pp. 82–83).

It will be noted that most attempts to furnish instances of mixed-mode phenomena are centered on traditions dominated by the doctrinal mode. Cases of religious traditions based on imagistic dynamics, and yet which incorporate some doctrinal-mode features, seem to be much thinner on the ground. It is possible, although by no means certain at this early stage, that this is because the imagistic mode is inherently robuster. It is never endangered by the tedium effect, or, per-haps, by other debilitating influences that (as we see below) commonly threaten the doctrinal mode. Consequently, the imagistic mode makes little use of the mo-tivating gimmicks of doctrinal transmission (moving oratory, textual validation, reinforcement of belief through repetition, and so on). It may also be that in con-ditions of low-frequency transmission, the mechanisms of the doctrinal mode are simply impossible to deploy, for what enduring relevance could be attached to a speech or a text that is rarely encoded? There is no cause for complacency on this matter, however, as Roger Beck amply demonstrates (chapter 6). Beck's account of Greco-Roman Mithraism strongly suggests the presence of full-blown imagistic dynamics, and yet he identifies a number of features that seem to conform to a doctrinal-mode pattern. Once again, the specter of mixed modes seems to be raised, and in a rather exceptional way.

To a Melanesianist like myself, Beck's data on two Mithraic rituals are forcibly reminiscent of many aspects of New Guinea initiations, which of course have so far provided my most detailed examples of imagistic-mode dynamics (White-house 1992, 1995, 2000). Despite their distance in time and space, both kinds of traditions begin the process of induction into cult mysteries by assuming a quite widely disseminated common stock of cultural knowledge stored in semantic memory. In the case of Mithraism, a crucial part of that knowledge would seem to be what Beck calls "star-talk," a remarkably systematic body of astronomical ex-pertise. In the case of New Guinea fertility cults, an equivalent corpus would be that pertaining to the domain of zoology. Celestial systems and natural tax-onomies respectively provide somewhat fixed and shared reference points for the building of more esoteric and essentially mysterious religious knowledge.

The revelatory process, in circumstances like these, typically commences with ritual acts that are high in arousal, personally consequential, and in certain respects deeply surprising or puzzling. These are optimal conditions for the formation of flashbulb-memory effects. In the case of the "Archery of the Father" ritual in Mithraism, as in most New Guinea initiations, terror is induced by an act of mas-sive intimidation. But this intimidation is also one that violates normal cultural frames. One of the most obvious ways of doing that, perhaps, is to associate the role of torturer or intimidator with categories of close kin, real or fictive—particularly the role of father as in Mithraism or, in many parts of Melanesia, the maternal uncle. But a deeper process of puzzlement is also being triggered. New Guinea initiations encourage novices to believe that their everyday knowledge about the natural world (albeit extensive and complex) contains only the shadow of deeper mysteries. In Mithraism, it is apparently the novice's presumptuous con-fidence in his astronomical knowledge that comes under attack. What noninitiates know about the cosmos is revealed to be no more than the outward appearance of a much more complex, and only partially penetrable, system. Although the corpus of nonesoteric celestial knowledge is not invalidated, it turns out to be only a collection of shallow truths, a veil. The revelation of deeper cosmological understandings occurs through processes of SER, in which episodic memory for low-frequency, high-arousal rituals plays a crucial part. As Beck puts it (pp. 157–58, emphasis removed): "The rituals and the elaborate material apparatus of Mithraism . . . instantiate not a doctrine, but a system of symbols, the apprehension of which by the initiate constitutes the mysteries."

This apprehension, however, is not simple and immediate—nor does it come to any final and satisfactory conclusion. It proceeds slowly, generating ever more elaborate semantic schemas over the course of a lifetime. It would be too much to expect ethnography or historiography to unveil fully the mechanisms that drive and shape such processes. Nevertheless, we can, as students of human culture, specify the conditions and contexts in which ritual meanings are generated and transmitted and within which our cognitive faculties for memory and analogical thinking are activated. Beck does this with exceptional depth and breadth of expertise.

So how does any of this raise the question of mixed modes? Mithraic cults bear all the classic hallmarks of the imagistic mode, at least if my reading of Beck's data are correct, and yet at the end of his chapter he seems ready to classify some aspects of Mithraism as doctrinal rather than imagistic. Beck reads me as saying that the presence of information stored in semantic memory belies the operations of the doctrinal mode. It seems to me, however, that no kind of religious tradition could get off the ground without semantic knowledge about the world.[1] What makes Mithraic cults and New Guinea initiations imagistic is the fact that they both use ritualization as a way of challenging a corpus of semantic knowledge. They do this by obliging people to form enduring and vivid episodic memories for deeply discomforting and puzzling rituals and by encouraging novices to believe that these ritual events contain clues to deeper layers of knowledge, accessible only through mystical personal rumination. In all these respects, Mithraism is unambiguously clustered around the imagistic attractor position, with no evidence that doctrinal mode features are somehow mixed in.

Yet the issue of mixed modes also arises from Beck's account of the sociopolitical features of Mithraism. Patterns of leadership, spread, and standardization, he suggests, conform more closely to the doctrinal than the imagistic model. Here again, on closer inspection, we find that some of the problems are more apparent than real. The leaders of Mithraic cults are strongly reminiscent of ritual elders and experts in contemporary Melanesia and possess none of the qualities of dynamic leadership found among the messiahs, prophets, and priests of the doctrinal mode. And there are, therefore, no grounds to suppose that the leaders of these Greco-

Roman cults ever came to form a centralized religious authority, capable of monitoring and policing a religious orthodoxy across a wide region. Nevertheless, Beck's evidence does seem to me to raise a very interesting challenge in relation to patterns of spread and regional homogenization. Mithraism seemed to spread rather more easily and uniformly than the modes theory would predict. The reason seems to lie in the fact that the tradition was transported via large-scale, centralized military machinery, and so its imagistic dynamics were overridden by those of the Roman state. I consider below the question of whether the transmission of state values constituted an expression of doctrinal mode dynamics (suggesting that Mithraism formed part of the wider picture of contrasting modes, as argued by Luther Martin [2004]) or whether we need another kind of model to make sense of the Greco-Roman materials, as argued by Gragg in this book (chapter 5).

In sum, although the chapters by Clark and Beck support the predictions of the modes theory in a number of interesting ways, they also point to the presence of factors that lie outside the ambit of the original model and that would seem to have a major bearing on patterns of historical transformation. This becomes clearer still in some of the discussions of how modes of religiosity interact.

Interacting Modes?

It might be argued that although the imagistic mode is capable, at least in principle, of operating independently, the presence of a doctrinal mode presupposes the prior or simultaneous inputs of imagistic dynamics. This is suggested not only by the sequential emergence of modes of religiosity (imagistic first and doctrinal subsequently) in human history, but also by the simple fact that complex doctrine has to come from somewhere, and the imagistic mode provides the archetypal model for its production. Anita Leopold (chapter 7) argues at length that we can identify imagistic dynamics in early Christianity, specifically in second-century Gnosticism. In other words, Gnostic mysticism provided a body of revelatory knowledge that emergent doctrinal regimes later colonized and appropriated. Moreover, the reliance of the doctrinal mode on imagistic outputs might be seen as a permanent state of affairs rather than merely a formative developmental stage. These issues are raised in a number of ways by relatively recent European religious history.

Arguments and Icons: Divergent Modes of Religiosity contains a somewhat tentative discussion of Christianity on the eve of the European Reformation, to which several chapters in this book present intriguing challenges. My hypothesis therein is that Christian laities in the Middle Ages had an incomplete version of the doctrinal mode in that they lacked a systematic corpus of religious knowledge necessary to motivate ongoing involvement. Instead, their religious lives were animated and motivated by forms of religious activity that gravitated toward the imagistic end of the spectrum.

Ted Vial (chapter 9) eloquently argues, however, that my argument was based on a rather too hasty projection of patterns underlying the development of new religious movements in twentieth-century Melanesia onto rather different (and frankly more complex) patterns of historical transformation in sixteenth-century Europe. The Melanesian model consisted of an oscillation between relatively long-term periods of routinized religious activity punctuated by periodic outbursts of imagistic splintering, triggered primarily by the tedium effect. The reabsorption of these splinter groups had the effect of rejuvinating the mainstream, routinized tradition, at least temporarily. Vial points out that such a model is only one of many possible interactions between splinter groups and mainstream traditions. In highlighting a number of others, Vial shows not only that established religion and its splinter groups can confront each other in a variety of ways, but that there are great risks in assuming that these confrontations map onto a notion of interacting modes of religiosity in any straightforward and obvious way. In sixteenth-century Europe there is precious little evidence of imagistic outbursts of the sort more recently observed in Melanesia. We have, Vial concedes, rather clear evidence of the doctrinal mode of religiosity in the practices of both Catholics and Protestants in the sixteenth century. But we also find a wide range of practices that occupy an uncertain position with respect to the modes theory—contributing neither to a doctrinal nor to an imagistic mode of operation, yet playing a prominent role in late medieval religious life and in the processes of transformation that engulfed it during and after the European Reformation. Excellent examples include what Vial calls "apotropaic uses of ritual objects" (p. 152), which are neither high in arousal nor low in frequency, but which, at the same time, require and receive no elaborate exegesis or mnemonic support.

Ilkka Pyysiäinen (chapter 11) develops a strikingly complementary line of argument. A great deal of religious activity and thought, he observes, is difficult to reconcile with the two attractor positions proposed by the modes theory. These aspects of religion may invite little in the way of elaborate rumination, but neither do they attract authoritative interpretation; they encompass rituals and other practices that are familiar but not necessarily routinized; they may contain allusions to official doctrine, yet tend to condense and simplify it in the process. Pyysiäinen is referring here to the naturalness of much religious thinking and action—the fact that it does not require special pedagogical resources to acquire and pass on. The challenge is to connect this kind of transmission to rather more elaborate and costly operations of modes dynamics.

Intuitiveness and Ritualization

It has long been appreciated that some cultural representations are easier to acquire and pass on than others. In part, this has to do with the natural capabilities and limitations of human cognition. Most normal humans would expend comparatively few cognitive resources learning to hum a simple melody, yet would find complex mathematical principles extremely challenging to process, apply, and recall. With most computers, the reverse is true (see Sperber 1996): complex mathematical manipulations may require minimal computational resources, whereas music rapidly clogs up the hard drive. And yet, humans have proven more successful than any other species in overcoming their cognitive limitations. Through techniques of regular rehearsal and practice, for instance, we are capable of acquiring conceptual frameworks that deliver inferences extremely remote from anything intelligible to our intuitive systems. As a result, culture consists of cognitively challenging concepts as well as more intuitive, cognitively optimal concepts. Let us begin with a brief survey of the role of cognitively optimal thinking in the domain of religion.

Much of religion is founded upon intuitive (or "minimally counterintuitive") cognition (see McCauley 2000). As Tom Lawson notes (chapter 1), we now have increasingly detailed accounts of the "naturalness" of this kind of religious thinking. Notions of supernatural agency, for instance, are easily triggered by mental architecture that is geared up for the detection of agency in general. Stewart Guthrie, who refers to this as "anthropomorphic" thinking (1980, 1993), has assembled a great wealth of evidence that humans overdetect signs of humanlike agency on the strength of minimal inputs (his book title, *Faces in the Clouds*, concisely conveys the point). Pascal Boyer (e.g., 1990, 1992, 1993, 1994a, 1994b, 1996, 2001a, 2001b) has meanwhile led the way in showing how various kinds of concepts of supernatural agency minimally violate intuitive expectations and, so, are naturally easy to learn and recall. Just as certain notions of gods, ghosts, and witches are easily transmitted, we also find that particular features of ritual structure and content can be highly intuitive and, for that reason, easily acquired (see Fiske and Haslam 1997, Lawson and McCauley 1990, McCauley and Lawson 2002). And many other aspects of religious discourse, such as the uses of parable (see Turner 1996) or the teleological reasoning exhibited in creation myths (see Kelemen and Donovan 2003), incorporate features that are naturally easy to process and pass on.

At the same time, some forms of religious thinking are far from intuitive and may require a vast repertoire of pedagogic tools and mnemonic supports in order to be transmitted intact. To put it another way, some aspects of religion are cognitively costly (see Whitehouse 2004). Doctrinal systems typically place great value on the standardization of cognitively costly concepts and emphasize the dire consequences (whether real or imagined) of unauthorized innovation. Thus, we often find a profusion of what Justin Barrett (1999) has called "theologically correct" concepts in religion—the truth of which may be asserted with extraordinarily dogmatic insistence. Some religions, by contrast, foster active rumination on questions of theological and ritual meaning. This is a particularly pronounced feature of the imagistic mode of religiosity, which triggers haunting memories for intrinsically mysterious and life-changing experiences and, thus, sets in train a seemingly unending process of intricate exegetical reflection.

In short, cultural concepts in general, and religious thinking in particular, are scattered across a spectrum adumbrating degrees of intuitiveness. At one end of the spectrum are extremely simple concepts (simple, that is, if you are equipped with a distinctively human mind), such as a notion of "ghost" or "parable." These sorts of concepts, since they are so easily learned and recalled, are found in all human populations the world over and have probably been around for as long as modern humans have roamed the planet. At the other end of the spectrum are maximally counterintuitive ideas, such as the hypotheses of quantum mechanics or of academic theology. For such concepts to be produced and passed on, massive institutional support is required: pedagogical (e.g., theories and methods of instruction), infrastructural (e.g., classrooms, libraries, equipment), motivational (e.g., systems of sanctions and incentives), and so on. Most of culture, including most of religion, is stretched across the intermediate range of the spectrum. It requires nothing so grand as a university, but it does demand more than a humble proclivity to see faces in the clouds. In short, it depends upon a set of socially regulated conditions for adequate rehearsal or arousal capable of stimulating feats of memory that surpass those of "natural" cognition.

If culture is a continuum, it is not only in terms of degrees of intuitiveness. Cultural knowledge is also graduated by degrees of ritualization. From middle childhood onward, all normal human beings irresistibly hunt for possible intentions lurking behind the actions of others. Perhaps we are congenitally nosy creatures, but if we didn't constantly try to pry into the internal states of others, we would be unable to accomplish the extraordinary feats of communication and sociality that characterize our species (see Baron-Cohen 1995). Because of this attribute, we can cooperate in complex ways. We can entertain our friends, curry favor with our bosses, and lay traps for our enemies. What this requires is being attuned to the interests of other people and their likely perceptions of ourselves. This deceptively subtle, if compulsive, activity is confounded by actions that are closely stipulated in advance and, yet, are irreducible to any set of self-evident technical motivations. That is the essence of ritual.

A ritual is an action that cannot be tacitly attributed to the intentional states of the actor. If you try, you immediately run into problems. Consider the person who crosses herself with holy water. Clearly, this is not the same kind of action as washing one's hands or clothing. It may involve a sort of metaphorical cleansing, but that interpretation is different from a purely technical one. Nor does the idea originate in the actor herself. She performs that act because she has learned it from others and not because it suddenly occurred to her that this would be a novel and desirable thing to do. Art, unlike ritual, expresses precisely that kind of novelty. It, too, is irreducible to technical motivations, but it bears the mark of creativity. For the artist, unlike the ritual actor, is the author of the idea. If we attribute rituals to a creator, then it is always after the event in a crucial psychological sense. For the act itself must have become disconnected from the intentions of those who perform it before it can be truly designated an act of ritual.

Degrees of ritualization and of intuitiveness together provide a method of carving up religious phenomena and may help to account for varying degrees of cultural plasticity more generally. At the maximally counterintuitive end of the spectrum, cultural knowledge can vary rather dramatically across time and space, since it is relatively unhampered by the constraints of natural cognition. By contrast, more cognitively optimal concepts (e.g., concerning intuitive ontology, social-causal cognition, etc.) would constitute a more stable and cross-culturally recurrent bridgehead of inferential engines and their outputs. In the case of religion, which is (in general) the most highly ritualized domain of culture (see figure 13.1), maximally counterintuitive concepts are the outcome, I would argue, of doctrinal and imagistic modes of religiosity.

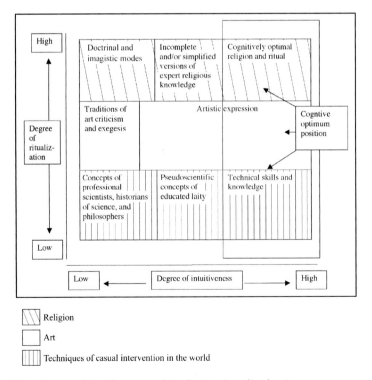

Figure 13.1   Degrees of intuitiveness and ritualization in cultural systems.

Implications for Historical and Archaeological Evidence

We may now be in a better position to understand the inherent instability of the doctrinal mode and its consequences for patterns of religious transformation. We noted earlier that the doctrinal mode may be vulnerable to the tedium effect—that is, a lowering of morale due to high levels of repetition. We have already identified at least three ways in which that problem might be addressed. One might be dubbed the "Melanesian solution": periodic reinvigoration of the mainstream tradition via imagistic splintering. Vial points out that this is not a prominent feature of European religious history, however. Another possible solution to the tedium effect is to increase the relevance of heavily repeated doctrine, along the lines described by Malley (2004, see above). A third way out is to adopt the kinds of high-arousal, revelatory practices described by Clark in her discussion of medieval monasticism. This involves a kind of "domestication" of imagistic strategies by the doctrinal mode, insofar as the revelatory experiences are mostly solitary, rather than collective, and the emphasis is on publicly stereotyped meanings rather than privately fabricated ones, thus privileging the interests of doctrinal reproduction over doctrinal invention. All these problems and their solutions[2] stem from what we might refer to as the "overpolicing" of doctrinal orthodoxy, at least partly through the heavy reiteration of cardinal principles and practices. But the doctrinal mode exhibits rather different vulnerabilities in circumstances of "underpolicing," for instance where transmissive frequency falls below a certain level necessary for effective learning and consolidation of complex, theologically correct teachings or for the triggering of salience/relevance effects. This is when the cognitive optimum effect kicks in and leads to a dumbing down or "naturalizing" of the religious orthodoxy. Such a scenario has often provided the stimulus for movements of reform and religious revival in European religious traditions, as Pyysiäinen observes in detail. All this suggests that the doctrinal mode is not a static model for religious transmission, but a suite of variables that operate in dynamic tension, with potentially predictable consequences for patterns of splintering and historical transformation. We have much more ground to cover in formulating specific predictions and owe a particular debt of gratitude to Pyysiäinen in illuminating the way forward, but we are now heading in a direction that should in principle lead to a fuller explanation for the twists and turns of religious history, not only in Europe but elsewhere.

Consider, for instance, Douglas Gragg's discussion of Roman religion as an assemblage of "cognitively optimal" practices (chapter 5). According to Pyysiäinen's formula, such conditions should be ripe for movements of doctrinal reform, and this is precisely what Gragg describes—a set of "protodoctrinal" tendencies "with the potential of developing into an example of full-blown doctrinal modality under the right set of pressures" (pp. 75–76). We know of at least one instance of such a development toward the end of the classical era, namely the establishment and official incorporation of Christianity. But that still leaves the problem of explaining why a full-blown doctrinal mode did not take hold as the dominant mode of religious organization and transmission throughout the history of the ancient Roman world. How did a vast, centralized polity, in other respects obsessed with control, come to exhibit such lack of interest in regulating and policing the religious practices and representations of its citizenry, at least during major portions of its history?

Although an adequate answer to that question lies beyond the scope of my expertise, and perhaps also of the modes theory as currently constituted, we can at least follow Gragg in explaining the success of Roman mystery cults with reference to imagistic dynamics. Gragg implicitly agrees with my interpretation of Beck's data on Mithraism as an exemplar of the imagistic mode and extends this argument to a much wider range of cases. Leopold likewise emphasizes the imagistic character of mystery cults in antiquity and also of Gnosticism in the second century. Yet Leopold goes further still. Gnostic cults, dominated by imagistic dynamics, were hotbeds of cosmological rumination—through their revelatory activities, they generated a wealth of complex religious ideas that were eventually susceptible to fixation through the routinized practices of the doctrinal mode. This appears to have underpinned the success of early Christianity. But it once again raises the question of why similar recodifications of imagistic revelation were not present (if indeed they were not) throughout antiquity. Clearly, this is an issue for classicists and ancient historians to resolve.

The Origins of Modes of Religiosity

As Donald Wiebe points out (chapter 12), the cognitive capacities required for the formation of doctrinal and imagistic modes are present in all human beings and have been for many millennia. Why, then, should one of these modes (the imagistic) emerge first in human prehistory and the other (doctrinal) become established only relatively recently with the growth of the early states? To explain this evolution we must have recourse to mechanisms outside the modes theory itself. For instance, we might seek to identify the factors that first gave rise to very much shorter cycles of transmission in the domain of religion and ritual and, thus, fostered the standardization of religious teachings across wide areas. Whatever those factors turn out to be, it will also be necessary to show that they were not activated during thousands of years of prior experimentation in the domain of religion, when the repertoire was apparently confined to imagistic or cognitively optimal practices. The need to look beyond the modes theory for a solution to this problem is, in Weibe's view, a serious defect. His concern here focuses partly on a rather narrow concept of causality, however, wherein "causes" appear to be construed as sufficient conditions. But even in simple mechanical processes, we use the notion of causation more liberally. We say, for instance, that the engine of a car causes it to accelerate, and yet we also know that an engine is not a sufficient cause of the car's propulsion. We must also have a road, a driver, a system of gears that connects the revolving drive shaft to the wheels, and so on. And it is possible to imagine circumstances in which a perfectly functional car is doomed to immobility, for instance because of a lack of roads. Until about 6,000 years ago, the doctrinal mode was rather like a car without a network of roads to drive along. Something happened that made a new kind of traveling possible, some shift in the ecology of religious life.

One possibility, explored elsewhere by Pascal Boyer (2001a, 2002) and Jack Goody (2004), is that the doctrinal mode was kickstarted by the advent of literacy. The appeals of this hypothesis are obvious. First, there is the argument of covariance: literacy seems to appear roughly around the same time as the doctrinal mode, and there are very few historical or contemporary cases of a religious tradition dominated by the doctrinal mode that does not either base its teachings around texts or model itself on another tradition which clearly does so. Second, there is the argument of standardization: religious guilds seeking to establish doctrinal uniformity could use writing as a means of stabilizing the canon, enabling them to squeeze out competitors in the religious market who lacked these methods of ideological regulation. Such arguments, however, raise, but do not resolve, the historical and logical priority of literacy in the emergence of the doctrinal mode.

In *Arguments and Icons*, I suggest that one of the most striking changes in religious ecology, aside from the development of writing systems, that seems to have accompanied the first appearance of the doctrinal mode in a number of locations, was a massive increase in the scale and frequency of agricultural rituals, occasioned by major technological and demographic changes at the time. It is possible that this, rather than the advent of literacy, is what primarily triggered the earliest emergence of routinized orthodoxies. The homogenization of a regional tradition required, first and foremost, a method of transmitting (acquiring, remembering, and passing on) complex, standardized teachings. Although literacy may have rapidly come to the aid of such projects, the latter's initial appearance and flowering need not have depended upon that. Indeed, the doctrinal mode may have been a major stimulus for the development of writing systems, rather than the other other way around.

Interestingly, the material presented in this book by Steven Mithen (chapter 3) and Karen Johnson (chapter 4) would seem to support this last interpretation rather than the Goody/Boyer position. Mithen suggests that the doctrinal mode may have appeared in western Asia as early as 8,000 to 10,000 years ago in a period classified by archaeologists as the Levantine Pre-Pottery Neolothic B, where we see the first evidence of centralization and regional homogeneity in religious practices and beliefs. During this period, Mithen goes on to observe, "There are no traces of literacy, although D. Schmandt-Besserat . . . argued that geometric clay tokens used at 'Ain Ghazal provided the foundation from which writing systems developed" (p. 31). Johnson, too, suggests that the doctrinal mode predates the development of writing systems on the Susiana Plain (specifically at Choga Mish and Susa) approximately 7,000 years ago. She writes,

> With respect to the sociopolitical features of Choga Mish and Susa, it appears that Whitehouse's model should predict a religious tradition that is more doctrinal in nature: the social cohesion was likely diffuse across the Susiana Plain; leadership was certainly dynamic through the cycling of chiefdoms into a state-level society; the communities were arguably inclusive in the attempt to exert influence over greater areas; the spread certainly seems efficient; large-scale accurately describes the sphere of authority; the degree of uniformity is admittedly difficult to discern; and the structure is obviously centralized. Yet, systems of writing are noticeably absent (p. 59).

Obviously, these kinds of conclusions are drawn tentatively on the basis of fragmentary data. Both Mithen and Johnson discuss the methodological challenges faced by archaeologists in seeking to make use of the modes theory and other theories like it that were not originally designed with a material that evidence in mind. Mithen observes, for instance, that few if any of the activities associated with contemporary Melanesian initiation practices, which I have frequently used to illustrate core features of the imagistic mode, would survive in the archaeological record. Indeed, it is tempting to say that the absence of material that remains associated with ritual practices is potentially a diagnostic feature of the imagistic mode. High-arousal, low-frequency rituals are usually secret and any ritual paraphernalia is liable to destruction immediately after use. In the face of these sorts of problems, Johnson searches ingeniously for solutions, postulating a variety of indirect indicators of relative levels of ritual frequency and doctrinal standardization. Ultimately, it is work of this sort, rather than armchair theorizing per se, that holds the key to discovering the origins of modes dynamics.

Epilogue

In closing, it seems appropriate to offer a very brief comment on the question of what constitutes religion. This issue was repeatedly raised in our conference at the University of Vermont, from which this book emerged, but seems to have largely faded from the agenda as participants have revised their papers for publication. What, in short, is the theory of modes of religiosity intended to be a theory of? To some extent, I fear this may be a red herring, and perhaps others have also come to that conclusion, but this is all the more reason to pin down the matter and put it to bed. Religion is not a phenomenon, like a new species or organism or a distant galaxy, waiting to be discovered. Religion is whatever we agree to say it is. For my part, I should be happy to agree on a minimal Tylorian definition that identifies religion as any set of practices that presupposes the presence of one or more supernatural beings.

Having religion, in the sense of having recourse to supernatural explanations for processes and events, does not necessarily require the activation of modes of religiosity. Indeed, as we have seen, the invocation of spirits and deities, the performance of rituals, and the transmission of myths can be as natural as smiling or blinking and would thus require no special training or mnemonic support. Modern humans, and probably also some of our premodern ancestors and cousins, have always had religion. But having religious coalitions—cults, churches, totemic groups, and the like—invariably requires the elaboration of modes dynamics. In the imagistic mode, cohesive ritual groupings irrevocably mark off their membership from those who are not (or cannot) be party to the weighty and mysterious knowledge of the initiated or enlightened. The emergence of such religious traditions does not require the presence of literate guilds and probably predates the invention of literacy by many millennia (see above). On the other hand, the large "imagined communities" that emerge with the development of the doctrinal mode are clearly more recent. Although it appears roughly around the time that early writing systems were invented, the truth is we do not yet know whether literacy caused or somehow fostered the creation of the doctrinal mode or the other way around. But what does seem to be clear is that having "a" religion, whether in the sense of belonging to a small, exclusivistic cult or a large, inclusivistic church, requires the presence of imagistic or doctrinal modes of religiosity. Once both modes of religiosity are firmly established in the cultural repertoire, they are hard to shift. And part of the success of religions that draw upon these organizational principles is that they never wholly or permanently commit to one or the other. One of the greatest remaining challenges for this area of research is to survey the range of ways in which modes of religiosity interact and to specify with greater precision how the vulnerabilities of the doctrinal mode are overcome and the strengths of the imagistic mode are harnessed by coalitions not of their own making.

Notes

1. A similar misunderstanding is apparent in Wiebe's critique (chapter 12).
2. Despite my somewhat functionalist language here, I should emphasize that we are dealing with processes of selection rather than of mechanistic causation. What works survives, but that does not mean that institutional innovation is driven (in the sense of intelligently motivated) by a deliberate search for workable arrangements.

References

Baron-Cohen, Simon. 1995. *Mindblindness: An Essay on Autism and Theory of Mind*. Cambridge, Mass.: MIT Press.

Barrett, Justin L. 1999. "Theological Correctness: Cognitive Constraint and the Study of Religion." *Method and Theory in the Study of Religion* 11: 325–39.

Boyer, Pascal. 1990. *Tradition as Truth and Communication: A Cognitive Description of Traditional Discourse*. Cambridge: Cambridge University Press.

Boyer, Pascal. 1992. "Explaining Religious Ideas: Outline of a Cognitive Approach." *Numen* 39: 27–57.

———. 1993. "'Pseudo-Natural Kinds." In *Cognitive Aspects of Religious Symbolism*, edited by P. Boyer. Cambridge: Cambridge University Press.

———. 1994a. "Cognitive Constraints on Cultural Representations: Natural Ontologies and Religious Ideas." In *Mapping the Mind: Domain-Specifity in Cognition and Culture*, edited by Lawrence A. Hirschfeld and Susan A. Gelman. Cambridge: Cambridge University Press.

———. 1994b. *The Naturalness of Religious Ideas: A Cognitive Theory of Religion*. Berkeley: University of California Press.

———. 1996. "What Makes Anthropomorphism Natural: Intuitive Ontology and Cultural Representations." *The Journal of the Royal Anthropological Institute*, n.s., 2: 1–15.

———. 2001a. *Religion Explained: The Evolutionary Origins of Religious Thought*. New York: Basic Books.

———. 2001b. "Cultural Inheritance Tracks and Cognitive Predispositions: The Example of Religious Concepts." In *The Debated Mind: Evolutionary Psychology Versus Ethnography*, edited by Harvey Whitehouse. Oxford: Berg.

———. 2002. "Review of *Arguments and Icons*." *Journal of Ritual Studies* 16: 8–13.

Fiske, A. P., and N. Haslam. 1997. "Is Obsessive-Compulsive Disorder a Pathology of the Human Disposition to Perform Socially Meaningful Rituals? Evidence of Similar Content." *Journal of Nervous and Mental Disease* 185: 211–22.

Goody, Jack. 2004. "Is Image to Doctrine as Speech to Writing? Modes of Communication and the Origins of Religion." In *Ritual and Memory: Toward a Comparative Anthropology of Religion*, edited by Harvey Whitehouse and James Laidlaw. Walnut Creek, Calif.: AltaMira Press.

Guthrie, Stewart. 1980. "A Cognitive Theory of Religion." *Current Anthropology* 21: 181–203.

———. 1993. *Faces in the Clouds: A New Theory of Religion*. Oxford: Oxford University Press.

Kelemen, D., and E. Donovan. 2003. "Purpose in Mind: Teleological Attribution and Religious Cognition." *International Conference on the Psychological and Cognitive Foundations of Religiosity*, Emory Conference Center, Atlanta, Georgia.

Laidlaw, James. 2004. "Embedded Modes of Religiosity in Indic Renouncer Religions." In *Ritual and Memory: Toward a Comparative Anthropology of Religion*, edited by Harvey Whitehouse and James Laidlaw. Walnut Creek, Calif.: AltaMira Press.

Lawson, E. Thomas, and Robert N. McCauley. 1990. *Rethinking Religion: Connecting Cognition and Culture*. Cambridge: Cambridge University Press.

McCauley, Robert N. 2000. "The Naturalness of Religion and the Unnaturalness of Science." In *Explanation and Cognition*, edited by Frank Keil and Richard Wilson. Cambridge, Mass.: MIT Press.

McCauley, Robert N., and E. Thomas Lawson. 2002. *Bringing Ritual to Mind: Psychological Foundations of Cultural Forms.* Cambridge: Cambridge University Press.

Malley, Brian. 2004. "The Doctrinal Mode and Evangelical Christianity in the U.S." In *Ritual and Memory: Toward a Comparative Anthropology of Religion,* edited by Harvey Whitehouse and James Laidlaw. Walnut Creek, Calif.: AltaMira Press.

Martin, Luther H. 2004. "Performativity, Discourse and Cognition: 'Demythologizing' the Roman Cult of Mithras." In *Persuasion and Performance: Rhetoric and Reality in Early Christian Discourses,* edited by Willi Braun. Waterloo, Ontario: Wilfrid Laurier University Press.

Sperber, Dan. 1996. *Explaining Culture: A Naturalistic Approach.* Cambridge, Mass.: Blackwell.

Turner, Mark. 1996. *The Literary Mind: The Origins of Thought and Language.* Oxford: Oxford University Press.

Whitehouse, Harvey. 1992. "Memorable Religions: Transmission, Codification, and Change in Divergent Melanesian Contexts." *Man,* n.s., 27: 777–97.

———. 1995. *Inside the Cult: Religious Innovation and Transmission in Papua New Guinea.* Oxford: Oxford University Press.

———. 2000. *Arguments and Icons: Divergent Modes of Religiosity.* Oxford: Oxford University Press.

———. 2003. "Why Do We Need Cognitive Theories of Religion?" In *Religion as a Human Sacrifice: A Festschrift in Honor of E. Thomas Lawson,* edited by Brian C. Wilson and Timothy Light. Leiden: Brill.

———. 2004. *Modes of Religiosity: A Cognitive Theory of Religious Transmission.* Walnut Creek, Calif.: AltaMira Press.

Whitehouse, Harvey, and James Laidlaw, eds. 2004. *Ritual and Memory: Toward a Comparative Anthropology of Religion.* Walnut Creek, Calif.: AltaMira Press.

Index

imagery: at Çatalhöyük, 36; medieval
theology about, 140n20; in modes of
religiosity, 62
imagistic mode of religiosity, ix, 10, 19,
45, 158; connectedness, 78; in
conversion from mission to Aladura
church, 168; counterintuitive
concepts, 61; episodic memory in,
198; first appearance, 206; in
Hermann of Scheda's description,
163; material record for, 49;
psychological and sociopolitical
features, 11; as religious form, 126;
reservations on, 125; Roman ritual
and, 73–74
imagistic, problems with term, 152
"I" mode, 175
implicit memory, 73
inclusiveness: in Mithraism, 99; of Roman
religion, 74
individuals: versus group, 175–76;
identifying inclinations, 158
Industrial Revolution, 181
initiation rites: on Mainz vessel, 90, 94;
for mystery cults, 76–77
Inside the Cult (Whitehouse), 202, 204
intimidation in ritual, 219
intuition, violation of, 174–75
intuitiveness, 222–25
intuitive ontology, 4
Iran: map, 50; material evidence for
religion, 49–60
Irenaeus, 112–13, 116, 119n9
Isis, 76

Jerf el Ahmar, 17, 28, 30
Jericho, 19, 28, 31; buildings for religious
activity, 34; excavations, 17; plaster
statues, 32
Jesus, 112; Gnosticism and, 111; visions
of, 129, 130
Jew, dialog with Christian, 161

Jewish scriptures, Christian use of,
112–13
Johann of Saxony, 146
Johnson, Karen, 229
Jordan Valley, 26, 27
Juda (Hermann of Scheda), 161;
conversion, 162–64
justification by faith, 152

Karacadağ Hills, 29
Karunki parish (Sweden), 186
Kebara Cave, 25
Kebaran hunter-gatherers, 22–24
Keil, Frank, 4
Kenyon, Kathleen, 17, 19, 28
Kfar HaHoresh, 31, 35
king of rites (rex sacrorum), 85n30
Kivung religion, 203
Kleinberg, Aviad, 169n11
Klein, Stanley, 189
Knapp, B., 48
knowledge, in Gospel of Truth, 112
konventikkeliplakaati, 181
Konya Plain, 35
Kraemer, Hendrik, The Christian Message in a
Non-Christian World, 107
Kuijt, Ian, 27, 28, 38
Kwaio people, 34

Laestadianism, 115, 173, 177–83;
communion exclusion, 186;
conservative, 179
Laestadius, Lars Levi, 177; Dårhushjonet,
182; Sami religion and, 180
language: of Gnosticism, 113–14; in
medieval Europe, 145; and modes of
religiosity, 158; as population division,
181
lares, 71
Larsson, Anders, 181
Läseriet ("Readerism"), 181
Late Natufian, 26

ontology, intuitive, 4
oral cultures, 175
Orphic inscriptions on gold plates, 114
Orphism, 77
Oschoffa, Joseph, 166
Oshitelu, Josiah, 170n17
otherness, contact with, 8
outillage mental, 8
outsiders. *See* syncretism
Ovid: *Fasti*, 75; *Metamorphoses*, 75

Pacific Islands aboriginals, reaction to
    Christian conversion, 188
paganism, 88
pageantry, 154; in Roman ritual, 73–74
paintings, relationshp between Umiliana
    and Mary, 135, 136
Pajala, Laestadius as vicar, 179
Paliau movement, 205
Papua New Guinea, 143, 154; missionary
    Christianity, 115; model found in,
    155; Pomio Kivung movement, 82
passwords, for Bacchic initiates, 77
pastors, Protestant, 147
Peel, John, 159, 168, 169
Pemmerler, Hans, 152
penates, 71
Pentikäinen, Juha, 179
Persephone, 102n34
"person files" of deceased, 32
Petrus Alfonsi, 160–62; doctrinal mode in
    rationality, 164
Pfeiffer, John E., 207
pictographic script, emergence, 46
Pietism, 155, 181
pilgrimage, 159
plaster statues, at 'Ain Ghazal, 32–34
Plato, 92
Plautus, 77
Plutarch, 119n1
Poimandres, 110
political organization: exploitation of
    religion, 80; and modes of religiosity, 20

Pollock, Susan, 53
Pomio Kivung, 155
Porto Novo, Dahomey, Celestial Church
    of Christ, 166
prayer, Hail Mary, 133
Prehistory of the Mind (Mithen), 1–2
preliterate societies, 20
Premonstratensian order, 164
Pre-Pottery Neolithic A (10,000 to 8500
    BCE), 27–28
Pre-Pottery Neolithic B (8500 to 6500
    BCE), 30–31
Price, S., 71
priesthood, 20, 145; absence in Pre-
    Pottery Neolithic B, 35; in Roman
    religion, 74–75
priesthood of all believers, 144, 152
"priest-king," 57
primitives, mental activity of, 8
private devotions, prohibition in Finland,
    181
procession on Mainz vessel, 90
Proclus, *Commentary on the Republic*, 92–93
Proof of the Apostolic Preaching, 112–13
proselytization, 146
Protestants, 144; characteristics of
    doctrinal mode, 152; early approach to
    religious education, 146–48; revivals,
    180; sacraments, 149–50
Proto-Elamite language, first documents,
    57
Psalms, 128; tone for chanting, 138n4
psychology: culture and, 209–10;
    doctrinal mode features, 11; features of
    Mithraism, 97; relationship with
    history and anthropology, 2–3
Pyysiäinen, Ilkka, 115, 222, 226

raptors, 35–36
rationalist theology, 182–83
reading, in monasteries, 128
reason, tension with revelation, 185
reductionism, 3

About the Contributors

Roger Beck is an emeritus professor of classics at the University of Toronto. He is a specialist in Greco-Roman religions and has written extensively on the cult of the sun god Mithras. He is also interested in ancient astronomy and astrology and in the ancient novel. He is convinced that the cognitive science of religion is the next big thing and is enthusiastically importing it into his home discipline.

Ulrich Berner is professor of history of religions at the University of Bayreuth. He is coeditor of SAPERE (Scripta Antiquitatis Posterioris ad Ethicam Religionemque pertinentes). His main specialization is European religious history from late antiquity to the Renaissance. Additionally, he is a participant in the collaborative research center on "Local Action in Africa in the Context of Global Influences" at the University of Bayreuth.

Anne L. Clark is associate professor of religion at the University of Vermont. Her research focuses on Christian religious life in the later Middle Ages. She has published on the visionary texts of medieval women and currently is working on women's religious communities and their ritual objects.

Douglas L. Gragg is a historian of Greco-Roman religions. His research has focused primarily on religions of Rome, including early forms of Judaism and Christianity, and has drawn heavily on insights and models derived from semiotic and (more recently) cognitive theory.

Karen Johnson is a doctoral student at the University of Michigan in the Interdepartmental Program in Classical Art and Archaeology and in the Culture and Cognition Program.

E. Thomas Lawson is emeritus professor of comparative religion at Western Michigan University. He is the author of *Religions of Africa: Traditions in Transformation* (1984) and, with Robert N. McCauley, *Rethinking Religion: Connecting Religion and Culture* (1990) and *Bringing Ritual to Mind: Psychological Foundations of Ritual Forms* (2002). In addition, he has contributed chapters to many books, articles to a wide variety of journals, and a large number of entries to encyclopedias. He is executive editor of the *Journal of Cognition and Culture* and codirector with Harvey Whitehouse of the newly established Institute for Cognition and Culture at Queen's University, Belfast.

Anita Maria Leopold is a doctoral student in the Department for the Study of Religion at the University of Aarhus, Denmark. She has published a number of articles on issues related to Gnosticism and syncretism and is the editor of a forthcoming anthology on syncretism as a theoretical problem.

Luther H. Martin, a professor of religion at the University of Vermont, is the author of *Hellenistic Religions: An Introduction* (1987), an editor of *Theoretical Frameworks for the Study of Graeco-Roman Religions* (2002), and author of numerous articles in this area of the history of religions. In addition, he is the author of many articles on theory and method in the study of religion, an editor of several volumes of essays on this topic, as well as an editor of a volume titled *The Academic Study of Religion during the Cold War* (2001). He is currently engaged in research on Greco-Roman religions from the perspective of cognitive science.

Steven Mithen is professor of early prehistory and head of the School of Human and Environmental Sciences at the University of Reading. He moved to Reading in 1992 after studying at the universities of London, Sheffield, York, and Cambridge. His research interests include the evolution of cognition, prehistoric hunter-gatherers, and the use of computer simulation in archaeology. His books include *The Prehistory of the Mind* (1996) and *After the Ice: A Global Human History* (2003).

Ilkka Pyysiäinen was educated in theology and comparative religion at the University of Helsinki, Finland. He earned his Ph.D. in 1993 with a thesis on Buddhist mysticism. Since then he has dedicated himself to the exploration of religious cognition. He has published numerous articles and his books include *How Religion Works* (2001), *Current Approaches in the Cognitive Science of Religion* (edited with Veikko Anttonen, 2002), and *Magic, Miracles, and Religion* (2004). He currently works at the Helsinki Collegium for Advanced Studies.

Ted Vial is Batten Associate Professor of Religious Studies at Virginia Wesleyan College. He is author of *Liturgy Wars: Ritual Theory and Protestant Reform in Nineteenth Century Zurich* (2004) and has published articles in *Numen* and the *Harvard Theological Review*.

Harvey Whitehouse is professor of anthropology and director of postgraduate studies in the Faculty of Humanities at Queen's University, Belfast. He is codirector with E. Thomas Lawson of the newly established Institute for Cognition and Culture at Queen's University, Belfast. He is currently the recipient of two major British Academy grants. His previous books include *Inside the Cult: Religious Innovation and Transmission in Papua New Guinea* (1995), *Arguments and Icons: Divergent Modes of Religiosity* (2000), *The Debated Mind: Evolutionary Psychology Versus Ethnography* (2001), and *Modes of Religiosity: A Cognitive Theory of Religious Transmission* (2004).

Donald Wiebe is professor of the philosophy of religion at Trinity College, Toronto. He has published numerous articles on theory and method in the study of religion in journals, collections of essays, and proceedings, as well as four books on this topic, the most recent being *The Politics of Religious Studies* (2000). He is also editor of the series *Toronto Studies in Religion* (Peter Lang Press).